THE CRISIS OF BRITAIN'S
SURVEILLANCE STATE

THE CRISIS OF BRITAIN'S SURVEILLANCE STATE

Security, Law Enforcement, and
The Intelligence War in Cyberspace

MUSA KHAN JALALZAI

Algora Publishing
New York

Library of Congress Cataloging-in-Publication Data —

Jalalza'i, Musa Khan.
    The crisis of Britain's surveillance state: security, law enforcement, and the
intelligence war in cyberspace / Musa Khan Jalalzai.
        pages cm
    Includes bibliographical references and index.
    ISBN 978-1-62894-078-7 (soft cover: alk. paper)—ISBN 978-1-62894-079-4
(hard cover: alk. paper)—ISBN 978-1-62894-080-0 (ebook) 1. Electronic
surveillance—Great Britain. 2. Terrorism—Great Britain—Prevention. 3. Great
Britain—Racism. I. Title.
    HV7936.T4J35 2014
    363.25'2—dc23
                        2014025359

Printed in the United States

ABBREVIATIONS

ABH	Actual Bodily Harm
ACC	Assistant Chief Constable
ACG	Asian criminal gangs
ACPO	Association of Chief Police Officers
ACR	Area Control Room
ADC	Area Data Centre
AFO	Authorized Firearms Officer
ALO	Architectural Liaison Officer
AWC	Afghan War Criminals
BBC	British Broadcasting Corporation
BI	Ballistic Intelligence
BNP	British National Party
CCNIPS	Chief Constable of Northern Ireland Police Service
CDII	Central Directorate of Interior Intelligence
CG	Criminal gangs
CI	Counter-intelligence
CIA	Central Intelligence Agency
CIA	Central Intelligence Agency
CIC	Commissioner of Interception Communications
CID	Criminal Investigation Department
CIS	Coalition Information Sharing
CJA	Criminal and Justice Act
CMP	Commissioner of the Metropolitan Police
CNI	Critical National Infrastructure
COBRA	Cabinet Office briefing room a (in Downing Street)
COMSEC	Communications Security
CONTEST	Britain's Counter-terrorism strategy
CPG	Crime and Policing Group
CPR	Cardio Pulmonary Resuscitation
CPS	Crown Prosecution Service
CPU	Case Progression Unit
CRB	Collision Report Book

CRB	Criminal Records Bureau
CRO	Criminal Records Office
CSA	Crime and Security Act
CSI	Container Security Initiative
CSIS	Canadian Security Intelligence Service
CSO	Community Support Officer
CSU	Community Safety Unit
CT	Cyber Terrorism
CTSP	Counter terrorism and Security Powers
D&D	Drunk and Disorderly
D&I	Drunk and Incapable
DARPA	Defense Advance Research Project Agency
DCC	Deputy Chief Constable
DCI	Detective Chief Inspector
DDPS	Directorate of Defense Protection and Security
DGIIA	Defense Geographic and Imagery Intelligence Agency
DGSE	General Directorate of External Intelligence
DI	CIA Directorate of Intelligence
DIA	Defense Intelligence Agency
DIS	Defense Intelligence Staff
DISC	Defense Intelligence and Security Centre
DNI	Director of National Intelligence
DPA	Data Protection Act
DSC	Defense Select Committee
EE	Electronic Espionage
EFQM	European Federation of Quality Management
EG	Evidence Gatherer
EOA	Enquiry Office Assistant
F&A	Finance and Administration
FAM	Finance and Administration Manager
FBO	Football Banning Order
FCC	Force Command and Control
FCMD	Force Crime Management Department
FCO	Foreign and Commonwealth Office
FIA	French Intelligence Agency

FISA	Foreign Intelligence Surveillance Act
GCHQ	Government Communication Headquarter
GEO	Government Equality Office
GIMP	Government Interception Modernization Program
HC	House of Commons
HO	Home Office
HRA	Human Rights Act
HSO	Health Service Ombudsman
IA	Information assurance
IAEA	International Atomic Energy Agency
IC	Intelligence community
ICC	Interception Communications Commissioner
ICT	Information and computing/communications technology
IISS	International Institute for Strategic Studies
IMINT	Imagery Intelligence
IPA	International Police Association
IPCC	Independent Police Complaints Commission
IRA	Irish Republican Army
ISAF	International Security Assistance Force
ISC	Intelligence and Security Committee
ISI	Inter-Services Intelligence
IT	International Terrorism
JIC	Joint Intelligence Committee
KP	Khyber Pakhtunkhwa
LAN	Local Area Networks
LICACD	Lawful Interception of Communication and the Acquisition of Communications Data
LPSDS	London Police Special Demonstration Squad
LWJ	Long War Journal
MASINT	Measurement and signature intelligence
MI5	Security Service
MI6	Secret Intelligence Service
MILINT/MI	Military intelligence
MPDPG	Metropolitan Police, Diplomatic Protection Group
MPUSU	Metropolitan Police Undercover Surveillance Unit

NAT	North African terrorism
NATO	North Atlantic Treaty Organization
NCCSI	National Commission for the Control of Security Interception
NCDEF	National Coordinator Domestic Extremism force
NCF	National Crime Force
NCI	National Criminal Intelligence
NCIS	National Criminal Intelligence Service
NCNPD	International Commission on Nuclear non-Proliferation and Disarmament
NCTC	National Counterterrorism Center
NDS	National Directorate of Security
NETCO	National Extremism Tactical Coordination Unit
NHS	National Health Service
NIC	National Intelligence Council
NICEM	Northern Ireland Council for Ethnic Minorities
NIE	National Intelligence Estimate
NIM	National Intelligence Model
NPOIU	National Public Order Intelligence Unit
NPP	Nuclear Power Plants
NSA	National Security Agency
NSS	National Security Strategy
NU	National Unit
OG	Olympic Games
OSCT	The Office for Security and Counter-Terrorism
PC	Police Commissioner
PHIA	Professional Head Intelligence Analysis
PIA	Policing-Improvement Agency
PIC	Professionalization of Intelligence Cooperation
PLE	Politicization of law enforcement
PMO	Prime Minister Office
PNIC	Police National Information Centre
PNRA	Pakistan Nuclear Regulatory Authority
PRISM	Foreign Intelligence Surveillance Court
PSA	Police Superintendent Association
PSCRB	Passport Service, Criminal Records Bureau

PSD	Professional Standards Department
PSNI	Police Service of Northern Ireland
RIG	Radical Islamic Group
RIPA	Regulation of Investigatory Power Act 2000
RPF	River Police Force
RRA	Race Relations Act
SAS	Special Air Service
SBS	Special Boat Service
SDSR	Strategic Defense and Security Review
SF	Special Forces
SFS	Scottish Faith Schools
SIPR-Net	Secret internet protocol router network
SOCA	Serious Organized Crime Agency
SV	Sectarian Violence
SYP	Scotland Yard Police
TERFOR	Tackling Extremism and Radicalization Taskforce
TIA	Telecommunications Interception Act
TJG	Takfiri Jihadi groups
TNDEU	The National Domestic Extremism Unit (NDEU)
TR	Telecommunication Regulations
TTP	Tehreek-e-Taliban Pakistan
UCII	The UK Chief Inspector of Immigration
UK	The United Kingdom
UKBA	UK Border Agency
USOCE	United States Office of Counterintelligence Executive
VAR	Vehicle Accident Report
VASCAR	Visual Average Speed Computer and Recorder
VDRS	Vehicle Defect Rectification Scheme
VHF	Very High Frequency
VIN	Vehicle Identification Number
WMDC	Weapons of Mass Destruction Commission
WP	Works and Pensions

TABLE OF CONTENTS

INTRODUCTION

Great Britain is in a great crisis, one that is only getting worse with every attempt to patch things up. From the phone-hacking scandal to the recent secret surveillance programs through TEMPORA, ECHELON and PRISM, public exposures of widespread intelligence and surveillance collaboration with America's NSA and CIA, and with the secret agencies of Canada, Australia, New Zealand and Europe, the overwhelming picture of intrusion into people's personal lives has caused a breakdown in trust, between the citizens and the state. Further, the actual deterioration of the security situation has led to a very negative response in the communities. The arrival of hundreds of thousands of immigrants, and weapons experts from Asia and Africa, some of them with links to professional criminal gangs, and sectarian mafia groups, has caused deep rifts in British society.

The country faces numerous social, political and economic crises. Unemployment and homelessness are on the rise, and hundreds of homeless and jobless people are joining criminal networks every year. The Local Government Councils are deeply involved in corruption and discrimination cases. Unaffordable rent and welfare cuts have bred a benefit-fraud culture. Borough councils award contracts to corrupt construction companies for road and housing projects, in exchange for kickbacks or incentives of various kinds. Education has become a joke, false student visas, and unregistered colleges caused a security challenge.

Drug addiction, prostitution and human trafficking, terrorists and organized criminals trafficking from Pakistan, India and European states, modern slavery, and burglaries, have become more commonplace, while smugglers and marriage centers sponsor the arrival of thousands of extremists, terror suspects, gangsters and trained prostitutes from Asia, Africa and Europe, into Britain. Consequently, Britain has become the center of foreign espionage and intelligence networks. Intelligence networks of various states have established strong roots in the country. Trust has ultimately been undermined between the state security apparatus, law enforcement agencies, and the citizens. The process of citizen's alienation from the state continues. The attitude of the police and Borough Councils has totally changed. Police and Asian communities view each other with mutual scorn. They do not trust each other, and do not want to cooperate on anything, including the fight against crime, extremism and terrorism.

On 30 October 2013, *The Guardian* reported the deteriorating health condition of Britain's children and women. According to Sir Michael Marmot's report, much of the rest of Europe takes better care of its families. Life expectancy is one measure. Half of the children live in poverty. The way NHS kills is very odd. NHS hospitals kill thousands of patients every year.

The culture of hate, racism, extremism, discrimination, and sectarianism has recently taken new roots in the country's various districts. Some religious clerics are preaching hate, especially in mosques during Juma prayers (Friday's congregational prayers). These are people who want to weaken Islam and create clefts among world religions, while Islam in fact, does not support this way of religious practice. These fanatics have established their own schools with their desired syllabuses teaching hate, violence and sectarianism. At present, they run more than 130 schools across the country. The case of Northern Ireland is fairly similar. In Northern Ireland, there are different sectarian schools, established with their own sectarian syllabuses.

Sectarian affiliations in government department are considered a serious threat. Organized crime firms are doing business in their own way. A report of the Science and Innovation Program of the Police Service for 2010–2013, warned that between 25,000 and 30,000 criminals are engaged in organized crime, generating over £20 billion every year. Narcotics drugs are openly and easily smuggled in taxies, train compartments and cars. Criminal and containerized trade, and black market economy continues to challenge the traditional financial market in Britain.

The United Kingdom is under threat from home-grown extremist and international terrorist networks. The incidents that occurred from 2011 to 2013 and the court decision against some violent extremist elements can be classified as a new wave of subversion. The August 2011 riots and other incidents raised public concern. Research institutions and newspapers carried out surveys and ran articles to identify the causes of unrest and campaign of killing and burning.

The causes were clear and evident. The police failed to control criminal gangs. The Government called for the arrest of more than 20,000 criminals and extremist elements, to ensure the security of the Olympic and Paralympics Games, in 2012. The police arrested thousands, but the situation remained the same. Britain's home-grown extremist returning from Syria, Iraq, Yemen, Nigeria, Somalia, Sudan, Afghanistan, Pakistan and Bangladesh, are posing a growing threat to the security of the country. In July 2011, government announced the revised Prevent Strategy with three objectives. The main target of the strategy is; to challenge ideologies that support terrorism and those who promote it.

The conflict in Northern Ireland has entered a new phase as both the sects (Protestant and Catholic) adopted new strategies of destruction and violence. In August 2013, more than sixty police officers were injured by dissidents. Due to the changing security environment, and deteriorating law and order, since the London terrorist attacks in 2005, successive governments have been proposing constructive changes into the National Security Strategy, but the fight against terrorists and extremists is continued with full swing.

Parliament introduced several counter terrorism measures, attempting to tackle the issue within the traditional law enforcement mechanism, but the rate of terror-related crime is still going up, and networks of hundreds of criminal gangs are taking roots in every town and city. Police arrest dozens of terror suspects under anti-terror laws every year, but they are unable to dent the terror networks.

Britain's approach to counter terrorism is mostly based on intelligence-led policing. In the past, the arrest of hundreds of people under various counter-terrorism laws, created mistrust between law enforcement agencies and the citizens. In Britain, various governments passed dozens of counter-terrorism laws from 2001 to 2012, but these laws have never been fully implemented. Extremist organizations are still dancing in the streets, and send threat letters to their opponents.

On 18 October 2013, a London based Somali extremist group, Al Shabab warned that British Muslims, who criticized the murder of a British soldier in East London, would face severe punishment. Police in London offered protection to several critics of the organization, but there is a general perception, that the police cannot protect such people from the wrath of extremist groups. Following the killing of the soldier, Prime Minister David Cameron announced a new task force, TERFOR (Tackling Extremism and Radicalization Taskforce) in 2013. TERFOR is made up of Ministers, Intelligence experts, Police Chiefs and Religious Leaders. The task force helps communities in tackling extremism and radicalization on line. It seeks to stop extremists using schools and mosques to promote their transmogrified sectarian creeds, but the police are stymied as to how to tackle Asian, African and European criminal networks in the country.

The present intelligence mechanism and its role in law enforcement face severe criticism in society. Intelligence mechanism is weak and complicated. The intelligence collection process is based on egoism, and sources of information are untrained and illiterate. Most reports from such poor sources lead intelligence and police officers in the wrong direction. Intelligence sharing mechanism is weak. Communities are not consulted in policing-community programs, and countering terrorism operations. Political and sectarian loyalties, appointments, transfers, and tactical mistakes have skewered the professional credibility of the UK law enforcement agencies. Surveillance laws are being amended time and again, but in spite of all these efforts, no concrete progress has been achieved on the interception of extremist literature disseminating in the country. Surveillance is under severe criticism. Drones in the UK skies, helicopter, and other surveillance equipment have failed to detect and disrupt terror-related networks, and criminal gangs.

Furthermore, the issue of interception of communication has become more complicated as complaints from various circles, raise legitimate questions of violation of privacy. The Police are using every means of surveillance, every way of alienating the citizens from the state. From ambulance policing to helicopter policing, from car patrol to motorcycle patrol, close and distance surveillance, no strategy has proved effective in collecting reliable information regarding the criminal activities of serious organized crime groups. The "terror law" or the Regulation of Investigatory Power Act 2000, Communication Act 1985, and the Police Act 1997, allow the state security agencies to intercept communications, but it has antagonized law-abiding citizens.

At the same time, US intelligence agencies are engaged in widespread surveillance of Internet Communications, using the so called 'PRISM' program. President Obama issued assurances that PRISM does not apply to US citizens, and it does not apply to people living in the US. That revelation quickly led to the concern that the UK's Government Communications Headquarters (GCHQ) was gathering data on UK citizens via PRISM and TEMPORA, thereby, circumventing the protection offered by the UK legal framework. These actions by the United States NSA and Britain's GCHQ were severely criticized in the print and electronic media.

In another report, *The Guardian* revealed a white structure on top of the British embassy building in Berlin that contained spying equipment, created misunderstanding between the two states. The British ambassador to Germany was called in for a meeting at the Foreign Office to explain allegations, that Britain had been using its embassy for covert surveillance against Germany, an ally. The issue is very complicated and making trouble as the Police and intelligence agencies in the UK have undergone no specific changes. In 1964, the Police Act introduced modern policing, but the record of achievement, and the tactics of the police have not been satisfactory during the last fifty years.

An Independent Police Complaints Commission report

states that corruption has always been an issue. In the UK, the development of modern policing has been punctuated by high-profile scandals involving malpractice, bribery, sexual harassment and misconduct. In just one example, Transparency International noted in its report: "In March 2010, former detective Chief Superintendent Phil Jones was jailed for eighteen months for misconduct in public office and conspiracy to commit fraud by false representation."

The Leveson inquiry reports also exposed the prevailing culture of corruption within the police department, and the newspaper industry. On July 13, 2011, the Prime Minister announced a two-part inquiry investigating the role of the press and police in the phone-hacking scandal. Even before this, on 12 May 2013, Home Secretary said that public trust was being undermined by the "minority" of police officers who behaved corruptly. The Leveson enquiry report criticized Metropolitan Police for errors in the handling of the phone-hacking scandals, and for fostering a "perception" that some senior officers were too close to the *News International* newspaper.

The ex-Border Agency (UKBA) has also been in trouble. Border control mechanisms had failed and were under severe criticism. More than 140,000 illegal immigrants disappeared, with their records, inside the country. The Border Agency issued thousands of passports and indefinite visas to criminal gangs and terror suspects, who were wanted for criminal acts in their own countries. These and other suspects spread like a virus and have started up criminal businesses across the country. Nothing is known about their identity, religious and political affiliation, and countries of origin. Now immigration enforcement is desperately looking for these missing immigrants in every corner of the country to officially record them.

The Border Agency was eliminated in May 2013, due to its inability to intercept illegal immigrants and terror elements entering the country. In a debate in the House of Lords, on the performance of the Border Agency, Lord Marlesford was particularly vocal in his criticism.

In November 2012, the UK Chief Inspector of Immigration Mr. John Vine said in his first report, that UKBA hadn't even touched more than 450,000 asylum cases. On 3 July 2013, Mr.

Vine's final report revealed the fact that UKBA continued to ignore important data on asylum seekers. The Agency failed to deal with the backlog and has been frequently criticized by the House of Commons Home Affairs Select Committee for its inefficiency and corrupt culture.

In this thoroughly-documented book, I have tried to highlight the crises facing the British state, due to corruption, drug trafficking, racism, foreign intelligence networks, criminal gangs, and sectarian violence in Northern Ireland and Scotland. I have also discussed Britain's weak approach to national security, surveillance, and the intelligence war in cyberspace. The book further documents the failure of the British state and its law enforcement mechanism to tackle these existential threats.

The first chapter highlights the weak national security approach of British governments, drug abuse, violent crime, teenage delinquency, family breakdown, welfare dependency, poor urban environments, educational failure, poverty, and the loss of traditional values. The second chapter discusses the crisis of policing, state institutions and the weaknesses of the agencies. The army of 1 million illegal immigrants, the presence of terror suspects, and the government's lack of coherent view of the nature, and priority of risk to the state, have also been discussed in detail.

The third chapter, however, highlights the police and its tactical mistakes, police–community relations, corruption and racism, political interference within the police department and discrimination. Chapter four focuses on racism in the police department. Recent accusations of sexual harassment by the police have been a matter of concern for the government and the police as well. Misunderstanding between the government and the police department, the Leveson inquiry report about the corruption of police officers, and policing tactical mistakes have also been discussed in detail. Chapter five discusses major criminal gangs and their networks across the UK.

Chapter six highlights extremism and social stratification, and the roots of violent extremism in society that harm the political and economic stability of the country. Contradictory statements and thousands of complaints about the poor performance of the police department, racism and corruption, combined to undermine the credibility of the force. Chapter seven discusses how Britain's hospitals, health care providers and NHS kill innocent patients. Chapter eight investigates sectarian conflict in Northern Ireland and Scotland, which have marked out the boundaries of community through religious identities.

Chapter nine explores the roots of segregation between the Protestant and Catholic communities, and the future of communal violence. Chapter ten looks at the politics of Intelligence and surveillance mechanisms. Non-state actors and extremist groups have intensified their efforts to disrupt the national security infrastructure. The failure of the coalition government to train more cyber warriors and prepare to hold its own in the war against cyber terrorism is questioned. Chapter eleven discusses the intelligence war in cyberspace.

Chapter twelve highlights the politics of intelligence surveillance inside and outside Britain and the issue of the professionalization of intelligence cooperation in Afghanistan. In chapter thirteen, I conclude by exploring the risk of nuclear terrorism in the UK.

My main theme is to elucidate the weaknesses of the government and its wrong-headed approach to National Security. By these measures, the British state is failing. My aim is to help readers understand the causes behind the failure of Britain's surveillance society, the controversial intelligence mechanism, various tactical mistakes of the police, and the future of violent extremism. Finally, I am highly indebted of friends in the British Police Department, Councils and communities, who helped me in identifying the crisis of state and society in the United Kingdom. I would also like to thank my friends in media, and other institutions for their intellectual contribution. In the tail end, my publisher, Mr. Andrea and my editor Mr. Martine helped me in making my manuscript standardize and extremely useful.

Musa Khan Jalalzai
London, the United Kingdom, June, 2014.

CHAPTER 1. BRITAIN'S INCOHERENT APPROACH TO NATIONAL SECURITY

The term National Security encompasses within it, economic security, military security, and security of natural resources. Britain faces the threat of domestic and international terrorism, nuclear weapons proliferation, espionage, and vulnerability of the Critical National Infrastructure. To address all these issues, the country needs a coherent approach to National Security Mechanism. Researcher and security expert Peter Laton, in his paper on Australian security strategy, has described three concepts of National Security:

> A national security strategy document does not have to follow the grand strategy conceptual approach. For some nations in particular circumstances there may be more suitable organizing constructs to use. The conceptual approach a national security strategy takes however, greatly determines the nature and the utility of the document so this seemingly esoteric matter requires some thought. There are three broad conceptual approaches—grand strategy, opportunism, and risk management—that policymakers can potentially use when formulating national security strategies. . . The principal issue however, is the policy that animates these three distinct conceptual approaches.[1]

1 "An Australian National Security Strategy: Competing Conceptual

National Security is understood as the ability to counter foreign invasion and imposed threatening environment. Terrorists, according to historian Frank Furedi, become any foreign people you don't like. In general terms, National Security means the protection of state from all kinds of threats. In a seminar organized by two Indian universities in 2011, Professor Shrikant Paranjape told the audience:

> The concept of national security has assumed wider dimensions and has become very complicated. In many nations, ethnic nationalism has emerged and ethnic groups are demanding right to self-determination. These internal challenges have exposed the limitations of military-oriented traditional concept of national security.[1]

Experts understand that National Security mechanism should be addressed in a broad vision. Researcher Charlie Edward argues that creating a National Security Strategy is not an easy process, but says the creation of such a strategy is considered the first step in understanding a government respond to the threats.[2] Britain's Annual Reports of Intelligence and Security Committee for 2011–2012 also discuss the requirements of National Security in detail, but the country's threat level from international terrorism has also been specified in the Intelligence and Security Committee Annual Report for 2012–2013.[3] The report warned about the capabilities of al Qaeda and its allies to carry out attacks in Britain:

Approaches," Peter Layton, *Security Challenges, Vol. 8, No. 3, spring 2012.* http://www.securitychallenges.org.au/.

1 *Linguistic Genocide in Education—or Worldwide Diversity and Human Rights?* Tove Skutnabb-Kangas, Routledge, 01 Feb 2000, *Defining National Security: The Non-Military Aspects,* Joseph J. Romm, Council on Foreign Relations, 1993, and also, "The "Annual Report of Intelligence and Security Committee for 2011". Press statement of the Joint Committee on the National Security Strategy (2012). Also, "Top Five Threats to National Security in the Coming Decades," Sandra Erwin, Stew Magnuson, Dan Parsons and Yasmin Tadjdeh. *National Defense Magazine,* India. November 2012. Also, *Law Enforcement Intelligence,* Nov. 2004.

2 "The concept of national security has assumed wider dimensions and has become very complicated." Professor Shrikant Paranjape, Shivaji University, 12th and 13th October 2011. "Intelligence and Security Committee Parliament Annual Report 2012-2013".

3 "Annual Reports of Intelligence and Security Committee for 2011–2012".

> Al Qaeda's core has continued to operate despite significant pressure in the Federally Administered Area (FATA) of Pakistan. The threat from Al Qaeda has diversified: although all Al Qaeda affiliates retain significant intent, their capabilities an opportunistic [attack are] very. . . In North Africa, state weakness in the developing democracies of Tunisia, Libya and Egypt leave room for the development of extremist Islamic groups. The threat in Northern Ireland from dissident republican groups remains high, and we have seen numerous attacks on the police and other security personnel.[1]

In his recent report for Britain's most trusted think tank (Demos), Charlie Edward notes that the times has come for a truly seamless, cross-government approach to National Security. On 12 May 2010, the United Kingdom's National Security Council was formed as an essential vehicle to coordinate the country's National Security apparatus. The National Security Council is responsible for the collective development of National Security Strategy, and for the associated Strategic Defense and Security Review. A statement from the Prime Minister's Office confirmed the NSC establishment and said; the council would coordinate responses to threats faced by the United Kingdom and integrating at the highest level, the work of relevant government entities with respect to National Security. In 2011, government published Justice and Security Green Paper and stated that; the first priority of the coalition government is to safeguard National Security. The coalition declared that it would use all its national capabilities to build Britain's prosperity, extend nation's influence in the world and strengthen security.

The role of Intelligence and Security Committee is vital in overseeing the performance and budgetary process of our intelligence community. Under the Intelligence Services Act 1994, the Intelligence and Security Committee of Parliament (ISC) was also established to review the expenditures of MI5, MI6 and GCHQ. The Justice and Security Act 2013 made some amendment to the structure and powers of Intelligence and Security Committee. The act gave more powers to the committee. Moreover, the committee oversights the intelligence works of

---

1 Ibid.

the Cabinet Office, including the Joint Intelligence Committee (JIC); the Assessments Staff; and the National Security Secretariat. In the Defense Ministry, this committee also provides the oversights of Defense Intelligence, and the Office for Security and Counter-Terrorism in the Home Office.

Notwithstanding all these security measures, the British state is still in deep crisis; the crisis of social concordance, financial instability, government-community relations, poor investment climate, sectarianism and ethnic divides, all are interlinked. Britain is one of unitary states in which central government substantially direct all provincial governments and their activities. There are wide-ranging differences in the structure of services in centre and provinces. Each province has representation through an administrative department and a Secretary of State. Multiculturalism has also died while drug abuse and children trafficking exacerbated. In 2010, in a social reform debate, the Parliament highlighted major causes of the crisis of British state:

> Drug abuse, violent crime, teenage delinquency, family breakdown, welfare dependency, poor urban environments, educational failure, poverty, the loss of traditional values, teenage pregnancy, dysfunctional families, binge drinking, children who kill: all have been cited as proof that we have a broken society.[1]

Though, Britain understands that no foreign state poses threat to its security, but threats like failed states, organized crime, home-grown extremism, international terror networks and climate change are deeply existed with strong roots. After the 9/11 terror attacks, however, with a relatively short space of time, terror groups targeted Afghanistan, Iraq, Madrid, London, Saudi Arabia, Pakistan, Turkey, France, Germany, Nigeria, Somalia, Kenya, Yemen, Libya, Syria and Greece. These groups and other networks operate in Britain, collect funds and send young people for jihad to various states. Terror related incidents of 1980s, 1990s and 2000s, in which home-grown extremists were deeply involved, forced government to announce a multi-dimen-

---

1 "The problems of British society: Is Britain broken?" British Parliament http://www.parliament.uk/business/publications/research/ key-issues-for-the-new-parliament/social-reform/broken-britain/.

sional national security strategy in the country.[1]

Due to the changing security environment, and deteriorating law and order situation, successive governments tried to bring about constructive changes into the National Security Strategy of the country, but the threat of terrorism is there, and fight against extremists is still continue with full swing. Many studies in the United Kingdom have focused on the causes of radicalization and extremism, but have neither proposed a long-term solution nor adopted multicultural countering measures. On the issue of alienation, marginalization, fragmentation, and religious ferments, many scholars depended on hypotheses instead of real concept of prevention. While highlighting motivational factors, their analysis turn around Islam and Islamism, and much of the research on the issues of extremism and radicalization has often been policy-oriented and problem-driven.

If we look at the process of radicalization in Britain, we will find it more irksome. Alienation, poverty and wrong perception of religious way of life, have already caused violence and disruption. In Britain, news reports revealed recent attitude of local Christians towards Muslims, together with some violent incidents caused rage and alienation. The social concept of "us" and "them" or "we" and "you" and specifying Muslim as other, left a wide-ranging negative impacts on British society. When Britain's National Security Strategy was published in 2010, it faced criticism from various circles in national and international press. In his foreword in the National Security document, Prime Minister David Cameron suggested:

> In an age of uncertainty, we need to be able to act quickly and effectively to address new and evolving threats to our security. That means having access to the best possible advice, and crucially, the right people around the table when decisions are made. It means considering national security issues in the round, recognizing that when it comes to national security, foreign and domestic policy are not separate issues, but two halves of one picture. The first change was to make sure the government takes decisions properly. That is why we set up a national security council on the very first day of the new government, and appointed a Na-

1 *Daily Times*, 10 November 2011.

tional Security Adviser. National Security Council brings together key ministries and military and intelligence chiefs. It meets weekly and is driving a culture of change in Whitehall, placing a powerful structure right at the heart of government to make sure our limited resources are deployed to best effect. . . The National Security Council has overseen the development of the proper National Security Strategy, for the first time in this country's history.[1]

In 2011, with some amendments, it was re-published, but again it came under severe criticism in intellectual circles. In their criticism, experts raised some questions about the weak National Security approach of government and security agencies. However, in 2012, government published the updated and improved version of National Security Strategy, and claimed that the new version was much broader than the 2011 version. Joint Committee released a press statement in which the Chair of the Committee said:

> We welcome this year's annual report on the National Security Strategy and Strategic Defense and Security Review which is much broader and more wide-ranging than last year's report. However, we regret the fact that it is not as complete, transparent and strategic as it could be. We hope the government will take the opportunity in next year's report to focus more on the strategic aspect of events; for example this year's report ignores the strategic impact of the Euro-zone crisis.[2]

We have experienced the failure of terror laws many times as the threat level in the country always remained potential. The presence of British forces in Afghanistan also caused the wrath of Jihadist groups as they have often threatened the government on its terror related policies. On 2 May 2011, *Dawn* reported al Qaeda warning to Western world in Afghanistan:

---

1 "A Strong Britain in an Age of Uncertainty: The National Security Strategy", presented to Parliament by the Prime Minister, by Command of Her Majesty October 2010, and also *The Guardian*, London 8 May 2010.
2 "The Government's 2012 Annual Report" acknowledged that it seeks to respond to JCNSS. The British Parliament, Joint Select Committee, and Committee on National Security Strategy welcomed improvements to Government's annual report on the NSS and SDSR, 07 December 2012.

> The soldiers of Islam, whether in groups or individually, will not relent, despair, surrender, or weaken and will continue to plan until you are afflicted with a catastrophe that turns your children's hair grey prematurely.[1]

In the above mentioned changes in Counter-Terrorism Strategy, government placed considerable emphasis on eradicating the root causes of home-grown extremist networks, and their links with international terrorism. National Security Strategy "CONTEST-II" further concentrated on preventative measures. As we experienced no specific improvement in law and order situation in the past, how can the government win the trust of communities by introducing varieties of counter terrorism legislations?[2]

At present, Britain is confronted with National Security challenges due to its political and military involvement in Iraq, Afghanistan and the Arab Spring. The threat of terrorism and proliferation of weapons of mass destruction dominate security agenda. A Smith Institute research report (2007) highlighted the interdependency of threats:

> The threats emerged from the rapidly growing interdependence that is the defining feature of our world: an interdependence that is deepening through multiple channels of communication, trade, investment, migration and the impact of economic pressure on the supply of natural resources and climate stability.[3]

In a DEMOS report, it was revealed that the National Security structure is weak in its design, because, the report noted, government spends a lot of resources on fighting international terrorism. Security experts say; various government departments, infrastructure and the structure of the police and intelligence have undergone no specific changes in the past two decades. According to former Director General of Indian Intelligence agency (RAW), Maj. Gen VK Singh, in most democratic nations, intelligence agencies are under the executive control of an elected government, and are accountable to the legislature, which in most

---

1 *Dawn* 02 May 2011, and also, *Dawn*, *Daily Outlook* Afghanistan, 11 June 2012.
2 Ibid.
3 Dr Paul Cornish, 2007. Smith Institute research report.

cases; approve not only their funding, but their charter as well.

In his recent book, Major General VK Singh describes the check and balance system in intelligence infrastructure of a country: "Intelligence and security agencies exist in all nations. However, they suffer from peculiar diseases. After some time, they become so big that they after devour their creators. This phenomenon occurs more often in totalitarian regimes or military dictatorship than in democracies, when the other organ of the state — legislature and judiciary — and the fourth estate act as a check on the executive. Without this system of check and balance, there is a great danger of intelligence and security agencies becoming a law into them."

Intelligence has been defined in many ways. Some define it as the ability to learn about, learn from, understand and interact, but Michael Herman (2011) understands that intelligence is a classified knowledge that support its own state's information security by advising on and setting standard of defensive, protective security measures. In his recent book, he describes intelligence in these words: "Intelligence supply assessments of intelligence threat; engages in counter espionage; and seeks evidence of hostile countries' intelligence successes through counterintelligence penetrations of their organizations." Without reform, intelligence agencies become out of control, and involved in various private business.

The threat of terrorism or violent extremism has not been imported from abroad — it is Britain's own products generated from its indirect and direct involvement in South Asia and the Middle East. These foreign-policy-led involvements also cultivate the seeds of numerous violent security threats. Therefore, the police and law enforcement agencies have grown tired of tackling these ever-recurrent threats.[1]

Government introduced some reforms in the police department, which were not sufficient. The reforms came under criticism from all sides because there was a lack of concordance among the responsible institutions, the intelligence and law enforcement agencies at the local, provincial and national levels, on law enforce mechanisms, and ways of tackling terrorism

---

1 *Daily Times*, 8 Nov 2012.

and sectarian violence. Intelligence Surveillance, sky watch or the installation of over six millions spy cameras cannot serve the purpose. The problem needs a more constructive approach. Moreover, voluminous reports are prepared by the law enforcement agencies' research departments, and by private and government funded research institutions, to propose a professional approach to law enforcement across the country, but no one has set the government in the right direction.

The roots of violent extremism have spread in society, harming the political and economic stability of the country. The most violent terrorist threat currently comes from the groups who distort religion and attempt to justify their attacks on the shared values of this country. Contradictory statements and thousands of complaints against the weak response by the police department and its racist and corrupt practices call the credibility of the force into question. The issue of possible aerial bombs and E bomb attacks has been matter of great concern, and the risk of chemical terror attack is still real.[1]

In Northern Ireland and Scotland, sectarian conflict marked out the boundaries of community through religious identities. These sectarian identities are further exploited by political groups.[2] Recent intellectual and political debates raised some questions about the issue of sectarianism and domestic politics in these regions.[3]

Former Prime Minister Gordon Brown established his own concept of National Security. In 2008, his government designed and published a National Security Strategy to technically deal with the growing terror threat in the country, but failed. In a statement to the House of Common, Gordon Brown elucidated the main concept behind the announcement of National Security Strategy and said, "the nature of the threats and risks we face have in recent decades, changed beyond all recognition; therefore, as the new strategy makes clear, new threats demand new approaches."[4]

---

1 Ibid.
2 *The Telegraph*, 03 April 2012.
3 "Identities and Social Action. Connecting Communities for a Change", Community Development Foundation. Alison Gilchrist, September 2010.
4 *Daily Times*, 8 Nov 2012.

In a Green Paper, the coalition government admitted that Britain has been the victims of terrorism but those involved in plots were home-grown extremists. The coalition criticized the Labor government for its outdated state of multiculturalism. On the issue of greater integration of British society, the Green Paper revealed differences between Labor and the Conservative party.[1]

The present strategy of the Labor government was condemned by various quarters, and they warned that the threat to this country comes from those who use Islam for political purposes. *The Telegraph* reported opinions of both the government and opposition:

> In opposition, the leaders of two parties making up the coalition were vehemently critical of labor plans for a substantial extension of the state's surveillance powers. Yet now they flip-flopped, and are making precisely the same supportive arguments as their predecessors.[2]

In response to the government allegations, on 06 January 2011, *the Guardian* reported Labor Party leader and shadow Home Secretary, Ed Balls accused the government for playing party politics on Control Order. In a statement he regretted that Prime Minister and Deputy Prime Minister were trying to make political deal, on Control Order, which puts the political preservation of the coalition above the preservation of National Security.[3]

During the Blair years, Liberal Democrat leader Charles Kennedy opposed him on the Iraq war. Prime Minister David Cameron warned that the old approach to National Security is inadequate. On Afghanistan, Iraq, African turmoil and the Arab Spring, there were wide-ranging differences of opinions, while the Opposition time and again accused Deputy Prime Minister Mr. Clegg of playing politics on national security.[4]

When the government planned to introduce secret court proceedings to allow intelligence agencies' evidence to be con-

---

1 On 8 March 2012, *Herald of Scotland* reported Westminster's Joint Committee on the National Security Strategy criticized government's lack of understanding the security implications of the collapse of Euro-zone.
2 *Daily Telegraph* 03 April 2012.
3 *The Guardian*, 06 January 2011.
4 *Daily Telegraph*, 3 April 2012

sidered in civil cases, the Opposition expressed their political reservations and said that the Security Service will not be allowed to ride roughshod over the principle of open justice. A war of words on the publication of the Green Paper also intensified, while the Defense and Security policy came under attack for lacking strategic vision.[1]

In August 2011, the inquiry of the Defense Select Committee into the 2010 Strategic Defense and Security Review (SDSR) and the National Security Strategy (NSS) criticized the SDSR and refused to accept the views of the Prime Minister and other politicians.[2] There were some complaints in intellectual circles, that political parties do not consider the security implications of some issues properly. On 08 March 2012, Herald of Scotland reported Westminster's Joint Committee criticized government's lack of understanding the security implications of the collapsing of Euro-zone.[3] The UK intelligence community (GCHQ, JIC, JTAC, SIS, SS, DI and intelligence staff) was also in hot water due to the changing opinions and stances of government and opposition leaders on the issue of National Security.

The UK based think tank (Demos) in its comprehensive report warned that: "government is at risk of being overwhelmed by the growth and complexity of challenges including terrorism, home-grown unrest, global instability and international drug trade.....This is the result of an overly fragmented approach to security."[4]

The Joint Intelligence Committee on the National Security Strategy criticized the National Security Council failure to discuss the possible collapse of Euro-zone or the possibility of Scottish independence. The committee also criticized the government failure in providing sufficient information about secret National Security Risk Assessment. In his research report (2008), Mr. Kevin A. O'Brien warned:

---

1 *Daily Mail*, 03 April 2012
2 August 2011, the inquiry of Defense Select Committee into the 2010 Strategic Defense and Security Review (SDSR) and the National Security Strategy (NSS).
3 *Herald of Scotland* 08 March 2012
4 Britain needs a strategic vision for national security, "Demos Report", http://www.demos.co.uk/press_releases/britainneedsastrategic visionfornationalsecurityclaimsdemos.

> Perhaps the greatest—and, as yet, unseen—challenge facing the national security establishment in future will not come from outside, but from within: the involvement of generation-Y in the workplace.[1]

The Chatham House report on Cyber Security and the UK's Critical National Infrastructure warned about the weak national response mechanism and incoherent approach to national security issues:

> Yet there appear to be widespread dissatisfaction across the CNI with the quality and quantity of information-sharing between the public and private sectors. There is yet, however, little sense either of governmental vision and leadership, or of responsibility and engagement within the CNI that could encourage a well-informed and dynamic political debate on cyber security as a challenge.[2]

To tackle cyber terrorism effectively, coalition government needed to train more cyber warrior and enter the war against cyber terrorism with full confidence, but the difference of opinions between the opposition and government put the issue in procrastination. On 22 February 2012, *The Telegraph* news report warned about the possible nuclear attack and its consequences. The report quoted Common's Defense Committee report that warned:

> A nuclear device detonated up to 500 miles above the earth's surface could generate an electro-magnetic pulse (EMP) with "devastating" effects on power supplies, telecommunications and other vital systems."30 Chairman of the Defense Select Committee, James Arbuthot also warned and said: "I personally believe that this is quite likely to happen, because it is a comparatively easy way of using a small number of nuclear weapons to cause devastating damages.[3]

As information war intensified across Europe and Britain,

1 "The Changing Security and Intelligence Landscape in the 21st Century". Kevin A. O'Brien, October 2008. International Centre for the Study of Radicalization and Political Violence (ICSR)
2 "Cyber Security and the UK's Critical National Infrastructure", Paul Cornish, David Livingstone, Dave Clemente and Claire Yorke, a Chatham House Report, 2011.
3 *The Telegraph*, 22 February 2012.

the Chatham House report warned about the possibilities of future cyber attacks in the country:

> In addition to the pace of change it is also clear that cyber threats to public and private organizations are becoming increasingly significant. These threats are broad in scope, ranging from increases in the level of sophisticated malicious software (malware), to disruptive activity by online activist and nationalist group, to organized crime and sophisticated electronic espionage operations aimed at stealing valuable and/or strategically significant intellectual property.[1]

Non-state actors and home-grown extremist elements are creating security problems time and again while the government response to their challenging stance is very poor. Intelligence agencies need to introduce new scientific techniques in tackling these groups. In the words of prominent Indian scholar B Raman:

> As conventional threats to nation-states from non-state actors such as insurgents and terrorists. . . have increased, there has been realization that techniques and tradecraft, which served us fairly adequately against predictable state adversaries, may not be adequate against often unpredictable non-state actors, and that new analytical tools are required to meet the new threats.[2]

As non-state actors and extremist groups intensified their efforts in disrupting the national security infrastructure, and national critical infrastructure, the United Kingdom needed a competent leadership and clear sense of direction. In his Demos report, author Charlie Edwards argued, successive British governments rarely took a strategic approach to National Security. When the government fails to respond to the day-to-day increasing security threats, it proposes changes to the infrastructure of National Security Strategy.[3]

---

1 "Cyber Security and the UK's Critical National Infrastructure" (2011). This Chatham House report warned about the inadequate national response mechanism and incoherent approach to national security issues.
2 *Weekly Outlook India*, 24 January 2005.
3 Government 'lacks a clear and coherent view' of security risks to UK, Need for radical reform of national security architecture, argues new "Demos report".

Corruption in the police department and thousands complains against the misconduct of police officers, though, is not security issue, but it affect the departmental credibility of the force. The recent accusations of sexual harassment against the women police officers are matter of concern for the government and the police department as well. Misunderstanding between the government and the police department, the recent Leveson inquiry report, policing tactical mistakes and yellow journalism have already been too irksome for British citizens.

Counter terrorism efforts intensified in 2012 and 2013, while security agencies began checking the background of more than 500,000 people to prevent possible terror attack during the Olympic Games in London. Police and MI5 were struggling day and night to provide a peaceful environment to the participants, while head of MI5 briefed the whole cabinet about the threat of terrorism. The Home Secretary also updated the cabinet and colleagues about legislative efforts to address the issue of security during the Olympic Games.[1]

Both the Home office and MI5 created threatening environment by their thunderous warnings. On 19 September 2011, Home Secretary Teresa May admitted that Britain is facing terror threat from Northern Ireland and said; the country experienced 40 attacks in 2010 and 16 in June 2011. A leading thank Tank also warned about the growing threat to Olympics from "Lone Wolf" terrorists. In 23 February 2012, a London-hosted international conference on Somalia warned about the violent nature of misunderstood jihadist culture and attitude of Lone Wolves and extremist elements.[2]

A government Counter Terrorism report also warned that Somalia, Nigeria, Sudan and some Arab states represent a potential front for counter terrorism in Britain. The looming threat, according to the contents of the report, poses new challenges as extremist forces dispersed across Asia and Africa.[3] These unnec-

1 Chatham House report for 2011.
2 "On 19 September 2011, Home Secretary Teresa May admitted that Britain is facing terror threats from Northern Ireland and said the country experienced 40 attacks in 2010 and 16 in June 2011."
3 "The Impact of UK Counter-Terrorism. Legislation on Peace Processes and. Mediation with Armed Groups," Chatham House (2010), criticized the risk-based approach and the proposed sharp cuts to police

essary warnings of possible terror attacks prevented thousands of people from participating in or viewing the 2012 Olympics; more than one hundred thousand tickets remained unsold.

As Britain has already benefited from friendly relations with the United States, specifically, on the issue of the war on terror and shared wide-ranging domestic information on counter terror efforts with its security agencies, on 14 March 2012, Prime Minister David Cameron and President Obama reaffirmed their commitment to continue close bilateral cooperation on global counterterrorism.[1]

Britain approaches to Counter Terrorism are mostly based on intelligence-led policing. In the past, the arrest of 2,000 people under various Counter Terrorism laws created mistrust between law enforcement agencies and citizens. In Britain, various governments passed dozen counter terrorism laws from 2001 to 2012, which means struggle is underway to defeat the forces of enemy.[2]

During the last ten years, Britain increased Counter Terrorism expenditures up to 250 percent from £1 billion in 2001 to £3.5 billion in 2010. This huge amount shows that the fight against terrorism in the country entered a crucial phase. Since 2001, the structure of Counter Terrorism policing underwent no considerable changes, which resulted in a significant failure.[3]

Muslims in the UK have made little intellectual contribution as they come from poor states and are struggling to re-establish their lives in a new environment. Most of them are illiterate and sectarian minded. What is the social, political and intellectual contribution of Muslim communities in Britain and how can their efforts be effective in the fight against terrorism? Writer

officers through recent reforms, experts say political parties are trying to inject politics into decision making.

1 Ibid.

2 *Daily Outlook* Afghanistan, 11 June 2012. On 19 September 2011, Home Secretary Teresa May admitted that Britain is facing terror threat from Northern Ireland and said the country experienced 40 attacks in 2010 and 16 in June 2011. A leading thank Tank also warned about the growing threat to Olympics from "Lone Wolf" terrorists who have the ability to plant bombs.

3 In 23 February 2012, a London-hosted international conference on Somalia warned about the violent nature of misunderstood jihadist culture and attitude of Lone Wolves and extremist elements. *Daily Outlook* Afghanistan, 11 June 2012.

Yahya Birt bemoaned their meager contribution:

> The marked weakness of the intellectual contribution of British Muslims to subsidiary debates around multiculturalism, citizenship, foreign policy objectives, civil liberties and security issues has become a critical problem.... This shortfall will prove all the more telling as the national discussion oscillates between culturalist and chauvinist explanation from the right, namely that Islam itself is a problem, and the reflex of the left, that disaffection is explained by disadvantage.[1]

The August 2011, and other incidents raised public concern and endangered the social transformation process. Research institutions and newspapers published surveys and research articles seeking to identify the causes of unrest and the campaign of killing and burning. This general sense of insecurity tainted the atmosphere in the lead-up to the Olympics and Paralympics in 2012.

---

1 *Daily Outlook*, 11 June 2011.

CHAPTER 2. THE CRISIS OF STATE AND SECURITY

On 09 October 2013, Chief of the Security Services, MI5, Mr. Andrew Parker's statement enflamed public opinion against the Muslim community in Britain. Among other statements that raised eyebrows, he said, "...there are several thousand Islamist extremists here who see the British people as a legitimate target. Al Qaeda and its affiliates in Pakistan and Yemen present the most immediate threat to the UK."[1] Experts in government circles termed it "just a policy statement," but it is an irrevocable fact, that British law enforcement agencies either purposely antagonized Muslims or do not understand the basic philosophy of multiculturalism. The MI5 Chief issued this statement in the wake of Edward Snowden's revelations of surveillance excesses, but it is hard to guess how he hoped to encourage social harmony and minimize conflict this way. Mr. Parker pointed to a specific mentality which justifies the killings of non-Muslims in British society. Mr. Parker said; 330 people had been convicted in terror-related cases between 11 September 2001 and 31 March 2013.[2]

Mr. Parker's statement was clearly indicative of his deep frustration as his agency failed to understand the process of so-

1 BBC News, *The Guardian* and Euro News, 9 October 2013
2 *Daily Telegraph*, 9 October 2013.

cial transformation, multiculturalism, integration and the concept of "big society" in Britain. Communities in the country face many challenges. Alienation and lack of social interaction allow religious bigotry, extremism and racism to prosper. British intellectual circles said that the MI5 Chief wanted to outline a new policy through this statement to his organization, but his words raised serious questions about his approach to intelligence-community relations.

Mr. Parker warned terror outfits in Northern Ireland that his spy agency has them clearly in their sights. Perhaps he was impressed by the Green Book of the Pakistan Army, which warns terrorist groups of that country in the same manner, or he is in deep frustration, as the growing threat of domestic terrorism and extremism has intensified.[1]

In Iraq and Syria, Britain nationals continue to fight alongside their Arab al Qaeda friends. However, on 24 April 2013, Russian security experts warned that Britain is at risk from international extremist networks, specifically from North Caucasus who have been allowed to live in the UK.

On 18 October 2013, in a threatening video message, the Al Shabab terrorist group warned that British Muslims who criticized the murder of a British soldier in East London would face severe punishment.[2] These and other threats forced Prime Minister David Cameron to announce a new task force, TERFOR (Tackling Extremism and Radicalization Task Force). It is represented by Ministers, MI5 experts, Police Chiefs, and religious leaders. TERFOR helps communities in tackling extremism and radicalization. It seeks to stop extremists using schools and mosques to promote their transmogrified sectarian creeds, but the police are simply not sure how to tackle Asian, African and European criminal networks in the country.[3]

The British welfare state faces an evolving threat from domestic extremist forces. The killing of a British soldier in East London proved that extremist forces have established strong networks in society. The current threat of violent extremism is serious and sustained. Immigration now is seen as a threat since

---

1 Ibid.
2 *Sky News*, 19 October 2013.
3 *Huffington Post*, 26 May 2013.

members of terror-related groups from Asia and Africa continue to enter the country in large numbers.

In 2013, a terrorist attack in Kenya caused much soul-searching as British citizens were found involved in the killing of innocent civilians. A former Taliban member who used to recruit young people for jihad in Britain was jailed. Pakistani by origin, Munir Farooqi was at the center of the game.[1]

The Kenya's attack and the subsequent arrest of a dozen British nationals in Asian and African conflicts suggested that the country's intelligence agencies are unable to tackle domestic radicalization. Spending money without solving this problem reduces the funding available for Britain's cherished welfare state. Because, families and jobless people complain that government introduces new formulas for cutting benefits every four months.[2]

Child-related benefits for the jobless were capped in July 2013. "Unemployed people who then choose to have more than two children should know that welfare is not going to further fund their choices," Tory Chairman told journalists.[3] Moreover; housing benefits have been denied to unemployed citizens under the age of 25. On 1 April 2013, Gerry Hassan reported the consequences of benefit cuts and the looming crisis of Britain's welfare state in his article:

> The bedroom tax will affect 660,000 households across the UK, who will lose an average of £14 per week. In Scotland, according to Scottish government research, when house building is at a 51 years low, 105,000house-holds will be affected. Eight out of ten households which it impacts upon have a disabled adult; 16,000 families affected have a child; this when according to the recent Breadline Britain study, 29% of Scots live in poverty and cannot afford the basic essentials of life.[4]

Dennis Sewell wrote a detailed article that elucidated important aspects of the welfare state in the United Kingdom. He criticized the system created by the Minority Report of the Royal commission on the poor laws drafted by Sidney and Beatrice in the 20th century:

1 *The Telegraph*, 09 September 2011.
2 *Dawn* 23 September 2013.
3 *Daily Mail*, 15 July 2013.
4 *Open Democracy*, 01 April 2013, Gerry Hassan report.

> We live in a country where the poorest members of
> society are literally trapped. We pay them millions not
> to work, simply maintaining them at subsistence level
> like prisoners of the state. Tied up with bureaucratic
> regulations and subject to crazy marginal rates of tax,
> there are few chances to escape for Britain's welfare-
> dependent. A million of those out of work have been
> jobless for a decade or more. They see their chances of
> getting a job in the future as so remote as to be barely
> worth considering. The chances of their children ever
> finding work are beginning to look slim too. The neigh-
> borhoods in which they live are falling apart. The equa-
> tor is palpable; crime rampant, local schools are very
> often failing or 'sink' schools. If you think I am exag-
> gerating, choose any area with a high level of welfare-
> dependency and go and look for yourself.[1]

Homelessness is on the rise, and thousands of homeless
people have taken to crime. High rent, welfare cuts and unemployment, racism and discrimination and criminal culture have
ruined their lives. In Borough Councils Chief Executives and officers receive huge funds for allocating homes to the citizens, but
unfortunately, their corrupt culture has made the availability of
houses to poor tenants impossible. Drug addiction, prostitution and human trafficking have become a profitable business,
while the UK-based smugglers and marriage centers continue to
destroy the culture of peace by bringing thousands extremists,
criminals, gangsters and trained prostitutes into the country.

The welfare state is going to shrink and shatter as these
groups have developed networks of criminal trade and established containerized market economy. There are no more funds
to support it. Sean Healy and Brigid Reynolds warn: "If the welfare state cannot be funded in the future then it will not survive.
In fact, the political acceptability of any development in the welfare state is closely linked to economic sustainability."

As we know, the welfare state in Britain slowly developed
through some important legislative acts. The state invested
open-heartedly in people and institutions, but the result has not
been fruitful since its inception. Author Franz-Xaver Kaufmann
has compared the variations of welfare state as implemented

---

1 *Spectator Magazine*, 25 November 2009.

in Britain, France, Germany and Sweden, and highlighted the historical journey of welfare state in the United Kingdom. He analyzed the period from 1603 to the Industrial Revolution, and world war on page 70 of his research paper:

> The personal union of the English and Scottish kingdoms since 1603 led to the union of the two parliaments in 1707, and since then the "United Kingdom" has been called Great Britain. England as the dominant member of the union became a kingdom as early as the tenth century, and the island location subsequently favored a very gradual development, shaped by dynastic conflicts but on the whole forward moving, towards a constitutional monarchy. The break with the Roman Church under Henry VIII gave rise to a state church that strengthened the identity of the kingdom, but which also led to bitter confessional clashes with Catholics, on the one hand, and the Puritans, on the other. After the end of the confessional conflicts and the absolutist intermezzo connected to them, the appointment of William of Orange by the parliament in London and the Bill of Rights of 1689 created the domestic political foundation for England's rise to a world power. The industrialization of England, and the attendant sociopolitical conflicts, therefore, constitutes merely one—central—domestic political aspect of the history of the British Empire, which came to a rather sudden end after the Second World War. The discussion that follows touches only tangentially in these international contexts.[1]

Historian Frank Field (2011) argues that Sir William Beveridge had tried to introduce welfare system in Britain by establishing an enquiry report in 1941, to redesign an effective strategy, but his enquiry report was delayed due to some necessary changes. Mr. Frank's argument tells us about the difficulties Sir William Beveridge enquiry faced:

> An enquiry was established in 1941 to propose how best to tidy up state welfare. Beveridge seized the opportunity, rewrote the script, and then redesigned the contours of British welfare. The publication of his report was fortuitously delayed. When it was produced in November 1942, it followed hard on the heels of the al-

---

1 *The Future of the Welfare State*, Healy and Brigid, Social Justice, Ireland, 2010, also, *Daily Outlook Afghanistan*, 8 May 2012.

lies' first major victory of World War Two. Implementing Beveridge was immediately seen as part of winning
the peace. The prize was security from the cradle to the
grave. Although largely a synthesis of ideas (including
Beveridge's) which had been around for more time, it
was the blueprint for conquering Want, one of the five
giants Beveridge declared should be slain by way of post
war reconstruction. Each giant was countered by: The
1944 Butler Act which reformed schooling, the commitment to full employment in the same year. The Family
Allowance Act of 1945, the 1946 National Insurance
Act, the 1948 National Health Act, aimed at achieving
that very objective, and established for the first time a
national minimum.[1]

After World War II, law-making in Britain brought about
a centralized welfare system. Various social policy reports of
1880s, 1890s and 1990s revealed self-governing, local and phil-
anthropic provision that was attempting in many ways to help
reforms. Author Jose Harris, in his research paper analyzes the
structural transformation of welfare provision that occurred in
1870s and 1940s:

> The structural transformation of welfare provision
> that occurred in Britain between the 1870s and 1940s
> was therefore of central importance, not simply in the
> history of social policy, but in the wider history of poli-
> tics, government, social structure and national culture.
> How did it come about that Victorian social welfare
> provision-largely purveyed through face-to-face rela-
> tionship within the medium of civil society-evolved
> into the most 'rational' and bureaucratic of modern
> welfare state?. . . Beginning with the reforming liberal
> government in 1905 and the period up to 1942 saw the
> emergence of the first notion of welfare state. . . The
> structure of the welfare state as we know it today was
> designed during the war time period following the Bev-
> eridge report (1942) and the white paper on employ-
> ment policy (1944).[2]

From 1964 to 1979, Labor was in power for thirteen years.
During the Wilson period, the rate of poverty minimized while
in 1967, the devaluation crisis began. In 1980 and 1983, the at-

---

1 *The Welfare State: Never Ending Reform*, Frank Field, 2011-03.
2 "Past & Present," Jose Harris, *Oxford Journal, No. 135*, May, 1992.

titude of the government changed and denounced the ILO on labor clauses in public contracts. In 1999, reduction in the child poverty began. In an interview before the 2005 election Tony Blair differed David Beckham on social policy. In 2006, 2007, 2009, 2010 and 2012 some changes were brought about in the welfare system.[1]

Majority of historian understand that Sir William Beveridge report's recommendations are considered the main foundation of British welfare state. As an economist, he outlined the basic foundation of welfare state. Author John Brown tells us about the feature Sir William Beveridge efforts and the establishment of Brittan's welfare state:

> The nature of the British 'welfare State', established in the 1940s through the acceptance of the Beveridge report's recommendations and assumption, has long been the subject of inconclusive debates, even though knowledge of its history has increased an official papers have become open to access under the thirty years rule. What aims, interests and forces shaped its development before and after the Beveridge report's appearance, from the liberal innovations in social policy before 1914 to the collapse of full employment in the 1970s.[2]

In mid 1970s, welfare state in Britain remained in crisis due to the unemployment of one million people. In April 1975, in its budget debate, the Labor Government decided to abandon the goal of full employment. The crisis of welfare state was not unique to Britain, but was experienced, to varying degrees of intensity, in all western industrialized states. In 1974–75, the oil crisis and price hikes further exacerbated the recession. In Britain, the administration of the welfare state underwent two reform processes; one in the 1960s and 1970s, and the second in 1980s and 1990s. The aim of these reforms was to "control" expenditure and restructure civil service and the Administration of welfare.[3]

Secretary of State for Works and Pensions Iain Duncan Smith deplored this stalemate: "Whole communities in Britain

---

1 *The British Welfare State: A Critical History*. John Brown, Blackwell, 1995.
2 "The Welfare State –Never Ending Reform", Frank Field, *BBC*, 03, 10, 2011
3 *The British Welfare State: A Critical History*, John Brown, May 1995

exist at the margins of society, trapped in dependency and unable to progress. In these areas aspiration and social mobility disappeared."[1] Journalist Steven explains the expectations of citizens and the inability of the state to feed them:

> Many people still assume that, once the fallout from economic crisis has worked through, and the economy starts to grow again, things will get back to normal. Citizens' expectations continue to rise, even though the state's ability to deliver is diminishing.[2]

Some say that the state is on the wrong track, some say that happiness and a peaceful life remain mere dreams; and some warn about the shrinking welfare state — but the story is more frightening. More than ten million people need full time benefit support. Unemployment, crime, and low quality education have threatened the existence of welfare state. It is now 70 years since Sir William Beveridge published his enquiry report, but the question is, whether Britain can recapture the spirit of compassion expressed therein.[3] In 2012, Sam Bradley analyzed some heartbreaking issues in his article and mentioned some immediate problems:

> The atmosphere of solidarity and unity that accompanied the construction of the welfare state during the post war period has now given way to colder feeling of mistrust, and as one ex-government Minister put it recently, a 'demonization' of the poor. . . We need not to be the tired, resentful, divided society we have become. . . We can bridge the gap between the country we are and the country we would like to be. It would be easy to attack government mistakes of the past 15 years. The UK's problems stretch back well before 1979. For much longer governments have failed to keep pace with revolutionary changes that have transformed the nature of work and society.[4]

---

1 *Daily Outlook*, April, 2013. State of the nation report: poverty, unemployment, and welfare dependency in the UK, Forward by, Secretary of State for Works and Pensions Iain Duncan Smith.
2 Ibid.
3 Ibid.
4 *International Business Times*, Sam Bradley, 05 December 2012.

Like most states in the world, British state does not have a formal document enumerating the core values of governance. British Parliament, comprised of the House of Commons and the House of Lords, is the sole law-making body. To regulate relationships within the state and prevent abuses of power by the state, the law is used as an instrument. The courts have their own role in disputes between citizen and the state. The concept of accountability has gone by the boards. The state institutions pay little heed to the central government. For example, the Home Office, Scotland Yard and Local Councils are operating as if they were independent businesses. Councils often threaten tenants by suspending their benefits.

Law enforcement has become controversial issue since the promulgation of Stop and Search laws and Regulation of Investigatory Power Act-2000. In the history of British law enforcement, there have been several efforts to reform and reinvent both the state and its institutions, but unfortunately, government's reform agenda faced opposition from within. Political intervention in the police department has created controversies. Upon the appointment of Mr. Winsor in the police department, 30,000 police officers moved out into the streets of London. They demanded a police force free of political interference. A cold war between the police department and Home Office started, and still continues to criticize each other. Meanwhile, the Border Agency ignored Whitehall.[1]

In 2009, the government proposed some reforms in the intelligence infrastructure, because security agencies had not been remodeled since 1949 and 1989. The aim of the proposals was to strengthen the function of the cabinet office as it works with all intelligence agencies. The Intelligence and Security Committee in its annual report for 2011-2012, stressed the need for protecting the state intelligence infrastructure. In October 2011, the Government published a Justice and Security Green Paper which outlines the proposals of reforms concerning the handling of sensitive materials in civil proceedings.

The Commissioner of Interception Communications in his annual report for 2011 emphasized the prevention and detection of serious crimes.[2]

---

1 *Daily Times*, 30 September, 2012
2 "Lords Hansard text for 17 January 2013", The UK Parliament.

As I noted in my previous papers, the power of the establishment in Britain is based on four elements: the banks, parliament, the press and the police, all of which have had their bouts of misuse of power in the past. Phone-hacking scandals and corruption, racism and tactical mistakes in the police force, led to the resignation of senior officers from their posts. The war of words had intensified between the police department and Prime Minister Office as; the Prime Minister was not satisfied with the performance of various police forces during the 2011 riots.

This crisis badly affected the performance of state institutions. Politicization of law enforcement further caused trouble. The Shadow Home Secretary warned that the police department faces a perfect storm of cuts in staff and chaotic reforms: "I am worried in particular about the risk of a growing gap between public concerns about the need for police action but also the capacity of the police to deliver.[1]

Border control mechanisms failed and came under severe criticism. As stated above, more than 140,000 illegal immigrants have disappeared along with their records. In a debate in the House of Lords, Lord Marlesford criticized the UKBA and in July 19, 2012, the UKBA was also criticized by Lord Avebury, who said, "The UK Border Agency is in meltdown and it is a situation that is steadily getting worse, as illustrated by the increasing number of successful appeals against their decisions on applications for leave to enter or remain in the UK."[2]

On 03 July 2013, the UK Chief Inspector of Immigration, John Vine, in his final report revealed the fact that UKBA continued to ignore important data of asylum seekers. In November 2012, in his first report, Mr. Vine revealed that UKBA hadn't even touched more than 450,000 asylum cases. The UK Border Agency failed to deal with the backlog and has been frequently criticized by the House of Commons Home Affairs Select Committee, for its inefficiency. In 2013, there were still 310,000 cases pending.

The threat of extremism and terrorism is not a new phenom-

---

1 *Daily Times*, 21 September, 2012
2 *Daily Times*, 17 July 2012.

enon. Britain repeatedly experienced terror attacks during the last several decades. Apart from Northern Ireland-based sectarian groups, radicalized Muslim groups are using a distorted version of the Islamic faith to justify their own style of violence. The threat of North African terrorism is not new either. Britain-based Somali, Sudanese and Algerian groups are sending their members to Africa for jihad. Every year,

The virus of sectarianism and racism is rapidly spreading in many state institutions. The police department is at the center of numerous deficiencies and controversies. Britain needs new reforms and a new scale of distance measure. The way in which law enforcement and security agencies tackle national security and law and order management, with a huge budget and sophisticated modern intelligence and surveillance technology, is now unaffordable as the country's economic and financial blood pressure is going out of control. These are major factors exacerbating in violence and crisis of the state.

Security, stability and a peaceful environment are fundamental goals of all states. To achieve these goals, a competent and professional intelligence system is vital. Intelligence analysis, collection and the process of information helps law enforcement agencies in protecting national security, but in Britain, the way intelligence is collected has become a joke.[1] Mistrust between government, communities and the police; controversies regarding the basic function of police; and the day-to-day changes in strategies at the Home Office, prove that some political circles are trying to influence the present security infrastructure.

The establishment of powerful criminal gangs of European communities is another challenging problem. From the Home Office to the Metropolitan police, organized crime agencies and intelligence-led policing, every law-enforcing agency has its own agenda and separate programs. Unfortunately, no proper coordination and exchange of information exists. This culture of policing without intelligence may create more problems in near future.[2]

Drug trafficking in the United Kingdom supports black market, and creates criminal culture and law and order issues. According to the National Crime Agency statistical report:

The use of illegal drugs, particularly Class A, im-

1 *Daily Times*, 19 September 2012.
2 Ibid.

pacts the social and economic well being of the country including its reputation overseas. The Government's organized crime strategy sets out that drug trafficking to the UK costs an estimated £10.7 billion per year. Drug smuggling by organized criminals is a major threat. Class A drugs, specifically heroin, cocaine, crack cocaine and ecstasy, are widely available throughout the UK. . . .The UK illegal drugs market remains extremely attractive to organized criminals. The prices charged at street level are some of the highest in Europe, and are sufficient to repay the costs of smuggling the drugs into the UK.[1]

The use of other drugs in colleges and schools is also matter of great concern. The NCA report noted that at present, more than 270 tones Cannabis is required to meet the user demand: "Cannabis is still the most widely used illegal drug in the UK and the UK wholesale cannabis market is worth almost GBP 1 billion a year. SOCA estimates that 270 tones of cannabis are needed to satisfy annual UK user demand. Most of this is herbal skunk cannabis. Despite increasing domestic cultivation most cannabis in the UK is still imported via all modes of transport.

In Afghanistan, and at the London School of Economics and Political Science (LSE), experts criticized the United Nation (UN)'s anti-drug policy, asking the international community to undertake effective strategies in combating drug production and trafficking. In a recent report, a five-member team of Noble Prize winners—including the British Prime Minister and the former US Secretary of State, pointed out the severe consequences of global drug smuggling, especially in Afghanistan. The report noted: "International anti-drug strategy through military option and pressures has left negative consequences and unexpected losses," the report concluded. The report points out that 90 percent of the drugs in the world are produced in Afghanistan. The country has also won the title of the world's largest producer of opium 15 times.

The British law enforcement agencies perform different roles in different fields. Intelligence agencies help enforcement of law

---

1 "National Crime Agency's statistical report" on the use of drugs in Britain. The Government's organized crime strategy sets out that drug trafficking to the UK costs an estimated £10.7 billion per year.

in many ways, but war in Afghanistan and the Middle East diverted their attention from countering domestic terrorism to international terrorism. The collective failure of the UK police to provide an appropriate and professional service to the communities, and to serve citizens because of their color, culture or ethnic origin, has become a hot debate in the national press.

The Home Office showed commitment to the Macpherson inquiry for the implementation of an inspection report on police–community and race relations, which clearly warn that the police cannot achieve success without the support of communities, but the Home Office, did not fulfill its commitment nor did any positive change in the police attitude towards communities, occur.

The Home Office, Policing-Improvement Agency and Independent Police Complaints Commission receive thousands of complaints from the public against the police misconduct, but one sees no improvement in the attitude of the force. Police stop and frisk thousands of people in the streets, but no major criminal has so far been arrested. The 'moral crisis' at the heart of policing is now so acute that it ought to be a matter of great concern.

The employment of illegal immigrants within the police department, as civilian staff member, who perform many functions to assist the police, has created new controversies. It seems that the virus of corruption has also penetrated the police rank and file. In Northern Ireland, the police service is being supervised by policing on board and in Scotland each police force is overseen by a local authority, but all these efforts to make the police departments work smarter have failed. Meanwhile, prejudice and discrimination on the basis of religion and race are rapidly spreading in the department.

To intercept corruption and the infiltration of incompetent people into the department, it was reported that on November 15, 2012, Wales and England police had to manage elections in all their sections. Policing experts warned that this would be considered the biggest shake-up since the establishment of the force. Some government circles viewed these changes as the empowerment of local communities to decide policing priorities.

The Home Secretary hinted at police reforms to reconnect

the police and communities. A National Crime Agency was also established in 2013. The spending review of the present government declared 20 percent cuts, which according to the Association of the Chief Police Officers (ACPO), will lead to 28,000 jobs being slashed during the last 4 years.[1]

Experts say the Cabinet Committee dealing with major crises such as terrorism or natural disasters should be replaced with a new National Security Operation Centre. Another suggestion concerns the degree of transparency in the health sector, and in the intelligence infrastructure. Accountability must be maintained and there must be some changes in the health and security Acts, to streamline the activities of state institutions.47

In the Security sector, reforms also face tough resistance. Security sector reforms are not only about the integration of relevant security branches, but increasing the capacity and effectiveness of security in a democratic government.[2]

The story of Britain's security sector reforms is very disturbing and complicated. The game of police reforms and budget cuts, and opposition from the police department entered a crucial stage. Politicians, police officers and the administrative machinery are engaged in an ongoing contest. Politicians want their own piece of the pie while the opposition sternly resists it. Political appointments caused friction between the opposition and government. Sectarian affiliation in the police department is another challenging problem. In Northern Ireland and Scotland, sectarianism has divided communities. Each police officer is loyal to the state and to his own religious group as well. Corruption is another serious issue. An Independent Police Complaints Commission report states:

> Corruption has always been an issue for policing. In the UK, the development of modern police has been punctuated by high profile scandals involving malpractice and misconduct.[3]

1 *Daily Times*, 08 November 2012
2 *Security Sector Reform and Democracy in Transitional Societies*, Hans Born/Marina Caparini/Philipp Fluri, Geneva Centre for the Democratic Control of Armed Forces. Proceedings of the Democratic Control of Armed Forces Workshops at the 4th International Security Forum, Geneva, November 15–17, 2000.
3 "Independent Police Complaints Commission Report", Corruption in

The Leveson inquiry reports exposed the prevailing culture of corruption within the police department and newspaper industry. On July 13, 2011, Prime Minister announced a two-part inquiry investigating the role of the press and police in the phone-hacking scandal.[1]

The administrative ruction between the UK border agency and home office over the failure of border controls further created misunderstandings, about the operational capabilities of the agency. The UK border agency Chief Brodie Clark's reputation was smeared by some media reports, when he failed to deliver professionally. His agency lost more than 140,000 files of immigrants, which caused deep concern in the government circles. From rendition, phone hacking scandals, to the weak security approach of intelligence agencies, all issues needed considerable attention, but politicians and bureaucracy kept silent.

Members of parliament, experts and elements within the government circles demand more collaboration between forces, to play their role more effectively. The government's planned to recruit thousands of part-time volunteer police, and at the same time its desire to cut 20 percent of the police force further caused controversies. The Home Secretary also outlined plans for a reserve police force to bolster the UK's 141,000 frontline police officers. In June 2012, the Home Secretary faced strong opposition from the police department on the proposed appointment of Mr. Winsor. Mr. Winsor proposed cutting bonuses and introducing compulsory fitness tests in his wide-ranging review of policing.

Some police officers started to resign over this decision. Political parties and policing experts also demanded reforms in COBRA, according to the BOW Group recent report. The coalition government attempted to change the status quo of COBRA, but the issue is still on the agenda. Dr James, the author of the report says that the ad hoc nature of COBRA should be replaced with a new National Security Centre designed for crisis management. On the issue of reforms in the intelligence networks,

the police service in England and Wales: Second report – a report based on the IPCC's experience from 2008 to 2011.
1 Leveson Enquiry: *Culture Practice and Ethics of the Press.* http://webarchive.nationalarchives.gov.uk/20140122145147/http:/www.levesoninquiry.org.uk/.

several politicians expressed reservations.

Security sector reforms in Britain need to be accountable for the overall security context, and address fundamentals and specifics as well. The core security actors that play a vital role in maintaining security and enforce the law include the army, police, intelligence infrastructure, private security agencies, border agency, border force, internal and external security agencies and New Scotland Yard. The Office for Security and Counter-Terrorism, Crime and Policing Group, the Government Equality Office, the UK Border Agency, Identity and Passport Service, Criminal Records Bureau, Border Force and several other competent agencies are playing a vital role in protecting national security and national critical infrastructure.

CHAPTER 3. METROPOLITAN POLICE: FIXING THE WINDOW

In the United Kingdom, the organizational structure of policing is excellent, and the mission of the UK police has become broader and complex. In England, Wales and Northern Ireland, there are 44 geographic forces, each led by a Chief Constable, who under statute controls the force. Every Chief Constable is accountable to law and to Home Secretary. In British Model Policing, police officers are citizens in uniform. The basic duty of the police is to prevent crime and disorder. There are two approached to reduce crime and make the police more effective: intelligence-led policing and problem oriented policing. In Britain, eliminating and detecting crime and preserving public peace have been the most important role of police force since its inception. In a speech to the Police Superintendent Association, Home Secretary Theresa May said: "The mission of the police is to cut crime, no more and no less. Cutting crime isn't just about the number of arrests which are made, the number of incidents responded to or the number of successful prosecution."[1]

In police laws, every member of the police department is a constable, whatever his actual rank is, which means that officers

---

1 *Policing in the UK*: Report and a Brief Guide, PP-2, http://www.acpo. police.uk/documents/reports/2012/201210PolicingintheUKFinal.

and constables are equally authorized to make arrests.[1] Police has the authority to held suspects for twenty-four hours in the police station.[2] According to the Police Act 1996, section (30): "a member of a police force shall have all the powers and privileges of a constable throughout England and Wales and the adjacent United Kingdom waters."[3] For criminal investigations, the presence of CID is vital in every police station.[4]

The Scotland Yard Police Act of 1967 specifies the jurisdiction of the police — the force is responsible to the Secretary of State.[5] In the immigration field, the UK Border Agency has been an active police force since its inception. The force had been divided into five unified operations: border, international, immigration, intelligence and detention. Each operation was conducted by a director. The UKBA was eliminated in 2013, due to its inability to control the borders of the country.[6]

Historically speaking, British police force has undergone several administrative changes and reforms. The Bow Street Runners were London's first professional police which was established by Henry Fielding in 1749. Between 1754 and 1780, Sir John Fielding reorganized Bow Street like police station, with a team of efficient and paid constables. The River Police Force was to combat rising crime on the Thames.[7] Watchmen and other local forces helped in maintaining stability. Before the Metropolitan Police Act was passed, responsibilities for law enforcement were on the shoulders of unpaid constables.[8] In 1739, Sir Thomas de Veil established Bow Street as a courtroom. In 1798, the Marine Police Force was established. In this force, there were 220 constables and 1,000 volunteers, who assisted constables in arresting criminals. Within one year, they arrested two thousands

---

1 content.met.police.uk, the Metropolitan Police website: Mayor's Office for Policing and Crime. 2013.
2 Ibid.
3 Police Act 1996, section, 30.
4 Police Information.co.uk, and also, *The Police Use of Firearms since 1945.* Mike Waldren, 2007.
5 "Metropolitan Police Service 2009".
6 Cabinet Office, 2009, "Report about the function of UKBA by Parliamentary Ombudsman" February 2010.
7 Ibid.
8 *The Official History of Metropolitan Police,* Gary Mason, 2004, Carlton Books Ltd.

criminals. In 1839, the Marine force was amalgamated with the Metropolitan Police to form the Thames Police Division.[1]

In 1829, the Metropolitan police started patrolling the London streets.[2] In the initial stages it was consisted of two commissioners, 8 superintendents, 20 inspectors, 88 sergeants, and 895 constables. From 1829 to 1930, 17 Police Stations Local Divisions were also established (Tottenham, Mayfair, Marylebone, Chelsea, Holborn, Kensington, Kings Cross, Islington, Peckham, Greenwich, Westminster, Hampstead, Hammersmith, Wandsworth, West ham, Bethnal Green, Willesden).[3]

In 1835, the Municipal Act required all Boroughs to establish a regular paid police, and in 1839, Rural Constabulary Act allowed more police forces to be established by counties. In 1839, first county police force was established in Wiltshire. In 1840, the County Police Act was passed, and in 1856, Police Act of County and Borough made compulsory the police force in England and Wales. In 1857, General Police Act required each Scottish county to establish a police body. In 1860, In England and Wales, there were more than 200 police forces. In 1878, the Metropolitan Police Department was reorganized, and renamed as the Criminal Investigation Department (CID).[4]

The police force became more important since the Metropolitan Police Act of 1829 was passed by Home Secretary Sir Robert Peel. With the implementation of this act, the British police force came into existence. Due to the developing situation in and outside the country, in 1890, the size of the Metropolitan Police was increased from 1,000 to 13,000 officers. In 1907 and 1940, New Scotland Yard was extended further.[5] In 1914; Special Constable Act allowed the appointment of Special Constable in wartime. In the 19th century, an efficient police force was patrol-

---

1 *History of Policing,* Emsely, C. 2011, Ashgate. London.
2 *Metropolitan Police Service*—Marin Police Unit. www.met.police.uk.
3 *The Branch: History of Metropolitan Police Special Branch.* Rupert Allison, 1983, London.
4 City of London Police, 18 November 2013, http://www.cityoflondon. police.uk/about-us/history/Pages/British-Police-history.aspx.
5 *The New York Times,* May 15, 1964. According to Simon Basketter; Special Branch: Spying on Activists since 1883. *Daily Mail* also reported the secret activities of Special Branch. 2 July 2013. www.http://social-istworker.co.uk/art/33765/Special+Branch%3A+spying+on+activists+s ince+1883

ling Newcastle. The force was receiving guidance from mayor and council. In Liverpool, watchmen and other forces were policing people in cities and towns. In all police stations, detective officers are inducted. All these officers are responsible to the Detective Chief Inspector.[1]

As far as the modern British police role in law and order is concerned, I will also discuss the role of the police, its administrative structure and the deteriorating law and order in this chapter. There are different types of police forces and private security agencies in the UK, but majority work of the policing is being carried out by the territorial police force. The police acts 1996, 1967 and 2000, highlight the jurisdiction and responsibilities of the police.[2]

At present, more than one hundred forty five thousands police force in partnership with private security agencies and their intelligence infrastructure is in full operation in the country. Notwithstanding, operations of Immigration Enforcement, New Scotland Yard Police, Her Majesty's Inspectorate of Constabulary, Criminal Investigation Department, Metropolitan Police, Diplomatic Protection Group, National Crime Force and Home Office law and order strategies, no specific improvement in law and order in the country is seen. Criminal gangs are getting strong by the day, and the network of criminal market economy has expanded.[3]

In 2004, the police Superintendents Association submitted proposals to the Home Secretary, which envisaged a three-tier system based on two hundred seventy local police divisions and ten regional controllers, with regional police units for public order and major investigations, and presumably the national units and agencies like Serious Organized Crime Agency.[4] As a result of these developments, Home Office function was confined to countering terrorism by the Prime Minister in 2007. According to the Prime Minister announcement, Home Office tackles

---

1 *Scotland Yard's Casebook: Making of the CID, 1865–1993.* Joan Lock, 1993.
2 *Police Accountability in the United Kingdom.* Dr Rob Mawby and Dr Alan Wright. 2005.
3 "Policing in the UK: A Brief Guide".
4 *The UK's Domestic Response to Global Terrorism: Strategy Structure and Implementation with Special Reference to the Role of the Police,* Frank Gregory, WP 27, 2007, The Elcano Royal Institute.

immigration and policing as well. Police experts designed comprehensive strategy, intercepting Muslim communities from becoming violent extremists.[1]

The Association of Police Officers said; this strategy could help schools in intercepting radical ideas of extremist groups. After the London bombing in 2005 and 2007, consultations started related to the future response to terrorism across the country. The extended detention was proposed by the Senior Police Officers up to ninety days, to collect evidence properly.[2] The issue of stop and search, according to the section 44 of the terrorism laws 2000, become more complicated.[3]

Home Office figures breakdown by ethnic origin category show, that from 2001–2004; those stopped and arrested under anti terror laws of 2000 were majority of Asian origin. A Home Office report issued in Nov 26, 2009, discussed the police power under the terrorism act 2000, and gave details of stops and search outcomes in 2008 and 2009.[4]

That report, has full details of law and order situation in the country. The report brings together, complete statistical materials from police and other agencies. As per the recently published reports, in 2008 and 2009, police arrested more than one hundred ninety terror suspects, compared with two hundred thirty one in 2007. The police in the UK arrested 2,000 terror suspects from across the country since 2001. Among the 190 terror suspects arrested in 2009, 123 were arrested under section 41 of the terror laws 2000.[5]

Charges for terror arrest, the report noted, were not limited to offences under terror legislation; many offences were dealing

1 "The United Kingdom's Strategy for Countering Terrorism", March 2009, *The Independent* 16 April 2012. House of Commons Home Affairs Select Committee report, 5 July 2013. *The Guardian*, Dec 2011 and the cross-government report, published on 01 November 2011. House of Commons Home Affairs Select Committee, House of Commons Home Affairs Committee: Roots of Violent Radicalization, 19th Report of Session 2010–12, Volume 1.

2 Ibid.

3 *The Guardian* 8 July 2010.

4 A Home Office report issued in 26 November, 2009, discusses the police power under the terrorism act 2000, and gives details of stops and search outcomes in 2008 and 2009.

5 Ibid.

with under other legislation, e.g. conspiracy to murder, are not covered in terrorism legislation. The 2000 Act of terrorism provides with the police force an opportunity to exercise the power of search and stop. According to the report details, under this law, some 256,026 people were stopped and arrested in 2008 and 2009. This action of the police, as we have already mentioned earlier, created misunderstanding between the police and communities.[1]

Under section 43 of the Terrorism Act 2000: "The Terrorism Act also gives powers for individual officers to stop and search a suspect whom he/she reasonably suspects of being involved in terrorism activity." Information collected from the Metropolitan Police Service website shows that in 2008 and 2009, 1,643 persons were stopped and searched under this law.[2] The police stop and search program created more trouble for Asian and European citizens. People complained against the behavior of the police in trains, buses and roads. Some were humiliated, searched inhumanly and asked irrelevant questions.[3] On the issue of good policing and local support, the *Guardian* newspaper reported:

> The claim that policing has become dangerously over centralized is now a political commonplace. But it is not just a slogan. Good policing depends on local support, on the willingness of individual citizens to come forward as witness or to support dubious activity.[4]

The police authority needs to gain its mandate by consulting local people about the policing-community issues, seeking their views on matters such as the level of the policing, divisional and force policing plans and their experience of day-to-day policing. In Britain, there are different police forces, agencies and private security agencies, which play very important role in safeguarding the state and its institutions. In spite all these forces and their struggle in tackling violent crimes and extremism in the country, criminal gang's networks are still very strong and con-

---

1 "The United Kingdom's Strategy for Countering Terrorism", March 2009.
2 Section 43 of the Terrorism Act 2000.
3 Ibid.
4 *The Guardian*, 02 September 2009.

tinue to harass communities.[1]

The Secretive Police Force in the UK has been enrolled and promoted by the Association of Chief Police Officers (ACPO) is, at present, in the field, and mostly tackling extremism. Another unit of the police is National Extremism Tactical Coordination Unit (NETCO) that works under the command of the ACPO.[2] People working in the NETCO and WECTU have been inducted from the police department. The basic job of these forces is policing. NETCO, experts believe is a private body, but receive financial support from the government.[3]

NETCO and WECTU need the cooperation of other private security agencies, but unregulated and poor management of these security agencies, expert say, can create more trouble for law enforcement agencies. Generally, private security agencies provide security to the people and help the police in eradicating crime.[4]

Newspapers in the UK published interesting stories about these security agencies. According to *The Guardian* report, they tackle terror incidents even in educational institutions. In October 2006, Special Branch that worked closely with MI5 in the past was merged with Anti Terrorism Branch and restructured to form a new command of counter terrorism in the country. To expedite the war on domestic terrorism and extremism, another security unit, titles National Public Order Intelligence Unit (NPOIU) was set up by ACPO in 1999.[5]

In February 2009, newspapers reported ACPO changing the role of NPOIU and extending its mandate on tackling domestic extremist threat in the country. According to the *Daily Mail* report, the confidential intelligence can operate across the country

1"Home Office report for 2000, Consultation & Engagement Strategy for 2012–2016. Police and Crime commissioner for Cleveland". UK. http://www.cleveland.pcc.police.uk/Document-Library/Consultation/Consultation-Strategy-PCC-and-Force.

2 *The Telegraph*, 20 October 2001 and *The Guardian* 15 February 2009.

3 "The United Kingdom's Strategy for Countering Terrorism", March 2009.

4 *Organized Criminals Won't Fade Away*, Vanda Felbab Brown, August 2012. Brooking Institute USA.

5 *"Globalization"*, Rita Abrahamsen and Michael C William. January 2005. BBC News, 3 March 2012. *The Times*, 9 May 2012. Police Foundation, report 2009.

because within the NPOIU, a new unit of intelligence was set up. At present, multinational corporations and private sector are the strategic partners of the government and, for the police training, protection of important installations, the destruction of ammunition stockpiles and the removal of small arms, more private sector companies have been hired.[1]

However, it means the nature of security environment has changed ultimately. According to the DEMOs research paper, at home, the responsibility of private sector regarding national security has grown since privatization began in 1980s. As we are living in the twenty first century, this century offers a radically different political landscape for debating national security. Security experts say government and the police have come under an ultimate influence of multinational security agencies.

The recent debates on trust deficit between the UK police and communities, the police way of conducting operations, racism, discrimination and search and stop under the Counter Terrorism Act 2000, raised many questions.[2] Communities complain about the inactive presence and invisible participation of police in streets and towns, and, demand that delivering policing—whether in form of force or service should not be based on discrimination.[3]

The day-to-day increasing distrust between communities and the police is a matter of great concern, not only for the government in power but for the Home Office and policing improvement agency as well. The image of the London police has been tarnished by their performance during recent riots, as well.[4]

In 2011, riots tested the credibility of Metropolitan Police across the country, as they badly failed in protecting public properties. It was not the first time, in 1919, riots hit Britain society, and there were race-related riots in South Shields, Glasgow, London's East End, Liverpool, Cardiff, Barry, and Newport. In 1930, immigrants started protests in East London and in Notting Hill in 1950s. In 1980, in Black minority communities, racism,

---

1 Ibid.
2 *Daily Outlook* Afghanistan, 27 October 2011.
3 Ibid.
4 Ibid

discrimination and poverty sparked a series of riots.[1]

In these incidents, the police came off looking quite unprofessional. In 1981, 1982 and 1985, there were riots in various cities and towns. In 2004, more than 87,000 minority residents told newspapers they had been victims of racially motivated crime. The Race Relations Act 1965 outlawed public discrimination. Acts in 1968 and 1976 also outlawed discrimination in employment. In 2001, there were racial riots in both Bradford and Oldham in 2005. In 2008, the London Children Bureau released a 366-page report in which they recognized racist behavior in young children.[2]

Hassan Ali (2003) painted another image of Britain police in these words:

"Top police and the government have been at pains to argue that racism in the police is merely a reflection of wider society. This is nonsense. It is clear from the program that the 'canteen culture' of bigotry in the police is at a level way above most of British society — only matched by that in other authoritarian jobs such as the armed services and prison officers."[3]

Among all Asian and Africans ethnic groups, majority of their members have reservations about the behavior of the police force. They are in hesitation whether to report crime to the police or not, as they understand that police has shown no specific interest, in resolving their issues in the past. They are now thinking on ethnic line and complain that police is only for the white people. For example, they complain that in many occasions, the police favored whites instead of tackling an incident impartially. Home Office is trying to establish the fact that citizens' involvement in policing has become a central element in its reform agenda, but the story here is different.[4]

---

1 *Notes on the Management of Spoiled Identity.* Goffman Erving. Simon and Schuster, New York, 1986.

2 *Daily Mail,* 7 July 2008.

3 Hassan Ali in his article painted a racist image of Britain police in these words: "Top police and the government have been at pains to argue that racism in the police is merely a reflection of wider society." *Socialist Review* 2003

4 *Economist,* 28 October 2006. "The Forgotten Underclass." 28 October. "Racial Equality", August 2009, http://www.sagepub.com/upm-data/.

Citizens and the police department are thinking adversely. A report (2010) found that fifty percent of Muslims across the UK believed that racism had spread to all sections of society in the past several years. Pakistani, Indian, Afghani, Bangladeshi, Somali, Sudanese and other black and white colors feel, they are loyal British citizens, but police and other government departments treat them in a racial way. They complain that police often targets ethnic minorities with a specific behavior which later on, causes deep mistrust between communities and the police.[1]

The above mentioned trust deficit between the police and community are considered to be a bigger challenge for Home Office, Policing Improvement Agency, the National City Community and Police Relations Commission. These trust deficits cannot be understood unless the constraints on both sides are thoroughly explored.[2]

Researcher Marshall Carter supports my perception of police-community relations: "What the police and community think and feel about each other reflect their own past experience and the images transmitted through friends, education, the media and popular stereotypes." One another aspect of citizens complaints is that police has often responds to unrests in a non-professional way which is not acceptable in any way.[3]

In response to all complaints of minority communities, government also complains that minority groups never thought to mix their colors within British society, and regret that multiculturalism has made no specific progress. They stress the need that all communities are to be encouraged to mix. Institute of Applied Social Studies in Birmingham University recently completed a research paper which suggested the establishment of good relationships between the police and local community members, and stresses the need on police information sharing with community.[4]

---

1 *Police and Racism: What has been achieved 10 years after the Stephen Lawrence Inquiry Report?* Jason Bennetto, Equality and Human Rights Commission.
2 "Trust deficit between the UK Police and Communities". 27 October 2011. The Police Act of 1964 and Race Relations Act 2000.
3 *Police in the Community: Perceptions of Government Agency in Action in Nigeria.* Marshall Carter and Otwin Marenin. Home Office report for 2000.
4 *Building Trust Between the Police and the Citizens They Serve: An Internal Affairs Promising Practices Guide for Local Law Enforcement.* US Department of

The issue of policing and police community relations in Britain is very complicated. Some recent news stories of police involvement in corruption cases, phone hacking, its contradictory role after the London riots and racism further transmogrified its image. The police criminal justice system is under fire due to the increasing number of prison population, unrest within the prison system and deaths in custody. There are different police authorities in Britain and each one is comprised of 17 members, nine councilors, three magistrates and five independent, but this is not clear how much they are effective in maintaining law and order.[1]

The police Act of 1964 gives the police more powers, Crime and Disorder Act of 1998 deals with crime and disorder, local government Act of 1999 order the police to achieve best value in delivering policing in communities, Race Relations Act (2000) is related to race equality and public access to policing information, but, in spite of all these legal restrictions, instructions and responsibilities, no specific improvement occurred in the police way of tackling community problems. Police administration has never been able to closely observe diversity, colors and their ethnic relations.[2]

The increasing power of criminal mafia groups, the deep rooted black market economy, the presence of 400 war criminals from different ethnicities, unemployment, poverty, prevailing criminal culture in society, failure of multiculturalism, racism, and trust deficit between the police and community, are considered greater challenges for the British police administration. Population terrorism and the invasion of illiterate armies from Asian and European continents has irritated Home Secretary Theresa May that how can her administration tackle this irregular invasion. She is considering professional way to tackled this and other law and order issues, but she has tired now to counter the invasion of criminal mafia groups in the street of our country.[3]

Justice. Office of Community Oriented Policing Service, 2007.
1 *Introduction to Policing and Police Powers.* Leonard Jason-Lloyd. Routledge-Cavendish, 2005.
2 Ibid.
3 Race Relations (Amended) Act 2000. Race Equality Scheme Review 2007–2008. In 31st May 2005, the City of London Police produced and

Home Secretary has often stressed the need on police reforms which is clearly indicative of her inner pain regarding the police failure to restore confidence of the business community. Home Office, police and research institutions have carried out innumerable surveys to find out professional ways for bringing about social concordance and harmony to British society, but all these efforts proved less fruitful.[1] The recent consultation paper (Policing in the 21st Century: Reconnecting police and people) proposed the introduction of elected police and crime commissioners. This proposal was supported by the government, and in response to the proposal, government promised to elect individuals who will oversee the check and balance system.[2]

Recent news stories about the racist behavior of the UK police have badly affected the image of the force as they have been part of low quality policing culture since a decade.[3] While the story of 150,000 cases of illegal migrants denied the right to stay in Britain appeared in newspapers, some quarters in government and public circles criticized border agency for its inconsiderate policies.[4] In 5 July 2012, *The Guardian* reported immigration inspectors disclosed the existence of a backlog of thousands cases involving immigrants refused permission to stay in the country.[5] On 29 June 2012, *The Guardian*'s crime reporter, Sandra Laville, reported Northumbria police constable Stephen Mitchell was jailed for life after he admitted charges of rape and misconduct in public office.[6]

As already discussed, the leaking of information from police sources to people outside the organization appears to be the most common form of contemporary corruption, according to PSU intelligence. This activity may reflect an evolution in the

published its second race equality scheme for the period of 2005–2008 as required under the race relations Act 2000.

1 *Daily Outlook*, 27 October, 2011.

2 "Policing in the 21st Century: Reconnecting police and people", Home Office, Consultation paper, Policing in the 21st Century: Reconnecting police and people. 2010. https://www.gov.uk/government/uploads/system/uploads/attachment_data/file/175454/response-policing-21st

3 "Conflict Research Paper", March 2013.

4 *Belfast Telegraph* 06 April, 2012.

5 *The Guardian*, 28 April 2012, on 9 April, 2012, police arrested six men after they threatened to kill more policemen and soldiers. *Daily Outlook* Afghanistan, 01 March 2012.

6 *The Guardian*, 29 June 2012,

nature of corruption in recent years. After an official enquiry, more than 382 police officers were either dismissed or forced to resign. A government funded study recently revealed that majority of young people who took part in London riots were driven by a combination of excitement and police attitude. Vice Chairman of the Police Federation Simon Reed in his statement disclosed the fact that: "The police are the public face of a criminal justice system that is failing and that's why we are being blamed."[1]

On 24 May 2012, *The Guardian* reported police recorded 8,500 corruption allegations in three years while the police watchdog called for more powers for the police to more effectively investigate themselves.[2] The police watchdog revealed that more than 8,500 allegations about corruption were recorded by forces in England and Wales in the last three years, but only 13 police officers have been prosecuted and found guilty.[3] On 12 May 2013, Home Secretary said public trust is being undermined by the minority police officers who behaved corruptly.[4]

The Leveson report also criticized the Metropolitan Police for errors in its handling of the phone-hacking scandals and for fostering a "perception" that some senior officers were too close to the international news. Not only was corruption identified across all of the forces involved in the study, but it also showed some similar patterns and was apparently linked to some similar underlying factors. This suggests that corruption arises in a systematic and predictable way from the nature and context of policing.

The 9th May 2012 demonstration in London by police was a culmination of more than a year of increasing tension between the government and the police over the recent reforms. Police officers were angry over the issue of cuts and other benefits. According to the police federation more than 30,000 of its members participated in protest. Home office figure shows that more than 6,000 police officers were spared. The past experience of police low quality performance and some flaws in immigration system forced home office to bring some changes into the policing strategies.

---

1 *The Guardian*, 18 April 2009
2 *The Guardian*, 24 May 2012.
3 Ibid.
4 *The Guardian*, 12 February, 2013.

CHAPTER 4. RACISM, AND THE POLICE DEPARTMENT

On 21 April 2013, *The Guardian* reported dramatic revelations made by Scotland Yard's black and Asian police officers, on the 20th anniversary of Stephen Lawrence's death. The association declared that the Metropolitan Police was still a racist institution. The issue of institutional racism has been a continually difficult one for Scotland Yard's to tier. At the Macpherson inquiry, Lord Condon, then Metropolitan commissioner, was visibly discomforted when Richard Stone, one of Macpherson's advisers, repeatedly persuaded him to accept that his force was institutionally racist. Stephen refused to do so, and said, the tag would unfairly brand individual officers.[1]

However, on 25 October 2013, *The Guardian* reported the Metropolitan police being sued by a former constable, who claimed he was racially abused in a three-year campaign by supervising officers. Mr. Urijah Phillips revealed in the high court papers, that he was labeled "nigger" by two Scotland Yard officers. The allegations come three months after a damning report by the Independent Police Complaints Commission, which found that the Met police was failing to deal effectively with race related complaints. The police watchdog criticized Scotland Yard's

---

1 *The Guardian*, 21 April 2013

'unwillingness or inability' to tackle the issue, after examining a sample of 511 allegations of racist behavior against its officers, made between 1 April 2011 and 31 March 2012.[1]

On 04 December 2013, the *Manchester Evening Standard* reported Chief Constable Sir Peter Fahy voluntarily called in another force to probe claims, that officers in GMP's Professional Standards Branch (PSB) provided misleading evidence, while investigating black or Asian officers. The PSB, which investigate officers accused of wrongdoing, ignoring or suppressing evidence, cleared the black and Asian officers who had allegedly committed misconduct offences.[2]

On 05 January 2014, *Daily Record* reported 120 police officers accused of crimes, including rape, abduction and racism. *Sunday Mail* investigation also reported at least 14 officers were suspended from duty, while alleged offences were probed. The allegations include rape, sex attacks, violence, wife beating, theft, fire attacks, abduction, stalking, football disorder, and racism and data breaches. Thirteen of the 14 suspended were constables, and one was a senior officer of inspector rank or above. A further 105 police officers and one civilian worker were the subject of criminal investigations, but were only suspended. Government data shows there was a 62% increase in the number of racism incidents reported to Suffolk Constabulary over the past year, from 294 in 2011/12 to 477 in 2012/13.[3]

On 01 April 2014, *The Guardian* reported a new case of racism in the police department, which clearly indicated that police used PC Carol Howard in attempts to clean up their image after the killing of Mark Duggan in 2011:

> A black female firearms officer has said the Metropolitan police have failed to learn the lessons of the Macpherson report, which branded the force "institutionally racist" . . . PC Carol Howard, 34, one of only two black women out of 700 officers in the diplomatic protection group (DPG), told an employment tribunal that in the wake of the police shooting of Mark Duggan in 2011, she felt she was used to improve the image of the Met police. Howard is claiming direct discrimination

---

1 *The Guardian*, 25 October 2013.
2 *The Manchester Evening Standard*, 04 December 2013.
3 *Daily Record*, 05 January 2014.

on the grounds of race and/or sex and/or marital status and is also claiming harassment and victimization.[1]

The crisis further engulfed the Metropolitan police, following fresh revelations about the Stephen Lawrence case, intensified as the leader of its black officers' association called on the commissioner, Sir Bernard Hogan-Howe, to admit that the force was still institutionally racist. The Black police association complained that despite the training and community initiatives put in place over the past two decades, Scotland Yard has failed to tackle the mindset at the heart of failure over Lawrence. *The Guardian* reported that Stephen Lawrence inquiry report, and the public response to it, were among the major factors that forced Metropolitan Police to address its mistreatment of ethnic minorities.

These and other incidents cause segregation, and whites distanced from the non-white communities. Research scholar and director of Demos, Mr. David Goodhart (2014), compiled and edited various articles on racism in a Demos paper to expose the fake idea of multiculturalism in British society. In his report, a contributor, Mr. Rich Harris also revealed some facts and figures about the fall of white British population in various London Boroughs:

> Between 2001 and 2011, the number of white British residents in England fell from 42747136 to 42279236, a 1.1 percent decrease. That provides a benchmark to evaluate changes in individual local authorities, here confining the analysis to England. Of 326 local authorities, 113 had a fall Of 326 local authorities, 113 had a fall in their White British population of greater than 1.1 per cent. All 32 of the London boroughs plus the City of London are among these. For London as a whole, the average decrease in the White British population was 14 per cent from 2001 to 2011, of which the greatest decreases were in New Ham (37 per cent), Barking and Dagenham (31 per cent), and Red bridge (30 per cent)." As the White British have decreased in London and other parts of the country, the numbers of other ethnic groups have increased.[2]

1 *The Guardian*, 01 April 2014.
2 "Closing the gap between the seminar room and the wider public debate on integration". Edited by David Goodhart, Demos, 2014. Also, in

Racism is the theory that people of one race are superior to another race. People are divided by this theory, and it is used to stimulate hatred between various groups. "Race" is an invented concept, first used in the 17th century as mercantilist explorers from Europe were encountering groups of people who were clearly of different physical appearance.

There are many types of racism in the modern world, especially in the UK, and some of them have changed names or exist in new forms: Religious racism, cultural racism, scientific racism, colonial racism, institutional or systemic racism, and British racism. The British Crime Survey in 2004 revealed that more than 87,000 black or minority ethnic groups claimed they have been victims of racially-motivated crime.

Since 2008 when recession starts and still continue, white racism towards ethnic minorities have risen in private and Government departments. Racism in the police service is practicing on high level. People from minority groups don't like to join the police force because they have already experienced bad treatment. Asian and Black police officers have taken their cases to the courts against the institutional or systematic racism and, majority of them won the case. According to Dr. Joe R. Feagin, systematic racism includes all the well-institutionalized patterns of discrimination that cut across major political, economic and social organizations in the society.

While the Association of Black Police Officers of the Metropolitan Police said that systematic racism in still exists in the Met Police service, this should not be taken lightly. It is a very strong statement against their own police department, where a mainly white uniformed police service has no room for minority ethnic communities. In 2014, a special campaign to recruit at least 2000 police officers from minority communities failed, as no one from these ethnic groups desired to join the London racist Police force.

There is a huge gap between the Police and minority communities; it's not only a lack of trust, but it is because minority communities believe that the police department is full of deeply rooted racism and discrimination. Crime is on the rise, and one

---

March 4, 2008, *BBC* reported twelve more racist police officers were punished.

of the main reasons is racism and discrimination within minority ethnic communities. Private and Government sectors include educational departments, are involved in this disease. The Police do not want to remove the gap between them, local minority communities, and many times, police don't even show up if an incident takes place in minority areas. Many events have been reported where the police released the suspect or did not take further action against him, or dropped the case altogether, if the suspect is white and the victim belongs to a minority ethnic community.

Those people whose first language is not English, or whose origin country is not where they live, face strong discrimination, especially, in the institute where they work. They have no back up or support from any organization where they consider seeking help.

The British Government has done nothing to stop institutional racism, the Government changed many laws within the private or Governmental sector to stop intimidation, harassment or racism against the minority groups, and have spent millions of pounds on social awareness, but all failed. Systematic racism is created by the people who run the institute and whose ideology is based on right wing policy. Institutional racism is not an only behavior against the minority, but it is a mind set by some right wing groups whose motto to establish right wing policy and culture into institutions and once they find other minority groups working with them, they cannot ignore or tolerate them and start the activities which lead to harassment, bullying, racism or intimidation.

The United Kingdom is facing a sustained threat from racist elements in state institutions. On society level, racist attacks have exacerbated, while on government level, racist behaviors is confined to either text messages or unusual behavior. At present, various communities face violent racism and these trends are in increase. In 1950s, 1960s and in 1980s, discrimination, poverty and racism together with the behavior of police officers, sparked a series of riots across the country.[1]

In 2001, Bradford and Oldham experienced riots. In 2005, In

---

1 Department of Health Press Releases, 11 March 1999. *Psychiatry and Institutional Racism.* Bracken P. and Thomas P, 1999.

Birmingham, there was a clash between Black and Asian communities. Mr. Talat Ahmad (2012) quoted Sir William Macpherson's report on institutional racism and the ultimate failure of an organization to provide services to people: "Macpherson's report characterized institutional racism as "collective failure of an organization to provide appropriate services to people because of their color, culture or ethnic origin."[1]

Mr. Talat Ahmad also described the police attitude towards black minority communities and their complaints about the stop and search program of the UK police: "In 1999, when Macpherson report was published, black people were six times more likely to be stopped and searched compared with white people. By 2006/7, this had risen to seven times more likely. This number of stop and search then increased for all ethnicities between 2006/7 and 2009/."[2]

Moreover, *The Guardian* newspaper reported racism in judicial system which raised many questions. The London riots in 2011 proved the actual strength of racism in Britain. Prime Minister David Cameron further ignited the fire by motivating judicial zeal. With his exasperated message, courts in the UK expedited the cases of ethnic minorities who took part in the riots. *The Guardian* reported racial sentences in the courts:

"The difference in racial sentencing between courts was also considerable. Haringey magistrate court which dealt many of the Tottenham riot cases sentenced — before the summer disturbances—11 of the 54 black defendants it dealt with for public disorder or weapon offences to prison, as compared to5 of 73 white defendants."[3]

The 1965, Race Relations Act, the acts of 1968 and 1976, declared discrimination outlaw in public, and established the Race Relations Board. The Human Right Act 1998, made organizations in Britain, including public authorities, subject to the European Convention on Human Rights. Race Relations Act 2000, extended existing legislation for the public sector to the police

---

1 *Equal in Law, Unequal in Fact*, (Erik Castren Institute Monographs on International Law and H), by Timo Makkonen, 06 Jan 2012, also, *British Medical Journal*, 6 March 1999.
2 *Racism: A Very British Institution Feature*, Talat Ahmad. February, 2012.
3 Metropolitan Police still institutionally Racist. *The Guardian* 22 April 2003, also, Met Chief Accuses Media of Racism *BBC* 26 January 2006.

force, and required public authorities to promote equality. Human Rights Act introduced a range of positive political and civil rights. In article 3, Human Rights Act prohibits torture, and in article 6, it emphasizes the right to fair trial. In the determination of a person civil rights and obligation, HRA has declares that everyone is entitled to a fair and public hearing within reasonable time by an independent and impartial tribunal.[1]

In article 9, Human Rights Act (HRA) emphasizes the right to freedom of thought, conscience and religion. It guarantees the right of religion and belief in worship and teaching. Article 10 of the Human Rights Act supports the freedom of speech and expression. Article 14 prohibits discrimination. Racist element also penetrated into NHS and other departments. In many hospitals, in England, doctors and nurses continue to discriminate against Irish, Black and Asian communities. Members of Asian and Black communities are unable to book an appointment with his/her GPs within a week. They wait for months to see his/her GP. Some are died due to a long wait for treatment. There are many cases in which white doctors and nurses behavior occurred irksome. Sir William Macpherson in his report advised all institutions, to examine their policies and the outcome of their policies and practices, to guard against disadvantaging any section of communities.[2]

The prevailing culture of racism in Britain threatened social stratification and national security. In fact, successive government and state institutions never established social strategy to create a strong and well organized society in the past. In 19th century, racism took roots in Britain when British state started thinking differently. White men claimed that the British were the best race to rule the world. Black people living in Britain, as well as those living in their own countries under European colonial rule, had to cope with this kind of racism. Racism has been and is central to the experience of black and Asian people in Britain, over the centuries.[3]

1 "Race Row in Mental Health Service", *BBC* 21 May 2007. "Racism and the Police: An Insider View", *The Guardian*, 29 July 2013.
2 "Neighborhood Policing PCSO Practitioners Guide." This guide is one a series of guides produced by the Association of Chief Police Officers and the National Centre for Policing Excellence.
3 *Policing in the UK: A Brief Guide.* Association of Chief Police Officers. UK.

This author personally experienced racist behavior on several occasions. On 27 November 2012, due to the London police illegal surveillance activities against me, I registered my complaint with the Independent Police Complaints Commission. Notwithstanding the subsequent investigation by the ICCP, no change occurred in the attitude of the police. I wrote the following complaint letter to the ICCP and the Metropolitan police Commissioner:

Commissioner of Metropolitan Police, London

Dear Sir,

I want to set down a few lines about my vulnerable life-threatening position and my treatment by the Metropolitan police department and its agencies. I am under threat from the police due to my articles criticizing their tactical mistakes. Since 28 January 2012, when my book came on the market, there has been a considerable change in the attitude of the police stations and other related agencies, as they have been chasing me throughout the country for a year.

I am under surveillance, my house is under surveillance, my phone is tapped and, and my e-mails are being checked on a daily basis. I am being watched by distant radar surveillance, and watched close at hand through a surveillance instrument fitted into a car. My telephone conversations are being tapped, and I receive several "Blocked Number calls, which are cancelled without talking to me. On 15 November 2012 (10:30 AM), while I was talking to my publisher in Karachi, Pakistan, my telephonic conversation was being tapped consecutively. All these illegal and unlawful activities of the police agencies have already been reported several times to the Metropolitan Police Commissioner's office, but no action has been taken so far. The police are following me in the streets, markets, shopping centers, towns, libraries, hotels and roads every day. In these circumstances, I am fed up now and I want to either leave this country or commit suicide.

I am not safe at home or on the streets, because of the police. I am suffering from anxiety and I fear I can further suffer a mental breakdown. On 28th of October 2012, I left my house in Tottenham and moved to the house of my son and daughter in Hayes End, but the very next day local police became more active against me. In the evening, the same day, an under-cover police vehicle with two plainclothes police (a man and a woman) parked in front of my house in the street; when I entered the street they left the street immediately.

In the first week of November 2012, I went to Birmingham to rent a house there and spare myself the threatening behavior of London Police. I returned the next day and faced the sneering behavior of the police again. The local police stations (Hayes and Uxbridge) started investigating me and my son, to find out why I was visiting Birmingham? The police started visiting my house every day, asked several irrelevant questions. After three day they called me to The Hayes police station and treated me in a different way. I asked the 101 women's operator within the police station, why I was subjected to this behavior, she told me, "No, we give you respect," but she was also giving some instructions to a policeman in Hayes Police station.

Your Honor, what do you mean by the freedom of expression, and why my right of expression is being quelled? After the publication of my article ("The Way Britain Law Enforcement Agencies Operate") in *Daily Times* on 8 November 2012, I came under stern pressure from the police and its agencies. My criticism of the police is ultimately constructive.

Sir, I am under threat from the police and its agencies, and I fear they might implicate me in some falsified cases to further humiliate me and force me to relinquish writing against the department. I need protection and need personal security; otherwise, I will leave the country. I have no criminal record but if anything happens to me, the police will be held responsible for that.

Thank you.

Musa Khan Jalalzai

Hayes-End. London, 2012

As we have already discussed the issue of racism in Britain, violence has now spread across the country as white, black and Asian students have started attacking each other in schools, colleges and universities. In 2009 alone, *Daily Telegraph* reported over 40,000 thousand racist incidents were reported in schools across the country. The police have failed to control such incidents.[1]

The disease of racism has penetrated all state institutions, and Institutional Racism in the police department has badly affected its basic abilities, professionalism and functions. The issue of black, white and Asian unionism in the police department is matter of great concern. On many occasions, white police officers were found sending text messages with derogatory remarks to their Asian and black colleagues.[2]

Interestingly, in 2003, some racist police officers from Manchester, Wales, and other forces were forced to resign due to their racist behavior.[3] On 4 March 2008, BBC reported twelve more racist police officers were punished. The Police Reform Act 2002 was introduced with the aim to increase public confidence in the police complaints system, and ultimately, the police service as a whole. The Act introduced a series of fundamental changes to the existing police complaints system, but no change occurred in the attitude of police towards communities. The reform laws and accountability bills are just in paper, in reality, police follow century old way of policing.[4]

From 2002–2008, over 95,000 racist incidents were reported in schools and colleges across the country. Later on, the government introduced CD music in which tolerance was requested. On October 19, 2008; three Asian police officers filed racism charges against the London Metropolitan Police. *The Independent* reported a complaint by a black women police officer against her colleagues in Manchester. Chief Inspector Police Karin Mulligan complained of sexual harassment and racist behavior, while Muslim communities also complained against the same behav-

---

1 *The Telegraph*, 29 October, 2009.
2 Ibid.
3 Chief Inspector Police Karin Mulligan complained about her sexual harassment and racist behavior. *Daily independent*, 02 April, 2004.
4 *BBC*, March 2008, and also, *Internet Journal of Criminology*, 29 November 2006

ior of the police force. *The Muslim News* criticized the government and agencies for its misguided campaign against radicalization in addressing the problems of Muslim communities.

According to the report of the Internet-based *Journal of Criminology*:

> One of the main motivation of the British government's movement away from the multiculturalists agenda is that it is now seen as too simplistic and to have contributed to too many inward looking and, therefore, economically disadvantaged communities. These communities are said in popular and political discourse, particularly, post New York's 9/11 and London's 7/7 terrorist attacks, to have advertently contributed towards an ending environment for violent extremism and social unrest.[1]

Police officers arrest those belong to minority communities at a disproportionate level, even more so if they are black or Asian. Ethnic minority officer's experience frequent prejudices and discrimination, expressed through joking, banter and exclusion from full membership of their work team. Editor of *The Muslim News*, Ahmad explains women's role: "It is important to empower women to play a greater role in the public life, regardless of their religious persuasion, but the Government seems only intent in focusing on Muslim women to tackle extremism,"

Muslims across the United Kingdom also complained against the anti terror laws of 2000, specifically against the search and stop program. A leader of Muslim Community, Mr. Ahmad warned that the government appeared to have not learnt from the past. In the past, Ahmad claimed, government received no support from Muslim communities.

There are complaints against the police everywhere in the country. For example, in Plymouth, a Muslim complained that local police was ignoring his call for help against racist attacks. Abul Azad was threatened and attacked by racist elements. The section 71 of the Race Relations Act 2000 (Amended), stresses the need that all institutions require, to adopt a policy of the elimination of racism, promote equality and promote race rela-

---

1 *Internet Journal of Criminology*, on October 27, 2008, ANI reported a black intelligence officer was racially assaulted by two white men. He complained that his boss mistreated him in a racist fashion.

tions. As per the police behaviors, the London Mayor once ordered an enquiry into the racism crime of the Metropolitan Police. The enquiry was constituted while the police association of the black people called upon Asian and blacks, not to join police force.

A Muslim Police Commissioner in London, Mr. Tariq Ghafoor has also been the victim of racism. Tariq Ghafoor filed a case with the employment tribunal, leveling charges of racism and discrimination against the police department. However, one another Muslim police officer filed his case against the police racist behavior. IANS reported three senior Asian police officers, complained against the London police department. A Muslim woman, Yasmin Rehman was another victim of racism in the police department.[1]

On October 27, 2008, ANI reported a black intelligence officer was racially assaulted by two white men. He complained that his boss mistreated him racially. Moreover, *Daily Telegraph* reported Sergeant Gareth, humiliation by his manager that he belonged to the Black Police Association. Another Pakistani origin police cop registered his complaint against a white police officer, saying, that he abused him and laughed on his beard. His white colleague told him that he was superior to him because he was white. Mr. Iqbal told the press, notwithstanding his humiliation, he was sacked by the Bedfordshire police administration.[2]

In May 2009, West Yorkshire Police started an enquiry into the involvement of white police officers in the racism cases. This wave of racism, the *Sunday Telegraph* reported, could impact on West Yorkshire Police ability in tackling extremism in the country.[3] In one case, an ethnic minority officer claimed, he was called a "terrorist" by a senior officer because he was carrying a rucksack. Moreover, five police officers resigned and three were suspended while the BBC documentary reported racism in the police department.[4]

In 1990s, the government introduced the Intelligence-Led Po-

---

1 *Telegraph*, 09 September, 2008.
2 *Daily Mail*, 09 March 2009.
3 *BBC*, 22 October, 2003, and also, and 25 June 2008, *Daily Telegraph*, 31 August 2008.
4 *BBC* News, 25 August 2006.

licing Program in the country. The program has so far been failed due to the day to day increasing criminal incidents and racist attacks of police against civilians and their own colleagues. Violent activities of criminal gangs, racist incidents and sectarian hatred are clear examples of the police failure, in tackling the prevailing criminal culture across the country.

In 2000, perceptions changed regarding the investigation and crime control. The same year, National Criminal Intelligence Service with the help of Association of Chief Police Officers piloted National Intelligence Model Agency, an effective law enforcement agency to manage crime, criminals, and local disorder and community issues.

The first National Policing Plan of the British government covered the period from 2003–2006, required all 43 police forces to adopt National Intelligence Model. NIM ultimately changed the police face. Due to the lack of concordance between the police and intelligence agencies, on the issue of crime prevention, in 2004, the Cardiff University presented another picture of the police in the country. Cooperation among the communities, police and intelligence agencies on the issue of law enforcement cannot be ignored.[1]

Police need public support, but here in the UK, there are wide-ranging differences between the public and the police. The policing community aspect is weak, police is unable to convince people and unable to win the mind and heart of the local population. This is the basic weakness on the part of police. The Strategic Tasking and Coordination Group, in its all bi-annual meeting advised the police for intelligence collection, but, there are number of intelligence agencies in the UK, devoted to different aspects of intelligence.[2]

We do not blame these agencies that they have failed in tack-

---

1 "To what degree have the non-police public services adopted the National Intelligence Model? What benefits could the National Intelligence Model deliver?" Nick Osborn. Thesis submitted in partial fulfillment of the requirement for the award of the degree of Professional Doctorate in Criminal Justice of the University of Portsmouth, May 2012.

2 In December 2008, Root and Branch Reforms were introduced to the existing systems, for dealing with misconduct, poor performance and poor attendance within the police service. These reforms were introduced, to make the police force more effective across the country.

ling law and order across the country; we just want to suggest that intelligence information gathering must be on traditional manner. We understand sometime intelligence failures frequently lead to call for reforms. As we mentioned earlier, ruction over the issue of law and order between the police and agencies, further complicated as an official report revealed that police and agencies are not willing to share information on crime and racism.

On Nov 8, 2008, *The Guardian* reported the lack of trust among law enforcement agencies created more problems in the struggle against extremism and violent crime, across the country. The police lack of understanding the day to day worsening law and order situation and racism, within the force, causes more problems. According to *The Guardian* report: "The Association of Chief Police Officers issued guidance to police forces to encourage them to share critical sensitive information to allow local councils and police commanders to develop more sharply targeted interventions."[1]

Having supported the police force, the British National Party in its statement claimed that:

"Although the empirical evidence is overwhelming that knife crime and terrorism in modern Britain originate amongst the black and Muslim communities, the police are still branded as 'racist' when they try and take preventative measures against these crimes. The usual cries of 'institutional racism' have once again been heard with the news that black people are almost eight times as likely as whites to be stopped and searched."[2]

The use of ordinary stop and search tactics in England and Wales, raised sharply to more than one million in 2007–08, the highest figure since 1998. The rise has had a disproportionate impact on non-whites.

On 30 April 2014, the Home Secretary announced the revision of Police and Criminal Evidence Act Code of Practice-A, to clear the way for police searches and stops of people in buses and trains. The Home Secretary wrote to all chief constables and police and crime commissioners (PCCs), ordering them to adhere

1 *The Guardian*, 07 November 2008.
2 *The Guardian*, 17 July 2011.

to the code's requirement that they should make arrangements for public scrutiny of stop and search records. In her parliament address, the Home Secretary read her statement and said:

"With permission, Mr. Speaker, I would like to make a statement about the use of stop and search powers by the police. As I have told the House before, I have long been concerned about the use of stop and search. While it is undoubtedly an important police power, when it is misused stop and search can be counter-productive. First, it can be an enormous waste of police time. Second, when innocent people are stopped and searched for no good reason, it is hugely damaging to the relationship between the police and the public. In those circumstances it is an unacceptable affront to justice.

"That is why I commissioned Her Majesty's Inspectorate of Constabulary to inspect every force in England and Wales to see how stop and search powers are used. And it is why, last year, I launched a consultation to make sure members of the public — particularly young people and people from minority ethnic communities — could have their say.

"Today I am publishing a summary of the responses to the consultation and placing a copy in the House Library. The consultation generated more than 5,000 responses, and it was striking that those on the receiving end of stop and search had very different attitudes to those who are not. While 76% of people aged between 55 and 74 thought stop and search powers are effective, only 38% of people aged between 18 and 24 agreed. While 66% of white people thought stop and search powers are effective, only 38% of black people agreed.

"The police have powers to stop and question you at any time - they can search you depending on the situation. A police community support officer (PCSO) must be in uniform when they stop and question you. A police officer doesn't always have to be in uniform but if they're not wearing uniform they must show you their warrant card." (Oral statement of Home Secretary to Parliament Stop and search: Comprehensive package of reform for police stop and search powers."[1]

---

1 30 April 2013, Home Secretary announced the revision of Police and

According to *The Sunday Times* report, a Middle Eastern law-yer threatened the UK police of legal action, for their racist be-havior, with the Arab communities in the country. A lawyer filed an official complain over the lack of police action, when crime was reported to the police. The claim was prepared by Dead and Dear Solicitors, whose clients included the Saudi Royal Family, the king of Morocco, David Khalili, the wealthy Iranian art deal-er and Nadhmi Auchi, the newspaper reported. In 2008–2009, over 353 investigations were carried out, which were either in-dependently investigated by the IPCC or had IPCC oversight.[1]

The same year, the IPCC received 4,634 appeals, and mem-bers of the public chose to make 14,870 complaints via the IPCC, rather than raising them directly with the police force concerned. In December 2008, Root and Branch Reforms were introduced to the existing systems, for dealing with misconduct, poor per-formance and poor attendance within the police service. These reforms were introduced, to make the police force more effective across the country.[2]

The police lost the trust of community, because it started dis-tancing itself from the community policing process. Community leaders believe that Britain's police is just running about here and there, making noises to show that they are actively pursuing criminal elements, while, in reality, they have failed to provide good services to the community. The police have collectively failed in countering multicultural crimes in cities and towns. They need to respect color, culture and different ways of life.

Police and its intelligence agencies have so far badly failed in bringing illegal immigrants into their records. The UK Border Agency was arresting illegal people and deported them to their countries but, within a month, they were coming back. There is no clear strategy for tackling criminal mafia groups. Home Of-fice claims that policing has undergone a transformation over recent years, and that it has responded to social changes, and rising public expectations, but communities complain against

Criminal Evidence Act Code of Practice A to make easy the way police searches and stops people in buses and trains.
1 On March 13, 2005, *Sunday Times* reported a Middle Eastern lawyer threatened the UK police of legal action, for their racist behavior, with the Arab communities in the country.
2 Ibid.

the police's behavior, and its way of tackling suspects through counter-terror laws.[1]

How can we accept that the police service has made significant progress, when it failed in tackling the 2011 riots in London, in which they demonstrated a less than professional approach? Another irony is that, the police do not properly respond to the complaints of communities, and keep them in long queue during the complaints registration process. Social and administrative connections between the police and communities are weak and based on misunderstandings. We all remember the statements of politicians and public leaders pinpointing the flawed crime strategies of the UK police, over the last five years.

On a council level, these and other issues are being tackled through various organizations, while their results have always been contradictory. Funds are released to the NGOs, community groups and religious clerics for bringing about concordance and harmony to society but, in spite of all these efforts, criminal culture prevails, intolerance exacerbated, and racism has targeted several government and private institutions, including the police. This wrongly understood way of maintaining law and order and community trust, undoubtedly, has left adverse effects on society.

---

1 *Daily Telegraph*, 27 October 2009. On October 27, 2008, *ANI* reported a black intelligence officer was racially assaulted by two white men. He complained that his boss mistreated him racially.

CHAPTER 5. DISCRIMINATION, CRIMINAL GANGS AND CORRUPTION IN BOROUGH COUNCILS

The crisis of the UK's local governments is growing to the superlative degree of bad and ill. The Borough councils face numerous social, political and economic crises. Unemployment, corruption and homelessness are on the rise, and nepotism and racism have increased. Low wages and welfare cuts have created a criminal culture across the country. Drug addiction, prostitution and human trafficking have become profitable business. Streets of majority Borough Council have become the centers of criminal business of organized criminal gangs. The gap between the poor and rich, extremism, hatred, racism, discrimination and forceful eviction of tenants from their houses, are wider diseases that put the lives of elderly people in trouble.

The pattern of local government in the UK is very complex, as the distribution of functions varies according to administrative arrangements of the country. In London, all decisions are taken by parliament because London does not have devolved assemblies outside the city. In 1994, the UK was subdivided into nine regions, while only London has an elected mayor and parliament. Like many other boroughs, the London Borough of Hounslow has its own bureaucratic system, which is very complicated. The borough was established in 1965 under the London

Government Act 1963.

The prevailing culture of racism in Britain threatened social stratification and national unity. In fact, successive government and state institutions never established social strategy to create a strong and well organized society in the past. In the UK, councils are responsible for ensuring public money is safeguarded, properly accounted for and used to deliver maximum value to their communities. Consequently, their business must be conducted in line with the law and proper standards, but the case is different here. Corruption is an issue that has painted an ugly picture of local governments. Corruption is problematic precisely because it crosses the boundary between public life and private interests. Transparency International, in its report for 2013, has expressed deep concern over the prevailing culture of corruption. On 9 February 2014, Ben Chu gave amazing details of housing crisis in Britain. In his article, Ben Chu warned the looming crisis might cause social unrest:

> Britain has a nightmare, and its name is housing. At the heart of the nightmare is the sheer expense. The average housing costs five times the average person's annual income, not far off record high. And they're going up too. In December house prices were almost 10 per cent higher than they were a year ago, largely thanks to George Osborne's various mortgage subsidies. Rents have also been rising quickly too in recent years. Housing now eats up around 20 percent of the typical family's weekly outgoings, up from 16 per cent in 2000. Housing is expensive for the Government too, as it must help the less well-off affords their soaring rents and there are now 1.7 million people hoping to secure a state-subsidized home. Young people are finding it increasingly difficult to get on the housing ladder, and many are forced to live at home with their parents well into their twenties (or later) as they try to scrape together the enormous deposits demanded by the banks.[1]

Before this, on 7 February 2014, writing in *The Guardian* newspaper, Grainia Long quoted the UN report about the UK housing crisis and warned that the crisis has deepen:

> A United Nations report on the UK has concluded

---

1 *The Independent*, 09 February 2014.

that we are facing a critical situation in term of availability, affordability and access to adequate housing.
That conclusion will come as no surprise to anyone
who works in housing or to the people who are suffering the worst impacts of this crisis — those who have
been made homeless or who have to cut spending on
essentials like food and fuel just to keep a roof over their
heads.[1]

In the United Kingdom, Shelter is the best organized charity that manages houses for homeless people across the country. According to the Shelter website details that the crisis of
homelessness has deepen. Shelter has provided thousands houses to vulnerable homeless Britain and continues to support them:

More than two million people find their rent or
mortgage a constant struggle or are falling behind with
payments. Against the background of mounting debt
across the country, huge numbers of homeowners are
having their homes repossessed, because they are no
longer able to keep up with their mortgage repayments.
Second home ownership is pricing local people out of
many rural areas. Over 1.7 million households are currently waiting for social housing. Some homeless house-
holds--many with dependent children wait for years in
temporary accommodation. Families renting privately
on low incomes have to put up with poor living conditions and little security. The number of new households
is increasing faster than the number of house builds.
And at the sharpest end, many hundreds of people sleep
rough on the streets every night, cold and fearing for
their safety. Shelter believes this situation is unacceptable and warns that the UK is now more polarized by
housing as 1.4 million children in England live in bad
housing.[2]

In London Borough of Hounslow, there is a considerable degree of concern from residents about the involvement of council staff members in corruption cases. Residents of Hounslow
Council feel that mechanisms for scrutiny remain weak, despite growing instances of corruption. Numerous cases of cor-

1 *The Guardian*, 07 February 2014
2   The   Housing   Crisis,   Shelter,   www.http://england.shelter.
org.uk/campaigns/why_we_campaign/the_housing_crisis/
what_is_the_housing_crisis?

ruption are currently emerging in the administration of Miss Mary Harpley, Chief Executive of the Hounslow Council. For example, in the housing strategy for 2014, while the council accepted the multidimensional role of ethnic minorities and said it should support them and meet their needs, Miss Mary Harpley continues to maintain a strict bureaucratic and system based on discrimination.

When Asian complainants want to contact her by phone, she does not respond. The humiliation of old aged men and women of different ethnicities, and the harassment of poor tenants through various administrative means, and fake letters, raised serious questions about the allegedly multicultural policy of Miss Mary Harpley's office. In Hounslow West, a dozen ethnic minority residents told this author that officers of the housing department continue to harass them illegally, going so far as to suspend their housing benefits or prolong the processing of their claims. Tenants are being harassed through threatening letters.

An elderly man from Wellington Road South told me that the attitude of housing benefit officers and benefit manager is unmistakably regrettable, and that they have to endure sneers and scornful smiles continuously. The manager treats people racially. Miss Mary Harpley should know that a majority of the council residents have come from a war zone; they are oppressed, distressed, suffer from anxiety, torment and mental diseases. They have lost their families and loved ones, lost their houses and properties. They must be treated in a professional manner, not oppressed bureaucratically.

Mismanagement and the intractable bureaucratic culture in Miss Mary Harpley's council offices raised several questions about her administrative mechanism and fairness. Allegations of corruption, degradation, racism, discrimination and harassment of visitors have surfaced repeatedly, while racism and discrimination are obviously prevalent. That all this could be going on under Miss Mary Harpley's nose, but yet so far no action has been taken against corrupt officials or those who intimidate tenants time and again.

However, this seems to simply be a whitewash, with various stains on the council's reputation consistently emerging. In one case, according a local newspaper report, two officers of the Hounslow Council were accused of using labor and supplies from Hounslow Homes to repair their own residences. There were also allegations that a dummy company was secretly established to fraudulently siphon off funds.

The council issued a quizzical statement saying, "Such allegations are treated very seriously and investigated in accordance with the Hounslow Homes Disciplinary Procedure." It appears this was simply a move to placate residents. The Hounslow Chronicle once revealed that a major probe into alleged staff corruption was launched by the council's housing arm, which manages 16,500 houses in the borough. However, the council's spokesman was afraid to disclose whether any staff member had been suspended or sacked as a result of the probe.

In another case, the Fraud Squad of Scotland Yard was called by the council following concerns arising from an internal investigation thought to involve the housing service division; the squad made some arrests but further investigation is needed as to the depth of these crimes. Meanwhile, Miss Mary Harpley receives a generous salary while the council suffers a financial crisis. The council ironically stated, "It is astonishing that it appears Chief Executives are finding elaborate ways to hike their pay through the back door. A culture of bumper pay and perks has no place in local government, especially during this tough time across the public sectors." However, so far, little has been done."

Whilst this situation prevails, poor and helpless complainants will continue to suffer from injustice, Hounslow Council services will remain incorrectly oriented and inept officers will walk away knowing that Miss Mary Harpley's administration is in denial of the truth. We were told upon the appointment of Miss Harpley that she would introduce professional measures to tackle corruption and mismanagement, but she has failed to do so or to create a climate of ethnic concordance, residents complained.

Here, I want to share an amazing and a painful story of an Asian writer with my readers. The story reflects the culture of official corruption and racism in local government offices in the United Kingdom, where poor migrants are being treated with impertinence. Normally, migrants coming to Britain from war zones, like Afghanistan, Iraq, Syria and Pakistan, are oppressed, depressed, mentally tortured and patients of hyper-tension. They are looking for a better future of their families and children, and claim asylum in Britain on the ground that this country is the champion of human rights.

Though, the country's general attitude towards immigrants is not too bad, as it supports human rights, but sometimes, illiterate elements in Local Government Departments and private firms act differently. The following painful story is heartbreaking and dismal. This will give the readers torment. I mean the miserable circumstances of an Asian intellectual and writer who suffered anxiety, hyper tension, sugar and high blood pressure, due to the threatening behavior of Miss Mary Harply administration.

On 11 February, 2014, Prof. M. J Khan received a threatening letter from the housing department of Hounslow Council. The same day, Prof. M. J Khan approached the housing department of Hounslow Council, and explained his position, but he was treated by the manager in a depreciative way. Being a poor migrant, (British National), nobody wanted to hear his cry. He tried to reach Director Housing Department or any other responsible man, but he was denied.

He tried to meet Chief Executive, Miss. Mary Harpley to explain his position; he was not allowed to go upstairs. He requested to meet the housing manager, but the manager gave him only two minutes and told him that he could not solve his problem. We all know that the government's plan to fix "broken Britain" is predicated on blaming our national scapegoat: the undeserving poor. Leaked internal documents from the Department for Work and Pensions warned that it was tabling proposals to charge people who challenge a decision to strip them of their benefits. In 2013, more than one million people had their benefits stopped.

Prof M. J. Khan recounted to me his tale of helplessness, with a cheerless countenance. "When I met the manager, I said, 'Good morning,' but he turned his face and didn't respond to me politely. Next day, when I entered the council office, I said hello and good morning to the manager of the housing department, and he again turned his face away, then gazed at me scornfully.

On 17 February 2014, when I entered the housing department, I came across the manager of the housing department and said, hello, good morning Manager, he again turned his face. After all these humiliating acts by the manager, I suddenly realized that something was wrong with my skin," the professor said.

The manager treated him in a racist way, based only on his ethnicity, with no regard for his accomplishments and stature. Prof. M. J Khan went back home suffering hyper-tension and anxiety. He collapsed on the floor. His son rushed him to hospital. What happened there, I don't know, but after a week he rang up me and requested I visit his flat.

This is the only story I will describe in this chapter, but such incidents are rife within the departments of local government. The propaganda machine of the Hounslow Council is busy brainwashing communities, painting a different picture, but the reality is different. Communities face irksome situations when they meet staff members to pursue their claims. The problem of racism in London boroughs remains worrisome. In 2011, racist elements of various communities painted an ugly story of Britain's "multicultural" society. A recent survey report revealed that a third of Brits are racists.

The worrying figure emerged in a poll of 2,000 adults who were asked their feelings about immigrants living in the country; majority of them expressed racist views. The report also revealed that one in five accepts the fact people around them make disparaging remarks about ethnic migrants. The most tangible divide in all state institutions of the United Kingdom might not be the one along racial and ethnic lines, but along religious as well.

In another incident, an Asian man faced a racist attitude among the Middlesex Hospital doctors in West London. On 27 January 2014, he visited hospital to treat his chest pain, but faced the wrath of hospital nurses and doctors. He remained in constant pain and wrote the following complaint letter to the Chief Executive of the hospital:

Dear Chief Executive, Middlesex Hospital, London.

Today, I felt severe pain in my chest and immediately came to the Emergency ward at Middlesex Hospital and registered myself with the reception. I was in severe pain and needed immediate attention, but waited for one hour. Notwithstanding my hour-long wait, nobody attended me and, finally, I decided to contact the administrator or emergency nurse on duty, but nobody was available. Consequently, I returned to my house and decided to inform you about my neglect.

You must be aware that there are innumerable articles published in leading newspapers about the killings and humiliation of patients by the incompetent staff in the hospitals of National Health Service. Poor medication and violation of health rights is an old tradition here. The NHS is often condemned over its inhumane treatment of patients, like me, in an official reports that found hospitals failing to meet even the most basic standards of medication. Moreover, not only this, thousands of patients are left marooned, forgotten and killed. Violations of the right to health or basic human rights are not considered a priority for the NHS staff, while article 25 of the Universal Declaration of Human rights, 1948 states: "Everyone has the right to a standard of living adequate for the health of her and his family."

The World Health Organization (WHO), in its constitution declares that it is one of the fundamental rights of every human being to enjoy the highest attainable standard of health. The United Nations has defined the right to health in article 12 of its constitution and guarantees the right of everyone to the enjoyment of the highest attainable standard of health.

However, the Constitution of the NHS defines the right of patients and their access to health services, the quality of care, treatments and the right to complain if things go wrong. Notwithstanding all these guarantees and right to health declarations and thousands of public complaints received by the Ombudsman during the last year alone, the NHS staff, GPs and Department of Heath is adamant in avoiding consideration of this issue.

Sir, you must understand that we are highly educated and skilled people; but your attitude and the attitude of your illiterate nurses are dismal. If I find no proper and professional answer to my complaint, I will take you to court and then to the International Court of Justice, European Court of Justice and World Health Organization. This will not only damage the reputation of your trembling organization but the state as well.

Yours sincerely,

M.S. Khan, January 2014

Institutional racism has created communal problems in the United Kingdom. Councils and Hospital treat minorities with a scornful way. On 16 December 2013, the *Mirror* reported incidents of racism in the UK hospitals:

> "There were 694 racist physical or verbal assaults reported against NHS hospital workers during 2012/13, according to alarming figures obtained under the Freedom of Information Act. The highest number of assaults was at NHS Greater Glasgow and Clyde with 76 in 2012/13, followed by 32 at Leeds Teaching Hospitals NHS Trust, and 27 at Belfast Health & Social Care Trust. Some NHS trusts said that higher numbers might be partially explained by improved data reporting systems. The data obtained by BBC Radio 5 live shows that NHS staff are reporting more racist abuse and attacks from patients than ever before."[1]

The roots of gang culture in the London Borough Councils are matter of great concern. Scotland Yard warned that it will not tolerate any behavior by the officers and staff which could damage the trust placed in police by the public. The police warned that the force is determined to pursue corruption in all its forms and with all possible vigor. The roots of gangsters In Glasgow can be traced in 18th century, but print media didn't report gang crimes until the 1870s. According the newspapers reports, when Irish immigrants entered Glasgow in 1850, the culture of criminal gangs flourished. The gangs established their branches in towns and cities. In 1920, Glasgow gangs received wide-ranging media coverage. In 1930, Glasgow was named the hotbed of criminal gangs. The first notorious gang (Billy Boys) was established by William Fullerton in Glasgow in 1924. In 2008, more than 170 criminal gangs were operating in Glasgow.

---

1 *Daily Mirror*, 16 December 2013.

In Liverpool, criminal gangs existed since 19th century, but media did not reported specific stories about their activities. Manchester and London have the same stories. Sectarian or 'political' gangs have featured in British cities such as Liverpool in England, Glasgow in Scotland and Belfast in Northern Ireland. The gangs run various businesses across the UK, while some of London notorious gangs have expanded their networks to all major cities. On 31 January 2013, *Guardian* reported Met Police warned that gangs are spreading their wings so rather working in London; they are going into the counties, even Scotland to deal drugs. Twenty-nine people aged 18 to 47 were arrested in the latest phases of an operation said to be focused on the so-called GAS gang, based in Lambeth.[1]

On 23 October 2013, the *Birmingham Mail* revealed that crime gangs in Birmingham are funding terrorism.[2] In 2013, a police report also revealed Birmingham gangs now run 59 legitimate businesses; include drug dealing, robberies, car key burglaries and even gun-running. "Influential extremists continue to operate in Birmingham, promoting extremist ideologies in order to recruit people to their cause. A number of locations within Birmingham, such as gyms, restaurants and cafes, are used to facilitate extremist activity by allowing key figures spaces to operate and promulgate their message," the report concluded.[3]

In August 2011, the UK Police Chief admitted that tactical mistakes of his forces allowed vandals to loot and destroy shops, houses and markets across the country. Police commanders and decision makers faced harsh criticism. According to a private research report, police officers had abandoned the streets and markets to looters, due to the failure of their coordination and communication system during the riots. They were empty hands with no weapons and proper guidance.

A leaked review of the UK Police Federation noted the police failure during the riots so miserable and ineffective. The Police National Information Coordination Centre, which works with the Cabinet Office Crisis Management Team (COBRA), failed to manage the crisis. During the riots, police was unable to call

1 *The Guardian*, 31 January 2013.
2 *Birmingham Mail*, 23 October 2013
3 Ibid, 23 October 2013.

upon community for calming the disturbances. Police communication radio system, surveillance and airwave failed while lack of sufficient riots gear restricted the number of officers that could be safely deployed.

Communication between various police units had disrupted and mutual aid officers were dispatched without equipments. Government had no contingency plan for the officers on the spot. Senior police officers, like Sir Denis, accepted the weakness of intelligence sharing between police and community based organizations and said, unless the present policing problems are addressed, confidence of business community cannot be restored. According to a research finding: "Widespread frustration caused the summer riots in every major city, where disorder took place."[1]

The Guardian and London School of Economics interviewed 270 people in London, who had participated in riots in London, Birmingham, Liverpool, Nottingham, Manchester and Salford to find out the basic tactical mistakes of the police force during the riots? They recorded most of complaints related to people's everyday experience of policing. Internal report of the Metropolitan Police (2011) also appeared identified simmering tension between the communities and the police.[2]

The debate in the aftermath of August 2011 disturbances left the impression that those who took part in riots were recorded criminals. According to *The Guardian* report, police began to review its tactics for responding to public order events. Moreover, intelligence failure in the Scotland Yard was another issue needed the government attention immediately. Assistant Commissioner told reporters, which the police review, continue to be a significant undertaking.[3]

The Police National Information Centre failed to respond effectively. *Daily Mail* reported London Police Chief, Bernard Hogan, saying that former police commander had failed to put enough police in the streets. Having supported my view of intelligence failure, Mr. Bernard told MPs that tactics of the police were flawed while it needed to review. Scotland Yard, specifi-

---

1 *The Guardian* 04 December 2011.
2 Ibid.
3 *The Guardian* 05-December 2011.

cally, failed to tackle the issue on a professional way. The police officers involvement in phone hacking scandals also damaged the reputation of the force who received money for information from the News Corporation Management.[1]

Policing in the United Kingdom faced severe criticism from various communities, and failed due to its flawed strategies to tackle disorder. Ordinary men complain they have no access to Borough police commanders sitting behind iron curtains, even visitors are not provided with information about his where-about. The literacy rate in the police department is very low; therefore their level of awareness is limited.[2]

The lack of accountability in the police department has led to rampant abuse of power. Research and survey reports on the performance of police and its role in the 2011 riots raised important questions. Criticism of the police attitude towards communities in these reports is understandable, because police have failed to tackle crime, racism and violence across the country. There are some reports that police is not interested to disband criminal gangs across the country. Police stations have failed to positively respond to the complaints of citizens.[3]

In July 2013, Department for Communities and Local Government published a detailed report about the riots in 2011, in which UK's notorious criminal gangs participated. The report, titled; "Government Response to the Riots, Communities and Victims Panel's final report," reviewed the police and justice system, and the weaknesses of law enforcement institutions in detail. The report also explored means of effective law enforcement in the country. Though the report represents the government and its gratifications to communities, but it also painted an ugly picture of the inability of law enforcement agencies in tackling the gang-war in 2011:

> An effective justice system is paramount in sending
> strong warning signals to criminals, including rioters,

---

1 *Daily Mail* reported (12 Oct 2011) the London police chief, Bernard Hogan saying that former police commander had failed to put enough police in the streets.
2 Police Reform and Social Responsibility Bill 2010-2011.
3 "In Justice and Security Green Paper", October 2011, it seems the Cameron government has showed a lot of commitment to safeguard Britain's National Security and in delivering this duty.

about their behavior. In July 2012 we published the White Paper; Swift and Sure Justice: the Government's Plans for Reform of the Criminal Justice System. This set out, as part of a broader series of reforms, our plans to make justice swifter; to bring home to offenders the consequences of their behavior; and to ensure the system is made more transparent to communities, enabling them to effectively hold services to account. The Government is keen to learn from the disturbances and have tested a range of options for opening up the criminal justice system to operate more flexible hours to better meet the needs of court users including victims and witnesses. Models include extending the operating hours in the magistrates' and youth courts; extending the sitting hours of the Virtual Court (i.e. preliminary hearings in the Magistrates' Court held over video link where the defendant is located at the police station) and maximizing the use of prison to court video links for example by starting cases earlier in the day and operating weekend courts.[1]

In the Police Reform and Social Responsibility Bill (2010–2011), police accountability and governance, alcohol licensing, the regulation of protests around parliament square, misuse of drug, and the issue of arrest warrant in respect of private prosecutions for universal jurisdiction offences, have been highlighted. In spite of all these instructions in the bill, drugs are misused, police accountability is not existed, and people experience bad governance.[2]

These multicultural criminal gangs in the United Kingdom are a threat to investment and market economy. Some have got training from their countries of origin and some have been trained here. Members of these gangs belong to 40 nationalities; 17 Afghani, Turkish and Chinese are involved in blackmailing, mobile and ID thefts. However, other groups from South East Asian communities are involved in computer crime and human trafficking. As these gangs are involved in drug trafficking as well, in 2011, police arrested eight people in connection with

1 In July 2013, Department for Communities and Local Government published a detailed report about the riots in 2011, in which UK's notorious criminal gangs participated. The report is headed, "Government Response to the Riots: Communities and Victims Panel's final report." 2 The Police Reform and Social Responsibility Bill, 2010–2011.

drug crime in South East London.

Metropolitan Police Force identified some 183 criminal networks in the city in 2011. A news report asked; who they are and how they developed these networks"? The situation is getting worse. There are over 60,000 active members of these gangs across the country. Experts suggest that a single culture based law in the country needs to be amended according to the multicultural nature of crime. The present criminal law needs to be tightened and severe punishment is to be proposed for the criminals, otherwise the nation will have to prepare for the future street fighting.

Violence and knife crime has badly affected investment climate. Major newspapers in the country report thousands knife crime every month. According to some report, there were 60,000 knife crimes every year, while some reported thousands every week. Government is struggling to control knife crime across the country, but the way it wants to control is no more effective. In 2008, over 80 teenagers were killed ruthlessly.

The irony is that majority of the unemployed and illiterate black teenagers and adults are involved in knife crime in the country. Government lurks the real statistic about the violent knife crime in towns and cities, while there are thousands incidents in which hundreds of innocent young people have been killed or injured. In 2008 alone, over 14,000 injured people were taken to hospitals, the figures of killed people were not known. According to the latest heath statistics, every day in England over 40 victims of knife crime are admitted in hospitals.[1]

Hospitals admission data stated: "assaults and injuries from knives and sharp implements together with sword and dagger injuries, resulted in 12,340 people being admitted last year — 446 of who were not older than 24.This is an increase of 19 per cent on the 10,372 admissions five years ago." The latest figures from Northern Ireland and Scotland bring the total number of victims in Britain to 13,795 each year. While *The Telegraph* reported Up to 60,000 young injured people. Mostly male are stabbed and injured each year, the equivalent of more than 160 victims a day.[2]

1 Ibid, *The Telegraph*, 06 July 2008.
2 Ibid, 20 March 2007.

Kurdish and Turkish communities are in control of drug trade in some areas. Asian, Colombian and Arabs who are wealthy criminals have political links with their groups in their countries of origin. In Asian criminal gangs, Chinese Triad, involved in hacking, computer crime, gambling and fraud.[1]

Vietnamese gangs are involved in smuggling. Nigerian and the gangs of Ghana are masters of fraud. European gangs are involved in the business of prostitution. In London, the Hackney Bombers, Tottenham Boys, Kurdish Bulldogs, in Brixton, Peckham, Lambeth, Abb and the south London Stratham are the most dangerous criminal gangs. In the South, Stock well Crew is operating independently.[2]

The Daily Observer revealed new thing about the Muslim extremist groups in the UK. The newspaper revealed about the London most notorious teenage criminal gangs, who are being targeted for recruitment by Muslim extremist groups.[3] Having quoted Special Branch Police, the newspaper reported: "Poverty Driven Children, from Brixton, the Muslim Boys, from Camber well, and the Money Crew, from Hackney, were three gangs identified at a Scotland Yard meeting. All were thought to have members who claimed to be radical converts."[4]

On 03 May 2014, the *Observer* reported the food fraud of criminal gangs in the UK. According to the UK based experts, criminal gangs have retrieved technology to perpetrate widespread food fraud. According to the newspaper report:

> A rise in criminal targeting of the food and drink sector is being blamed on the huge mark-ups that can be made by passing off inferior products as premium goods, coupled with the fact that there is little oversight and lenient penalties for those caught. Concerns about the role organized crime is playing in the endemic diluting of virgin olive oil has seen the UK government appoint a specialist testing company to establish if

1 "National Youth Gang Survey Analysis. Demographics, age of gang members". National Gang Centre Report, http://www.nationalgang-center.gov/Survey-Analysis/Demographics.
2 "Turkish Drug Gang Wage War on Streets of North London". Palash Ghosh, *National Business Times*. 11 June 2013.
3 *The Evolution of Multiculturalism in Britain and Germany*: Panayi Panikos, Journal of Mutilingual and Multicultural Development. 2004.
4 *BBC News*, 03 April 2004.

the grade declared on the label is genuine. Olive oil is recognized by the EU committee on the environment, public health and food safety as the product most at risk of fraud by gangs, in particular Italian crime syndicates. Other foods attracting the interest of organized crime, according to the committee, include fish, milk, honey and rare spices such as saffron." The Newspaper reported.[1]

Moreover, all these gangs are operating in London, Birmingham, Bradford, Manchester, Liverpool, Leeds, Bristol, Glasgow and Nottingham. Terror experts are of the opinion, that terror and extremist groups in the country can use these groups in their criminal activities in near future. In 2007, with the participation of 1000 police force in London, Birmingham, Liverpool and Manchester, in a coordinated operation, 188 gangsters were arrested.[2]

There are thousands of criminal gangs operating in the UK. The list of most powerful criminal gangs I compiled is very interesting; Black British gangs, Chipset gang oulsdon gang, Chetto Boys, Peckham boys, Spanglers, Brixton Boys, Fire blades, Kingsland Crew, Much Love Crew, Asian gangs, Afghan Bad Guys, Afghan guys of Ilford, Pak gang of East London, Brick Lane Massive, Stepney Posse, Oriental Mandem, Holy Smokes, Tooti Nang Drummond Street boys, Paki Panthers, Sri Lankan Tiger, Arif Friends of East London and the Narco smuggling gang of Afghans and Pakistani smugglers. There are over 200 criminal gangs operating in London alone.[3]

---

1 *Daily Observer*, 03 May 2014.
2 *The Mirror*, 25 August 2011
3 *BBC News* 15 August 2011.

CHAPTER 6. EXTREMISM AND SOCIAL STRATIFICATION

During the last two decades, extremism has been a challenging problem in the United Kingdom. The last decade experienced growth in a range of extremist and violent behavior. Religious and political radicalism and violent extremism motivated by intolerance of other caused deep frustration in our society. Extremism in the name of ideology is defined as violence and incitement to violence. A number of recent studies in books and literature identified that the process of radicalization is composed of distinct and identifiable phases, charting the transition from early involvement to becoming operationally active. In Britain, various communities will not tolerate extremism as the country is socially stronger because of its multi-faith communities, which can tackle extremists together. As the UK faces a continuing threat from domestic extremist groups and individuals, members of communities need to notice extremist activity.

In May 2013, the murder of British soldier in East London raised many questions about the ineffectiveness of Prevent Strategy, countrywide surveillance and other law and order management efforts.[1] The Woolwich incident and other terror related acts became the center of debate in print and electronic

---

1 *BBC News*, 23 May 2013.

media. From 2005 to 2014, terrorists and home grown extremists targeted Britain's institutions and tried, to justify their ideology of jihadism. Though, they terrified civilian population by killing innocent people, but their dream of waging jihad in the country fade away. They received no support from communities.[1] The rise of extremism inspired by jihadism in Afghanistan, Pakistan and Africa is one of the today's most pressing security concerns. According to the Association of Chief Police Officers recent statement, this journey into terrorism is often described as a process of 'radicalization.

Security Service (MI5), in its website, introduces its own definition of domestic extremism with a clear concept: "Domestic extremism mainly refers to individuals or groups that carry out criminal act of direct action in pursuit of a campaign. They usually aim to prevent something from happening or to change legislation or domestic policy, but try to do so outside of the normal democratic process. They are motivated by domestic causes other than the dispute over Northern Ireland's status.[2]

The term of extremism is generally used for people who want to carry out criminal act. They are extremists and they are anti establishment. They want to establish their idea of jihadism and create an environment of fear. In a DEMOS report, the basic idea of takfiri jihadist organization has been described in detail:

> Across Western Europe, Salafism or Wahabism and Tablighi Jamaat are the two most high profile fundamentalist movements, although they are very different from one another. Salafism is a literalist Sunni Islamic Movement that emphasizes the importance of the Salaf or 'pious ancestors' as the example of devout Islamic life.[3]

The Guardian reported a National Unit (NU) that uses undercover officers to spy on political groups is, currently monitoring

1 On 12 April 2013, *The Guardian* reported Black and Asian police officers in Scotland Yard made a dramatic statement on the eve of the 20th anniversary of Stephen Lawrence's death by declaring that the Metropolitan Police is still institutionally racist.
2 MI5 Website details about extremism. https://www.mi5.gov.uk/home/the-threats/terrorism/domestic-extremism.html.
3 "Tackling home-grown terrorism requires a radical approach..." *The edge of violence*, Jamie Bartlett, Jonathan Birdwell, and Michael King. DEMOs, 2010.

more than 9,000 extremists. The National Domestic Extremism Unit (NDEU) is using surveillance techniques to monitor campaigners who are listed on the secret database.[1]

According to a report of the Prime Minister's Task Force on Tackling Radicalization and Extremism, since the 2011 revised 'Prevent' strategy, the government has defined extremism as: "vocal or active opposition to fundamental British values, including democracy, the rule of law, individual liberty and mutual respect and tolerance of different faiths and beliefs. There are some towns and cities in the UK where extremism is of particular concern. Chairman of the Charity Commission also warned that Islamic extremism is potentially the "most deadly" threat to charities in England and Wales.

"The problem of Islamist extremism and charities... is not the most widespread problem we face in terms of abuse of charities, but is potentially the most deadly," William Shawcross told the *Sunday Times.* "And it is, alas, growing." He said the regulator is taking action against charities sending money to certain groups in Syria and asked David Cameron to ban people with terrorism convictions from setting up charities. In view of certain thinkers modern society sacrifices a lot to bring transparent changes in the UK society. They definitely assist the deprived and savage people to modernize and bring tranquility and prosperity among them, but there are many people who hesitate to accept these realities, because their minds are limited to the confinement of fanaticism and religious torture cells, where our thousands of young people have been sordidly pushed in the deep valley of illiteracy, ignorance and viciousness.

Under the original CONTEST strategy, the UK government sought to set in motion a program to prevent violent extremism (PVE) under it's PREVENT strategy. However, since the tenure of former Prime Minister Tony Blair until this government, the move in policy has been very much geared towards preventing any forms of extremism — this forcing the strategy to take a far more ideological approach to Muslim belief and practice.

An in-depth study of people who support jihadist groups found that platforms like Facebook, Twitter and YouTube were

---

1 *The Guardian* 25 June, 2013.

still fuelling radicalization. The report, by the counter-extremist think-tank Quilliam criticized the government strategy of censorship and filtering, saying it was an ineffective, costly and counter-productive means of countering extremism.

"Currently there's a large focus for governments to use censorship, blocking and terrorist-related content," said Dr Erin Marie Saltman, research project officer at Quillam. "Censoring, filtering and blocking don't necessarily work. You can take down a website and it can go viral 10 seconds later."

"If a young individual who is a vulnerable individual goes online and wants to find out more? It is highly likely that (he is) going to reach propaganda and narratives," Dr Saltman added. "We need a much more effective system of counter-speech so that when young individuals have questions? They have a resource online that gives a different message that explains why going and fighting in a foreign country is not the right thing to do," he said.

Britain becoming a hub for right-wing extremism is evident by the spate of attacks on mosques, the increasing Islamophobia and its tolerance to groups such as the English Defense League (EDL). These attacks have included excrement being smeared on mosque walls and nail bombs being left inside places of worship.

The Government recently revised its strategy of dealing with online radical content, and said it acknowledged more needed to be done. "We have removed over 18,000 items of online terrorist propaganda and intervened more often than ever before to limit the opportunities for hate preachers to spread their messages," said a report from the Prime Minister's Task Force on tackling online extremism in December. Today we can easily find out the miseries and unsafe conditions which are undoubtedly the ultimate repercussions of extremism. Today the reputation and honor of our religion, and civilization is extremely in immense danger due to extremism.

In March 2014, an anonymous letter was made public which claimed to be a template illustrating how state schools could be taken over and pushed into adopting a more Islamic culture. There is a conveyor belt of individuals who are being 'radicalized' and the number of individuals at risk of becoming involved in violent extremism is increasing. Those who are at risk come from a diverse range of backgrounds, but the common denominator is a feeling of disengagement and disillusionment with mainstream political discourse, institutions and leadership.

Tony Blair also warned Western leaders they must put aside their differences with Russia over Ukraine to focus on the threat of Islamic extremism — and work with both Russia and China. In a speech at Bloomberg in London, he said powerful nations must "take sides" and back "open-minded" groups. Mr. Blair repeated his claim that Islam is a peaceful religion which has been hijacked by extremists, but it is encouraging that he has recognized the threat posed by militant Islam, even though a globalist agenda may be behind what he had to say.

According to the recent report of Kris Christmann, Research Fellow at the Applied Criminology Centre at the University of Huddersfield; "The radicalization of European Muslims is now a focal point of research and political debate on contemporary Al Qaeda-influenced terrorism in Europe. Considerable research efforts have been made to understand this new emerging paradigm in radicalized violence, and this review examines and synthesizes this research literature."

In view of these trends and developments in society, British government established National Coordinator Domestic Extremism force (NCDEF) in 2004 to tackle the menace of extremism across the country. Extremist groups use different tactics. They send malicious letters to their opponents, blackmail people and damage public and government properties. Speaking in the House of Commons, Home Secretary Theresa May praised the efforts of Jamaat Ahmadia. She said the organization's philosophy of love for all and hatred for none was exemplified by its condemnation of the horrific murder of Drummer Lee Rigby in Woolwich.[1]

Writing in *Daily Mail* on 26 May 2013, columnist Melanie Phil elucidated the government failure to understand the real threat of extremism that promotes violence in society:

> Accordingly, it poured money into Muslim Community groups, many of which turned out to be dangerously extreme. When David Cameron came to power, his

---

1 "Extremism has no place in 'open and tolerant'" Britain. Home Office 14 June 2013.

government raised hopes of a more realistic approach when it pledged to counter extremist ideas rather than just violence. This approach, too, has failed. The Government still has no coherent strategy for countering Islamic radicalization.[1]

However, in April 2009, Electro Hippies published a research paper by Paul Mobbs on the issue of Britain's secretive police force, which tackles extremism in society. The paper gives readers new information about the three police forces and their way of operation. While, before this, in 1999, a new police force, National Public Order Intelligence Unit (NPOIU) was established by the Association of Chief Police Officers (ACPO) to track public demonstrations. ACPO defined the role of NETCU, WECTU and NPOIU and stated that these secretive police forces would support the police service, to tackle domestic extremism, reduce crime and disorder. The National Extremism Tactical Coordination Unit (NETCU), though not a public body or a formal police force; but was privately established under the supervision of ACPO.[2]

The threat of African and Asian extremism to the interests of the United Kingdom is not new, recent events proved how the threat has evolved and, specifically, how the threat of extremism might express itself back to the country, or as a threat to the UK interests abroad. There are several African terrorist and extremist groups operating in Britain with their countrywide networks. Prime Minister David Cameron, in his address to parliament said: "we face a large and existential terrorist threat from a group of extremists based in different parts of the world who want to do the biggest possible amount of damage to our interests and way of life."[3]

Sectarian war between Muslim and Christian sects in Nigeria, Sudan and Somalia causes radicalization in Britain. In Nigeria, sectarian war started in 1987 on schools and university level. In 2002, with the establishment of Boko Haram sect, sectarian violence started dancing in the streets of Nigeria, in which Brit-

---

1 *Daily Mail* 26 May, 2013, until our leaders admit the true nature of Islamic extremism, we will never defeat it,
2 National police unit monitors 9,000 'domestic extremists. *The Guardian*, Wednesday 26 June 2013.
3 David Cameron to Parliament, 18 January 2013.

ish citizens also participated. In July 2013, Britain banned Boko Haram sect as a terrorist group. British Minister for International Security Strategy, Dr. Andrew Morrison, declared Boko Haram illegal, when he met Nigerian Minister of State for Defense, Mrs. Ulusola Obada. Morrison said proscription of Boko Haram was in order that the UK was in support of the federal Government, which recently designated the group as terrorist organization. The UK based Ansar-ul-Din website was linked to Abu Nusaybah who was arrested after talked to BBC about Michael Adebolajo, one of the suspect in the murder of British soldier Lee Rigby in Woolwich, London.[1]

Author N.D Danjibo, in his research paper, (Islamic Fundamentalism and Sectarian Violence: The Maitatsine and Boko Haram Crisis in Northern Nigeria), has discussed the troubled journey of the sect in detail. In page six, he has introduced the leader of Boko Haram, Mr. Yusuf in these words:

"The leader of the Boko Haram Movement, Yusuf, was a secondary school drop-out who went to Chad and Niger republic to study the Quran. While in the two countries, he developed radical views that were abhorrent to Westernization and modernization. Like the late Maitatsine, Yusuf got back to Nigeria and settled in Maiduguri and established a sectarian group in 2001 known as the Yusufiyya, named after him. The sect was able to attract more than 280,000 members across Northern Nigeria as well as in Chad and Niger republic. Yusuf began his radical and provocative preaching against other Islamic scholars such as Jafar Adam, Abba Aji and Yahya Jingir and against established political institutions."[2]

In 1997, while sectarian terrorism was at most intense point in Pakistan, my book (in Urdu Language) on "73 sects in Islam" came out in the market. In that book, I thoroughly discussed the history of all 73 Muslim sects in brief, and the emergence of violent sectarianism in South Asia and Africa in detail. In 1998, 1999, 2000, 2005 and 2006, I wrote four more books on the issue and warned that violent extremism, social alienation of young

---

1 *BBC*, In July 2013, Britain banned the Boko Haram sect as terrorist group.
2 *Islamic Fundamentalism and Sectarian Violence: The Maitatsine and Boko Haram Crisis in Northern Nigeria.* N.D Danjibo.

people and Talibanization in Pakistan can anytime develop into a bigger insurgent movement. In my last book, I clarified the fact that an unending civil war would divide the country on ethnic and linguistic lines.

The 1980s established Takfiri Jihadi groups with the financial assistance of the Arab world in South Asia now turned their arms on their Arab friends. From Al Shabab to Boko Haram and Houthies, members of all militant groups of the Arab and African region received training in the camps of Afghan mujahedeen and Taliban, in both Pakistan and Afghanistan. In Nigerian violence, though ethnic factor is dominant, but religious sectarianism emerged as the most potentially explosive social division. Violence introduced several social changes to the fragmented society and widened distances between Muslim and Christians in 1980. In Sudan and Somalia, Salafist extremist groups have been targeting government forces since three decades.

In Nigeria, in 1980, for the first time, the Maitatsine sect started attacking opponents which resulted in eleven day emergency in Kano. The Kano riots were suppressed by army in which 4,000 people killed. In 1981, when leader of Kano was deposed, extremist sects started attacking government installations and public properties. In 1982, followers of Maitatsine sect attacked opponents in which 188 civilians and 18 police killed. In 1984, members of the proscribed sect attacked Yola. In 1985 and again in 1988, more innocent people were killed and thousands houses were set to fire. Now, Boko Haram has established it network in Britain and receive financial support from the UK based Nigerian community.[1]

From 2010 to 2012, thousands innocent civilians were killed by sectarian armies of different sects while members of Boko Haram sect started the killings of Christians in various places. Boko Haram is an anti Western and anti Christian Muslim religious sect. In Hausa language, Boko Haram is translated as Western education is Haram or sinful. In July 2009, Boko Haram killed more than 1000 people. This Islamic fundamentalist group is basically called Jamaatul Ahlussunna.[2]

Boko Haram was formed by Muhammad Yusuf in the city of

1 Ibid.
2 Ibid.

Maiduguri in 2002 and converted into a Salafist takfiri Jihadist group in 2009. According to their religious philosophy, they abhor western education and working in civil service. The sect propagate the interaction with the Western world is Haram and opposes Christians. Boko Haram is trying to impose Sharia law in Northern Nigeria. After the killing of Muhammad Yusuf, Boko Haram carried out its first terror attack in Bomo in 2010 which resulted in the killing of four civilians. In 2012 Abu-Bakr Shekau took control of the group and under his leadership, group's terror cell killed more than 900 innocent people. Boko Haram is considered a terrorist sect in Nigeria and, according to a CIA report; the group is believed to be associated with Al Qaeda.[1]

A radical Islamic group, Boko Haram, that kills innocent civilian trains it members in various African countries and receives military and financial support from Chad, Niger and Sudan. The group has close relations with Al Shabab and other Asian terrorist groups. Boko Haram bombed many Churches in the past two year. According to the Long War Journal recent report, just two months after targeting UN Office in Abuja, the sect launched series of attacks in Northern Nigeria's military headquarter and in Maiduguri. The campaign of beheading non-Muslims in the name of religion including attacks on Churches and suicide bombing was condemned worldwide. In 2012, Human Rights Watch reported more 255 people were killed in various terror attacks.[2]

In Britain, Muslim communities have established separate schools for their children with their own proposed curriculum. Their sectarian clerics are teaching sectarian education in school. Extremist elements in a typical Middle Eastern conservative society tend to be religious fundamentalists who continue to hold a monopoly over religious discourse in society. Exploiting the apparent lack of a well-established tolerant religious education, extremists continue to manipulate the religious feelings of some ordinary people. Many Muslim individuals find it hard for example to question some of the extreme religious views they have been exposed to for decades. In view of the above mentioned extremist networks of African and Asian groups, it is

1 *IRIN News.* 20 January 2012 and also *The Guardian*, 25 September 2012.
2 *Arab Times*, 09, 05, 2014

an established fact that Britain has become a safe haven for terrorists, extremists, criminal mafia, warlords, war criminals and most wanted murderers, who have been involved in the killing of innocent people around the world. Among these wanted war criminals, Afghani and Rwandan are the most wanted people. More than 80 Afghan war criminals are living here.[1]

With the resignation of Britain's most senior Asian police officer, Chief Superintendent Dal Babu, it is clear now that racism and extremism are the most violent threat to the multicultural society of the country. Dal Babu accused Chief Constable that he could not understand the importance of ethnic minority. *Daily Telegraph* reported Mr. Babu was refused for promotion to chief officer rank. His resignation raised many questions that Metropolitan Police still need to understand the importance of multicultural society. The issue of Muslim integration into the British society has also become a complicated issue.[2]

Britain wants its Muslim population to integrate into its society, but Muslims don't want to share their value with their white countrymen. Muslim communities don't accept the process of integration due to their limited study of their religion. They view themselves, as a separate nation, because they are Muslim. The government and people of the United Kingdom want immigrants, specifically, Afghani, Pakistani, Somali, Sudanese and Bangladeshi to be better integrated in British society. They want Muslims to be professional in every field. Unfortunately, the case is different here, because, the schools, established by the extremist and banned organizations don't want social cohesion.

Britain's Muslim residents, and their attitudes towards Muslim identity and integration, and their reluctance to integrate into the British society, can be better experienced in parts of the country's private schools. As they are jobless, poor, ethnicized, sectarianized, living with lower household income, live in more ethnically segregated areas; therefore, they feel they are not part of this society. Racism in society and institutional level, on area level, on housing level, on the Borough level and on religious and

1 *The Telegraph*, 04 February 2013.
2 "Pursue Prevent Protect Prepare": The United Kingdom's Strategy for Countering International Terrorism, 2009.

political levels has further pushed them towards alienation and hate culture.

The attitude of young Christians, who have no specific study of their religion and don't know the importance of attending church and religious ceremonies, is more racist than that of their Muslim countryman. In churches, attendance is poor and in mosques, attendance is very strong — and increasing by the day. I think this is the main factor of keeping religious identity separate. Pubs and night clubs have ruined the lives of many young people. They work five days a week and spend all the money in two days.

They don't even have money for breakfast on Monday. As the UK government struggles to integrate Muslim communities into the British society, extremist elements show no specific interest and are going on opposite direction. Terrorist incidents in the United Kingdom have created more suspicions between Muslims and Christians. They treat each other as an enemy and do not want to participate in each other cultural, political and social programs.

According to the United Kingdom's Strategy for Countering International Terrorism: "The threat to the UK (and to many other countries) now comes primarily from four sources: the Al Qaeda leadership and their immediate associates, located mainly on the Pakistan/Afghanistan border; terrorist groups affiliated to Al Qaeda in North Africa, the Arabian Peninsula, Iraq, and Yemen self-starting networks, or even lone individuals, motivated by an ideology similar to that of Al Qaeda, but with no connection to that organization; and terrorist groups that follow a broadly similar ideology as Al Qaeda but which have their own identity and regional agenda. All these groups respond to local challenges and grievances."[1]

The recent disclosures of Wiki Leaks confirmed that Britain is the breeding ground for extremists and suicide bombers who have already been involved in suicide attacks in Somalia, Syria, Yemen, Pakistan and other states. Terror and mafia groups from Afghanistan, Somalia, Sudan, Pakistan, Bangladesh and the Arab world live here, learn here, get ideological refreshment and

---

1 The United Kingdom's Strategy for Countering International Terrorism, 2009

go back to their destiny. The Whitehall has badly failed in confronting these groups and their networks across UK.

The arrest of some extremist elements across the UK and their revelations created more complications as they were found more experienced in their actions. Prevailing sectarian tendencies and the existence of various sectarian and extremist groups in society have threatened the national security of the country. The story arrested extremists described to the police investigation team about their international links was shocking. These revelations, terrorism experts say, can affect Britain's friendly relations with the Muslim world as the country plan to re-invent its colonial influence in the region.[1]

In an interview with a local newspaper, the Home Secretary said: "I think for too long there's been complacency around universities." These comments came before the government's updated counter-terrorism strategy was released. Some intelligence reports indicated that terrorist attacks in Britain are likely because threat comes from home-grown terror networks. On 9 November 2010, the Home Secretary announced a review of Prevent, the counter-terrorist program but terrorism experts criticized the newly updated prevent strategy and viewed it as a failed attempt.[2]

Moreover, the networks of several suspected terror groups and their propaganda campaign across UK is matter of great concern. Somali militant group al Shabab has established its strong networks here. Algerian Armed Islamic Group, Taliban, Arab extremist groups, Pakistani and Bangladeshi sectarian groups have established strong terror finance links in towns and cities. As the government has kept silence about their illegal activities, analysts in Asia and Africa complain that Britain promotes its foreign policy objectives through the collusion with radical Muslim groups. Britain police, counter terror institutions and every new government are complaining about the prevailing extremist culture in the country, on one hand, and yet, on the other hand, they avoid taking any violent action against them due to

---

1 "Neighborhood Policing", PCSO Practitioners Guide. This is one in a series of guides produced by the Association of Chief Police Officers and the National Centre for Policing Excellence.
2 *BBC News*, 06 June 2011.

the fear of backlash in the African and Asian communities.

In Britain, political analysts understand that today or tomorrow, these terror-addicted elements can any time join terrorist organizations in Northern Ireland. As these groups have already established links in the province, they will face no hurdle in joining the violent waves in the province. They are British or EU passports holders, their families live here and they operate from a safe heaven. Their presence in various government departments including the police made them capable to influence the decisions making process in cabinet and parliament.

Due to their political pressure and disagreement among the cabinet members, a new review of the Prevent strategy was delayed in June 2011. Michael Gove and Lord Carlile, in charge the new Prevent review argued for crackdown on non-violent Muslim groups, while the Deputy Prime Minister said there must be distinction between violent and non-violent groups. In these circumstances, we can say that extremist groups are more powerful than the expectations of the government. They are intimidating women, homosexuals' non-Muslims and Muslims, in colleges and universities.[1]

In view of the recent sectarian clashes in Northern Ireland and in parts of England, political commentators believe that Britain is losing the battle against extremists and sectarian mafia by relaxing its counter terror policies. Home Secretary, Theresa May disturbed by the re-emergence of extremism and sectarianism in Britain. Prime Minister David Cameron once said his government cannot tolerate Islamic extremism, but in spite his harsh stand against these elements, the Prime Minister eats with them at the same table. Experts view this apologetically adapted policy of the Cameron government as a basic weakness in tackling extremism. The government fears lest the fire of ethnic and sectarian violence ignite across the UK. The issue of fake indefinite visas circulation across the country is considered a bigger security threat.

Another interesting story circulating across the country is the presence of 400 war criminals here. Anti-genocide campaigners complain that hundreds of war criminals from across

---

1 *The Guardian*, 04 June 2011.

Asia and Africa are living here with "impunity" because the country legal loopholes are the biggest firebrand in prosecuting them. At present, there are more than 400 war criminals living in the UK, suspected of war crimes, torture and genocide. In the Immigration Department, a special war crimes unit recently recommended action against them.

In 4 February 2011, *The Guardian* reported a list of war criminals in the country: "The 383 suspects include 105 from Iraq, 75 from Afghanistan, 73 from Sri Lanka, 39 from Rwanda, 32 from Zimbabwe and 26 from the Democratic Republic of Congo. They are believed to include senior officials from Saddam Hussein's regime, a senior Afghan intelligence service official alleged to be involved in torture and a former police chief from the Democratic Republic of Congo, who confessed in a radio interview to overseeing torture."[1]

The main cause of violent sectarian movements together is fear. Religious extremists are united by fear whether they are Christian, Muslim, or Jew. They adapted a new technique and have also been quick to use new technologies. They are improving their abilities, way of operations and attacks. In future, Britain will face more violence, more terror attacks and more sectarian clashes in Northern Ireland. The recent riots and economic terrorism on the streets of Britain and the way it was tackled raised many question about the performance and credibility of the police and its intelligence units.

During the 2011 violence and disorder, Britain's police officers encountered trouble and failed to protect public and government properties across the country. Though the factors behind these riots were numerous but the most concerning developments in the UK's political and social fields have been the emergence of racism, discrimination, Islam phobia and the prevailing criminal culture of recent years.35 The issues of burning the holy Quran, derogatory cartoons of Prophet Muhammad (PBUH), religious dress, the *Burqa*, the issue of *Halal* and *Haraam* food shops and acts of terrorism by some Muslim and non-Muslim extremist groups inside and outside the UK, have all caused plenty of misunderstandings among the followers of different faiths.

---

1 *The Guardian*, 04 February 2011.

The idea of cultural diversity as it relates to Great Britain has also evolved into a different creature in the past several decades. The concept of developing an integrated society is looking more and more unattainable. The threat to national security used to encompass demands for recognition of Scottish, Welsh and Irish nationalist values; now, multiculturalism has pitted widely divergent national and ethnic communities against each other. In the absence of a sophisticated and political response to cultural diversity and plurality, many white and black issues remained untouched. Blacks and Asians complain they are not treated equally, while whites say their country's citizenship has been contaminated. Mark Perryman (2009) views the issue from a different perspective:

> Debates about Welsh, Scottish, Irish or English identity were conducted in isolation from the multicultural question. Britain's broad pattern of allegiance within, across and between, was lost in the homogenizing tendency of nation building . . . however, it is clear a new discourse of multiculturalism is required.[1]

Yasmin Alibhai-Brown warned that black people are now retreating into tribal identities instead of thinking of themselves as British. They demand attention and resources for their particular patch. Ms. Brown notes that: "The English are understandably disgruntled that their ethnicity is denied while all other identities — Welsh, Scottish, Hindu, Caribbean and the rest — are celebrated."[2]

---

1 Mark Perryman, 2009, *Daily Outlook*, 05 September 2011.
2 *The Telegraph*, 23 May 2000.

CHAPTER 7. HOW NHS DOCTORS KILL PATIENTS THROUGH LIVERPOOL CARE PATHWAY IN BRITAIN'S HOSPITALS

Heart-breaking stories about the killing of patients in the UK hospitals are making headlines in the electronic and print media of the country. Patients are routinely neglected, humiliated and even killed by the incompetent staff in the hospitals of the National Health Service (NHS). Poor practices used by inexperienced GPs, nurses, and violations of the right to health care are endemic. The NHS has often been condemned over its inhumane treatment of patients. Official reports find hospitals fail to meet even the most basic standards of medication. [1]

Article 25 of the Universal Declaration of Human rights (1948) states: "Everyone has the right to a standard of living adequate for the health of himself and his family." The World Health Organization (WHO), in its constitution, declares that the enjoyment of the highest attainable standard of health is a fundamental right of every human being. The United Nation has defined the right to health in Article 12 of its constitution and guarantees the right of everyone to the enjoyment of the highest attainable standard of health.[2]

---

1 *The Guardian*, 13 October 2011, on 20 June 2012, *Daily Mail* published an investigative report by journalist Steve Doughty.
2 "The Universal Declaration of Human Rights", http://www.un.org/

However, the Constitution of the NHS defines the right of patients and their access to health services, the quality of care, appropriate treatments, and the right to complain if things go wrong. Notwithstanding all these guarantees and declarations of the right to health care, thousands of public complaints were received by the Ombudsman during the last three years. The NHS staff, GPs, and Department of Heath is adamant in their desire to consider this issue properly. In many cases, poor people treated by the NHS clinics and GPs were denied the most basic standard of medication, and patients are left hungry and thirsty and unwashed. The government has been in trouble to tell the public about the way of killing (Liverpool Pathway Care) innocent patients. More than 95% Britons don't know about the NHS secret killings through Liverpool Pathway Care. In effect and sometimes, in fact, patients were tortured, humiliated and abused. The government has strictly instructed GPs not to prescribe expensive medicines for patients. In 2010, a GP doctor (Pakistani) told me in East London, that GPs are strictly instructed by the government, not to recommend patients for expensive hospital treatments.

The National Health Service faces the same challenges. A news report in the *Daily Sun* exposed the NHS as a killing machine. "A shocking 72,000 patients a year are being killed by safety blunders in the NHS," the newspaper reported. On 20 June 2012, *Daily Mail* also published an investigative report by journalist Steve Doughty which provides a number of revelations:

> NHS doctors are prematurely ending the lives of thousands of elderly hospital patients because they are difficult to manage or to free up beds, a senior consultant claimed. Professor Patrick Pullicino said doctors had turned the use of a controversial 'death pathway' into the equivalent of euthanasia of the elderly. He claimed there was often a lack of clear evidence for initiating the Liverpool Care Pathway, methods of looking after terminally ill patients that is used in hospitals across the country. . . . There are around 450,000 deaths in Britain each year of people who are in hospitals or under NHS care. Around 29 percent—130,000—are of patients who were on the LCP. Professor Pullicino claimed that

far too often elderly patients who could live longer are placed on the LCP and it had now become an 'assisted death pathway rather than a care pathway.[1]

On 30 December 2012, Daily Mail reported the government plan to kill people through Liverpool Care Pathway. Every year, more than 130,000 innocent patients are put on the pathway. Doctor receive bonus for the killings of their elderly mothers, sisters and countrymen in hospital. The payments, the doctors receive are designed to encourage doctors to kill more patients open-heartedly without fear. On 31 December *Daily Mail* reported:

> Up to 60,000 patients die on the Liverpool Care Pathway each year without giving their consent. A third of families are also kept in the dark when doctors withdraw lifesaving treatment from loved ones. Despite the revelations, Jeremy Hunt claimed the pathway was a 'fantastic step forward. In comments that appeared to prejudge an official inquiry into the LCP, the Health Secretary said 'one or two' mistakes should not be allowed to discredit the entire end-of-life system. But Elspeth Chowdharay-Best of Alert, an anti-euthanasia group, said: 'The Pathway is designed to finish people off double quick. It is a lethal pathway. The pathway involves withdrawal of lifesaving treatment, with the sick sedated and usually denied nutrition and fluids. Death typically takes place within 29 hours. The 60,000 figure comes from a joint study by the Marie Curie Palliative Care Institute in Liverpool and the Royal College of Physicians. It found many patients were not consulted despite being conscious when doctors decided on their care. Records from 178 hospitals also show that thousands of people on the pathway are left to die in pain because nurses do not do enough to keep them comfortable while drugs are administered. An estimated 130,000 patients are put on the pathway each year. Concerns have been raised that clinical judgments are being skewed by incentives for hospitals to use the pathway.[2]

Hospitals receive bonus payments related to the number of patients placed on the Liverpool Care pathway. The payments,

---

1 *Daily Mail*, 20 June 2012.
2 On 30 December 2012, *Daily Mail* reported the government plan to kill people through the Liverpool Care Pathway.

according to government sources, are intended to encourage good quality care, by ensuring patients are being looked after appropriately at the end of life and not being aggressively treated, but the case is different here. Patients are abused, tortured and humiliated in various hospitals in the country.

Professor Pullicino revelations also justify the above mentioned news reports as he regrets that far too often elderly patients who could live longer are placed on the LCP, and that has now become 'Assisted Death Pathway' rather than a 'Care Pathway'. He cited pressure on beds and difficulty with nursing confused or difficult to manage elderly patients as factors. In the Independent Review of the Liverpool Care Pathway, the government defended the way of brutal killings of elderly patients:

> The Liverpool Care Pathway for the Dying Patient (LCP) is an approach to care, including a complex set of interventions, that resulted from a desire to replicate within the hospital sector the standard of care for the dying found in many hospices. It was in part a response to the belief of clinicians and others that care for the dying in the acute sector was deficient. The introduction and widespread use of the LCP must be seen in the context of a number of developments in society itself. One of these is a substantial shift towards the idea of patient choice, with people increasingly likely to question treatment plans for themselves and their relatives, and to question the authority of clinicians. A second factor is that death and dying is now beginning to be debated more openly.[1]

On 15 July 2013, the *Guardian* reported a government-commissioned review which heard that hospital staff wrongly interpreted its guidance for care of the dying, leading to stories of patients who were drugged and deprived of fluids in their last weeks of life.[2]

A *Daily Mail* reported (2002) about a hospital patient raped in her bed. The Scotland Yard Police investigation team confirmed the 71-year-old woman suffering from cancer was raped in a mixed gender ward at a London hospital. There are numer-

---

1 "Independent Review of the Liverpool Care Pathway", July 2013. https://www.gov.uk/government/uploads/system/uploads/attachment_data/file/212450/Liverpool_Care_Pathway.
2 *The Guardian*, 15 July 2013.

ous stories about mentally ill people and their vulnerability in hospital wards. Official figures of the Department of Health revealed recently that 50% of the UK hospitals placed more than 11,000 patients in mixed-sex wards in December 2010.[1]

On 17 July 2012, *Daily Mail* reported Kane Gorny, 22, death of thirst.

The young patient phoned police from his bed because he was so thirsty, but nurses and doctors ignored his requests for water and he died the following day. In a devastating verdict, deputy coroner Shirley Radcliffe said there had been a collective failing by staff at St George's Hospital, Tooting, and South London, who all refused to take responsibility for their roles. He phoned his mother, a civil servant from Croydon, Surrey, who recalled: "He sounded really, really distressed. He said, 'They won't give me anything to drink.' He also said, 'I've called the police . . . they're all standing around the bed getting their stories straight'."[2]

According to the Health Service Ombudsman report, most patients are not offered help with eating and bathing, they are left in urine-soaked cloths. A report of the Heath Service Ombudsman, Ann Abraham, about the NHS humiliation of patients is shameful:

Investigations into the discrepancies, malpractices and incompetency of the NHS staff and doctors revealed heart-breaking facts. They have failed to recognize the humanity and individuality of the people concerned and to respond to them with sensitivity and professionalism.... These stories, the results of investigations concluded by my Office in 2009 and 2010, are not easy to read. They illuminate the gulf between the principles and values of the NHS Constitution and the felt reality of being an older person in the care of the NHS in England. The investigations reveal an attitude — both personal and institutional — which fails to recognize the humanity and individuality of the people concerned and to respond to them with sensitivity, compassion and professionalism.[3]

1 *Daily Mail*, 2000
2 *Daily Mail*, 17 July 2012.
3 "Care and compassion"? Report of the Health Service Ombudsman

Daily Telegraph reported that a majority of NHS hospitals are being given financial rewards for placing terminally-ill patients on a controversial "pathway" to death. "At many hospitals more than 50 per cent of all patients who died had been placed on the pathway and in one case the proportion of foreseeable deaths on the pathway was almost 9 out of 10," the newspaper reported.

How can we forget the miserable cries of those patients who were brutally humiliated, forcefully discharged from hospitals, and died in helplessness, just in the last year? One of my friends experienced medical vandalism in GPs clinics. On 30 March 2011, he complained to the Department of Health, New Ham, Minister of State for Health, Simon Burns, Parliamentary Health Committee and his MP, Mr. Stephen Timms, about his illness and medication, but he received no positive response either from the health authorities or State Minister for Health. The man needed expensive medicines to cure his ulcer, but he was denied by his GP in East Ham, London.

The story does not end here; poor people are being forced to use the low-quality medication provided by the NHS doctors, and are advised not to dare to complain about the poor treatment they receive. The story of local GPs is more frightening; these less qualified and untrained General Practitioners can only prescribe Paracetamol or other cold remedies for every patient. In their surgeries, they are kings, behaving like Afghan warlords, and do not care whether patients are satisfied or if they want to go to an expensive private clinic, because to them, this is not an important matter. Just on one occasion, an NHS trust was fined when a mother died after giving birth to a child, when inexperienced doctors give her the wrong medicines. Moreover, an NHS Trust was prosecuted by the Health and Safety Executive after thirty-year-old Mayra Cabrera died from being given the wrong medicine at Marlborough Road Hospital in Swindon.

In a secret inquiry, some 1200 patients were found dead due to neglect by the hospital staff in 2009. An elderly woman, who was honored by the former Prime Minister for her work as a

on ten investigations into NHS care of older people, "Fourth report of the Health Service Commissioner for England Session 2010-2011", Presented to Parliament pursuant to Section 14(4) of the Health Service Commissioners Act 1993.

Land Girl during the Second World War, was found wallowing in filth in an NHS hospital. Later on, her daughter accused the Prime Minister of betraying the elderly citizens. A recent newspaper report revealed the involvement of NHS directors, former Ministers, nurses and doctors in a hospital scandal that killed hundreds of patients.

These are only the reported cases of murder, humiliation, neglect and medical torture in the United Kingdom's hospitals; unreported cases are in thousands. News stories about the GPs and their favoritism are innumerable. GPs may give preferential service to friends, relatives and people recommended by pharmaceutical dealers. Most GPs in London are not well trained; neither do they understand the pathological philosophy of diseases. They prescribe ordinary medicines, easily available in drug stores.

Keeping in view this worsening crisis in the NHS hospitals and GP clinics, the general public is calling for significant changes in the health sector, and proposes severe punishment for the health Minister and hospital Chief Executives, who never regretted on the killing of innocent citizens. They are killing more people than the people killed by the US and NATO forces in Afghanistan every year. The cross-party Commons Health Committee urged a rethink of the proposals, saying GPs should not be solely in charge of commissioning services for patients.

The Guardian reported on efforts made by the Health Secretary to rescue his controversial NHS plan. Health Secretary Langley was forced to announce the amendment of his plan. Shadow Health Secretary John Healey complained that the Prime Minister should have told voters about his NHS plans before the election. In February 18, 2010, Jenny Hope reported that if the NHS improved its safety record, more than 40,000 deaths a year could be avoided.

A new study, disclosed by The *Daily Telegraph*, (2011) also found that hospitals are making a third of elderly people who fall and break their hips wait too long for operations. Those who are admitted at weekends are more likely to face delays. This prompted a strong response from the Department of Health, which wants trusts to find out why patients are not receiving the same standard of care around the clock. (Hospitals in England are managed by acute trusts or foundation trusts.) Prof. Sir Bruce Keogh, the NHS Medical Director, told the *Telegraph* newspaper:

> Mortality rates in the NHS are going down, but hospitals with high rates and poor outcomes in the evenings and at weekends must investigate to see where performance may be falling short and look to those with the best rates to see how they can improve.[1]

The analysis of all 147 NHS acute trusts in England identified 19, where death rates are higher than expected according, to both the HSMR and the SHMI. Hull and East Yorkshire Hospitals does poorly on both measures and also on deaths after surgery. Nine trusts are identified "where out-of-hours mortality may be a particular problem"; it is within the expected range from Monday to Friday but rises at the weekend.[2]

On 2 December 2011, *The Guardian* reported public criticism of the watchdog responsible for overseeing the NHS or the public inquiry into the Mid Staffs hospital scandal, calling into question its leadership and "unhealthy organizational culture" while the National Audit Office said its failures had risked "unsafe or poor quality (patient) care."[3]

According to the BBC report (2012), a former London NHS trust executive, admitted that "institutional racism" is an issue within the health service, with very few senior figures from ethnic minorities in the organization. "Almost 1,000 patients are needlessly dying in NHS hospitals each month as a result of poor patient care." *The Guardian* reported. On 12 Jul 2012, the London School of Hygiene and Tropical Medicine study, one of the most detailed surveys of hospital deaths ever undertaken; found that all the deaths were preventable.[4]

According to an RT news report (2013), health system in Britain's hospital raises many questions: "A documents seen by the *Daily Mail*, a "key objective" of the project — which underwent a trial period in England's east—was "to shift the place of

---

1 *The Telegraph*, 2011
2 *The Telegraph*, 27 November 2011.
3 *The Guardian*, 2 December 2011.
4 "The London School of Hygiene and Tropical Medicine Study", 12 July 2012.

death" away from hospitals, thus "reducing...healthcare costs. . .
. I think it's got everything to do with money, with the cost of a
hospital bed being £200 a day," Dr Anthony Cole, acting chairman of the Medical Ethics Alliance, told the newspaper."[1]

National Health Service is full of smears. There are numerous stories of scandals in hospital across the country. Thousands elderly Britons are being starved, killed and humiliated.
Corruption has spread into every part of NHS hospitals. On 14
July 2013, *Huffington Post* reported up to 13,000 people died needlessly in just 14 hospitals since 2005. The Department of Health
refused to comment on the report's findings ahead of its publication, the newspaper reported. According to the *Sunday Telegraph*
report, the worst hospital, Basildon and Thurrock University
Hospitals had more deaths during the last 7 years. *Huffington Post*
listed 14 hospitals, comprised on; Basildon and Thurrock in Essex, United Lincolnshire, Blackpool, The Dudley Group, West
Midlands, George Eliot, Warwickshire, Northern Lincolnshire
and Goole, Tameside, Greater Manchester, Sherwood Forest,
Nottinghamshire, Colchester, Essex, Medway, Kent, Burton,
Staffordshire, North Cumbria, East Lancashire, and Bucking-
hamshire Healthcare, where the killing of innocent citizens has
become a tradition.

On 15 February 2013, *Daily Telegraph* reported Gary Walker,
head of a hospital, was investigated on high rate deaths, and
paid £500,000 to keep quiet when he was dismissed in 2010.
Mr. Walker alleged that he prioritized scarce resources on
emergency care despite pressure from above to meet targets
on non-emergency treatment "whatever the demand," while he
was chief executive at the United Lincolnshire Hospitals trust
(ULHT). The Newspaper reported. On 16 February 2013, *Daily
Telegraph* reported heart-breaking stories from various hospitals. Moreover, on 13 May 2014, the newspaper reported nurse
leaders pleaded with the Chief Executive of NHS to "show pru-
dence" after revelations that health officials were routinely pay-
ing five times the basic rate for train fares. Expenses claims from
the board of NHS England disclose 170 train journeys costing
more than £200 each during 2013/14, the newspaper reported.

---

1 *RT News report*, 2013.

On 12 May 2014, *Daily Mail* reported a former rugby player had weighed a healthy 11 stone before he was admitted to hospital. In just a few months, his weight had plummeted. His 75-year-old wife claims her husband was left to starve to death in the University Hospital of Wales, Cardiff. Staff members are accused of effectively giving him half of the 1,964 calories he needed every day. "The father of five, 69, became so thin while in their care that his fragile skin could be ripped open by simple sticking plasters, she said. Mrs. Ward, who was married to the retired builder for 53 years, said: "He went in to that hospital a walking man of a healthy weight and came out a skeleton in a wheelchair," the newspaper reported.

The media coverage over the savage killing of Sally Hodkin by psychiatric patient Nicola Edgington has, yet again, failed to expose the general collapse of NHS mental health services. On 14 October 2012, *Daily Express* reported a family who said that poor treatment led to their son's brain damage. And a document seen by the *Sunday Telegraph* stated that the hospital needs to scrutinize its last 50 child heart deaths.[1]

On 21 October 2013, RT news reported general practitioners in England receive £50 bonuses for placing patients on controversial 'death lists. "The move is yet another tactic aimed at cutting NHS costs, UK media reported. Each death which occurs outside an NHS hospital has been calculated to save the health system some £1,000 ($1,600) in England. On average, deaths which occur inside NHS hospitals cost the service around £3,065 (just under $5000), while those elsewhere cost £2,107 (around $3,400)" RT reported.[2]

The Health Minister warned hospitals could be hit with financial penalties if they cover up mistakes that cause injury, according to a *Guardian* report (19 November 2013): "Doctors, nurses and all other NHS staff will also be put under a similar obligation of honesty by having their professional codes of conduct beefed up. Medical negligence lawyers argue that hospitals often fail to tell those affected by errors what happened and why, and can withhold vital documentation."[3]

---

1 *Daily Express*, 14 October 2012.
2 *RT News*, 21 October 2013.
3 *The Guardian*, 19 November 2013.

On 21 March 2014, *The Guardian* reported that a leading health expert had announced an investigation into the mortality rates in six Welsh hospitals, where the figures are higher than expected, as part of a nationwide review of the data on patients' deaths. The Labor-controlled government in Wales came under severe criticism over it health record.[1]

On 02 February 2014, according to *The Guardian*, "David Prior, Chairman of the Care Quality Commission, demanded a radical shift in the culture of the NHS, to rid it of outdated working practices, cure it of widespread bullying and heal the damaging rift between managers and clinicians."[2]

Writing in the *Sunday Telegraph*, David Prior called for greater input from the private sector, the merging of hospitals and changes to the way the NHS is held to account — particularly, the scrapping of waiting targets. He highlighted the "alarming" revelation from a survey of 100,000 NHS staff that found one in four had been bullied. He described the NHS as having a culture that "stigmatizes and ostracizes" whistleblowers that raise concerns or complaints. On 16 February 2014, *Scottish Express* reported the behavior of illiterate and over-worked nurses and doctors during emergency hours:

> In some of the most worrying cases, calls were sent to the wrong hospital, pagers failed to receive vital alerts, while in others messages were incomprehensible. Other incidents saw an anesthetist too busy in theatre to attend a dying patient while other medics simply did not receive the emergency calls. And in one bizarre turn of events, doctors rushed to respond to an alert but, on arrival, were informed that no one actually required treatment and there had been a system malfunction. In Scotland, NHS staffs call the unique 2222 number if there is a sudden life-threatening incident, such as a patient suffering a heart attack. The crash team — including senior medics, nurses and anesthetists — is alerted, usually via a pager system.[3]

---

1 Ibid. 21 March 2014.
2 Ibid, 02 February 2014.
3 *Scottish Express*, 16 February 2014.

CHAPTER 8. SECTARIAN CONFLICT IN NORTHERN IRELAND

Sectarian violence in Northern Ireland is still far from resolved. Political parties of the province have never been agreed on power sharing formula, since the Good-Friday Agreement. This chapter will explore the problems and intentions of religious and political parties about the conflict resolution mechanism in the province. The conflict has entered crucial stage, and the government has failed with all its strategies to ensure the safety of citizens. There exists deeply ingrained sectarian violence, which, coupled with a range of social factors, continues to give rise to atrocities of dissidents against the Asian, European and African families. Some groups are trying to heal a sectarian divide and some seek unification with the South.

The roots of sectarianism are deep in society; even football game has also been divided on sectarian bases. Education and business go sectarian. The so-called Peace Walls further divided the mind and heart of communities as they are in hesitation to enter social interaction openly. Players threaten their colleagues of dire consequences. The issue of peace walls still needs to be resolved, because these walls define boundaries along sectarian lines. The physical segregation maintained by the walls creates an environment, in which daily life became dismal.

Notwithstanding, the existence of these walls, attacks on

the houses of immigrants continue. In night attacks, racist elements attack the homes of foreign nationals, usually from Africa or Eastern Europe — where attackers daub racist graffiti onto the property, ahead of smashing doors and windows before fleeing. The current war of attrition is leading nowhere except in the direction of greater conflict. Journalist Richard Seymour (2013) explores the fatalities of the conflict and difficulties of Asian and African residents in the province:

> The state that emerged out of the Good Friday compromise is still a sectarian one, with representation structured around nationalist or loyalist identifications. Resource competition is predicated on an assumed war between Protestants and Catholics. . . The loyalists have also branched out into racist terror, attempting to drive out Chinese residents. This and the recent escalation in evictions of Catholics from their homes perpetuate the logic of "the estate", which materially embodies at a base level the very sectarian divide that is institutionalized in Stormont. These localized ethnic-cleansing initiatives are therefore not simply the activities of "criminal elements", as police blandly suggest. Certainly, there are pecuniary motives, drugs wars and so on, involved. Chiefly, however, they are a form of racial-nationalist class politics, rooted to a degree in sections of the Protestant working class. And in the era of austerity, this is potentially lethal.[1]

In 2012 and 2013, more than 400 families became homeless in Northern Ireland, and a considerable number of residents were driven out of their houses, by racists and religious bigots. Northern Ireland and Belfast particularly, is scarred by a 40-year legacy of violence. The city's deep cultural and political divisions between Catholic and Protestant communities are reinforced by a network of "peace walls" — physical barriers erected to "keep the peace." At present, society in the province is undergoing a social and economic transformation, but many fear sectarianism may further destabilize the region. Education in the schools and religious institutions is heavily segregated. Majority of schools in the province are Protestant. Catholic children go to Catholic Church schools, and follow their own way of worship. Recent

1 "In an era of austerity, Northern Ireland looks more fragile than ever," Richard Seymour, *The Guardian*-29 December 2013.

reports revealed that more than 90 percent of children still go to separate faith schools. The irony is that, children of different religious backgrounds are not allowed to have a serious conversation with each other— so how will they ever become comfortable together, and how is there any chance for mutual trust to develop?. Children of Ulster are not allowed to have conversation with a member of rival creed.

The Education Act introduced the requirement of prayers in all state-funded schools. On 18 February 2014, *Belfast Telegraph* highlighted the issue in its detailed article:

> The British government had not carried out properly its sovereign responsibilities in relation to these civil rights matters. Furthermore, it was unwilling to accept advice or seek co-operation from the Irish government. There was a failure in relation to policing.[1]

However, Scottish faith schools have the practice of school-wide daily assembly and worship; some Catholic schools even have their own prayer. In a situation, where violence and opposition are built into the social structure, there are important problems associated with determining personal responsibility. It is difficult to determine, who is responsible and who is not, but one thing is clear — dialogue between the two sects may possibly play vital role.

In July, and in August 2013, there have been violent clashes between the police and protestors in Belfast city, due to the city council's decision to hoist the British flag over the city hall. This new episode in the unending violence left a deep scar on the mind and thoughts of a new generation. A survey of Northern Ireland's teenagers shows that religious and ethnic lines are gradually being crossed, but according to other sources, there is still a long way to go.

This conflict combines many factors: conflict of interest, conflict between political groups, sectarianism, ethnicity, discrimination and the interests of some European states that fuel sectarian violence where they can. Despite the progress that has been made in Northern Ireland, many issues related to peace remain outstanding. Nationalists continue to press for more prog-

---

1 *The Belfast Telegraph*, 18 February 2014.

ress in the area of human rights and equality, arguing in particular that, Northern Ireland needs its own Bill of Rights and an Irish Language Act. Professor Peter Bul, in his research paper (2006), describes religious differences:

> Sectarian conflict in Northern Ireland has often been described in terms of a clash of identities between the Protestant British, who wish to remain part of the United Kingdom, and the Irish Catholics, who desire the unification of the whole island of Ireland.[1]

Most people in Britain fear that terrorism in Northern Ireland and extremism in England might develop into a new form of security threat. The networks of international terrorism in the country support terror groups, and help them in preparing Improvised Explosive Devices (IED). War in the Middle East generated a series of major terror-related incidents in the country. Government and its counter terrorism strategies have so far failed to combat these terror threats or to undermine the secret networks of home-grown extremist groups. No doubt, the UK is trying to control the prevailing violence in the province, but attacks on police, civilians, infrastructure, transportation networks and the use of Improvised Explosive Devices have blown away all hopes of stability.[2]

The principal threat is from individuals, who represent a distorted version of religion to justify violence, and kill more citizens. They claim, they are right and their rival groups are wrong, but their agendas have no popularity in society. The current threat from these groups and their networks is serious and sustained. The issue of Northern Ireland is going to be more complicated in near future. British Parliament, in its 6 July 2010 debate also criticized the IRA, and its tactics.[3]

The conflict in Northern Ireland has entered a new phase as both the sects (Protestant and Catholic) adopted new strategies of destruction and violence, in the Province. For a better under-

---

1 *Shifting Patterns of Social Identity in Northern Ireland.* Peter Bul. The Psychologist, Vol, 19, Part 1, January 2006.
2 Richard English (2006). *Irish Freedom: The History of Nationalism in Ireland.* Pan Books.
3 British Parliament debate on terrorism in Northern Ireland, 06 July 2010, and also, Jordan, Hugh. *Milestones in Murder: Defining moments in Ulster's terror war.* Random House, 2011.

standing of the real problems of the people of Northern Ireland, we will have to resort to the historical nature of the conflict. In 1606, English and Scottish settlers grabbed the land of native Irish in the plantation of Ulster.[1] This act by both English and Scottish land grabbers resulted in an unending sectarian war in Northern Ireland, and it continued till 1798. A new political framework was formed in 1801, while the Irish parliament was abolished and Ireland became part of England.[2]

In the 20th century, limited Irish self-government was resisted by Protestants, and in Ulster they concentrated on the fear that Roman Catholics might dominate the land in future. In 1912, Home Rule was rejected by Unionists by entering the Ulster Covenant. Thus, they formed an Ulster paramilitary force and retrieved arms from Germany. In 1914, due to the World War I, civil war was averted and the question of Irish independence was deferred. In Dublin, in 1916, the Irish Republican Brotherhood protested while their fifteen leaders were executed.[3]

The 1920 Act of Ireland's government divided Ireland into two parts, Southern Ireland and Northern Ireland. This division of the land was confirmed while the parliament of Northern Ireland exercised its right in December 1922 under the Anglo-Irish Treaty of 1921.[4] During the Irish War of Independence, more than 550 people were killed from 1920–1922. In 1966, the Ulster Volunteer Force was formed under the leadership of an English soldier in the Shankill area of Belfast. In 1967, the Civil Rights Association of Northern Ireland was formed and, in 1968, protests against housing discrimination began.[5]

In Derry and Belfast cities, in 1969, People's Democracy began a four-day march which was attacked by Loyalists. In 1970 and 1972, political violence created the climate of fear and ha-

---

1 Marianne Elliott, *The Catholics of Ulster, New York, 2001, and also, Sectarian Violence in Northern Ireland*, Neil Jarman, Institute for Conflict Research March 2005.
2 Southern, N, "Britishness, 'Ulsterness' and Unionist Identity in Northern Ireland", *Nationalism and Ethnic Politics*, Volume 13, Issue 1 January 2007.
3 McDowell, R.B. *Crisis and Decline: The Fate of the Southern Unionists*. The Lilliput Press (1998).
4 Irish Free State agreement Act 1922, *The Times*, 9 December 1922, *Irish Times*, 10 January 2007.
5 Ibid.

rassment when 500 civilian were killed. From 1971 to 1975, more than 2,000 people were arrested of which 1,800 were Catholics and about 181 were Protestants.[1]

In 1981, three republican prisoners died while in 1986, and Sinn Fein split into two groups on the issue of the recognition of the legitimacy of the Republic of Ireland. In August 1994, the Provisional IRA declared a ceasefire. In 1996, when the Dockland area of Canary Wharf was bombed, the ceasefire was revoked. In 1997, the IRA again declared a ceasefire. In 1998, the IRA bombed Omagh and killed 29 civilians. On 10 April 1998, the Good Friday Agreement was signed between the government and major political parties. But in 2001, the issue of disarmament remained unresolved.[2]

In 2002, 2003 and 2004, several rounds of talks were held but in December 2004, when a $50 million bank robbery was linked to IRA, all negotiations were put on hold. The IRA killed a Catholic leader, Robert McCartney, in 31 January 2005. In 2006 and in March 2007, leaders of rival groups met and discussed the issue of violence in Northern Ireland. In 2010, Prime Minister Gordon Brown and Brian Cowen created a breakthrough in the Northern Ireland peace process.[3]

Since 2001, the attitude towards minorities in Northern Ireland has remained very strained. The increase in violence and discrimination has been more dramatic. In recent years, there has been a sharp rise in racist incidents. In David Cameron's Munich speech, he admitted that Britain has failed to provide a vision of a multicultural society.[4]

In 2009 and 2010, terrorists attacked the province 62 times. In 2009, 17 people were charged with terror offences, while in 2010, according to a statement by the Chief Constable of the Northern Ireland Police Service, some 74 people were charged in terror related incidents. What is important is that despite the

---

1 *The European Convention for the Protection of Human Rights: International Protection versus National Restrictions.* Mireille Delmas, translated by Christine Chodkiewicz, 1991.
2 Good Friday Agreement, *BBC*, 10 April 1998 and also, *The failure of Northern Ireland Peace Process*, Peatling Gary, Irish Academic Press, 2004.
3 *Daily Times*, 03 October 2012. "Irish Travellers, Racism and the Politics of Culture", Jane Helleiner. *Irish Times*, 05 July 2011.
4 Ibid.

large number of arrests, terrorist groups continue to recruit new members for future wars.[1]

People in Northern Ireland complain that the counter-terrorism strategy of government has failed in tackling the IRA terror networks, and complain, that the Real IRA and international terror networks are responsible for the recent terror-related violence. (The Real IRA is a clandestine faction of the Irish Republican Army that rejected the Good Friday Agreement. They are now called the Republican Taliban for their acts.)[2] The arrest of Irish terrorist Michael Campbell set off an alarm bell.[3]

The death of a young police officer in a bomb blast in Highfield Close in the Co Tyrone town on 02 April 2011, give us a threatening message that international terror networks resurfaced in the province. The police officer, named Ronan Kerr, was ruthlessly killed in a bomb explosion.[4] *Belfast Telegraph* reported Ulster Unionist leader Tom Elliott as saying that those behind the murder had one aim — to take Northern Ireland back to the dark days of the past. "The deliberate targeting of a new recruit to the police by these criminals is utterly reprehensible," he said.[5]

Police and security agencies are introducing different counter terrorism strategies time and again, but they have never focused on the basic roots of the conflict.[6] On July 2010, the coalition government, with a view to rolling back some of the stringent anti-terrorist laws, published a long-awaited 'Review of Counter-Terrorism and Security Powers'. But the Government and its strategies cannot prevent violent extremism and radicalization, by detaining extremist elements and putting them behind bars. *The Guardian* newspaper reported the government program of preventing Muslim youth from violence.

Leaders of Muslim communities also complain that the government program of intelligence gathering or surveillance is alienating Muslims, and deterring organizations from becoming

---

1 "Police Service of Northern Ireland". Annual Report of the Chief Constable, 2010-2011, Presented to Parliament Pursuant to section 58 of the Police (Northern Ireland) Act 2000
2 *Daily Times*, 09 June 2011.
3 *The Guardian*, 10 August 2010.
4 Ibid.
5 *BBC News* Report, 03 April 2011.
6 *Daily Times*, 09 June 2011.

involved in doing good works in the communities as well. The House of Commons Communities and Local Government Committee in its Sixth Report of Session 2009–10, on Preventing Violent Extremism, concluded: "The current international terrorist threat is quite different from the terrorist threat we faced in the past."[1]

Terrorist and sectarian elements along with their foreign partners are looking for various means to create a war like situation in the province. International extremist and terrorist groups are trying to penetrate into the region. War in Middle East (Libya, Iraq, Bahrain, Yemen, Afghanistan and Palestine) and mass migration from the region into Europe and the UK may further intensify the issues of law and order.

The emergence of newly developed terror networks and the fresh wave of terrorist attacks in Northern Ireland have become a bigger challenge for the law enforcement agencies. Britain again faces new challenges as extremist and radical groups are getting stronger, the police and law enforcement agencies are getting weaker, due to the departmental politics and Racism. Religious conversion is on the rise through specific funds across the country. There is a constant need to save the police department from institutionalized sectarianism, discrimination and ethnic politics. Unionism also affects the ability of the police in tackling racism and violent crime. The division of police department on various ethnic unions (Black and White) can further create challenging problems.

The United Kingdom spends over forty million pounds on tackling organized crime overseas, and over two hundred million Pounds on preventing crisis and conflict, compared with an annual armed forces budget of thirty five billion. The country is one of the global investors in preventing terrorism, but its contradictory approach to counter insurgency, stability, law and order management and good governance raised serious questions. Bad governance reduces the opportunities of investment and economic growth. The recent wave of street crime, gangsters, robberies and thefts has frightened investors.

Factors behind the present terror networks and their

1 The House of Commons Communities and Local Government Committee Sixth Report of Session 2009–10

strength are considered to be unemployment, poverty, housing, and illegal immigration, the networks of European, South and Central Asian jobless communities, the network of Pakistani criminal gangs and sex thirsty opportunists, the networks of international terrorism, the changing terror strategies of the domestic terror groups, and political turmoil in the Middle East and war in Afghanistan. The strongest Pakistani network of black market economy and criminal trade is the main source of terror finance in the country. Economic and industrial terrorism has established strong roots across the UK. The present unemployment crisis forced thousands Asian illegal and unemployed people to shift to Ireland and Northern Ireland in search of job. They can be the best prey to the IRA and other terrorist groups there.

Britain is the only country in Europe where over 90,000 people are involved in the selling, distribution and import of narcotic drugs. *The Guardian* reported recent study of the police, which highlights the boom in cannabis production across the UK in recent years with nearly 7,000 illegal farms and factories uncovered in 2009 and 2010. According to the report, largest cannabis factories were found in an industrial unit of Haddenham, Cambridge shire and 7600 plants were seized.[1]

The Guardian reported that Greater Manchester, West Midlands, and West Yorkshire had more than 1,000 factories. In another case, seven men were jailed who smuggled weapons and cocaine with a street value of £10m into the UK. These smugglers were from Liverpool, Bradford, Dundee and Corydon.[2]

Daily Finance reported that the Royal Bank of Scotland was fined £5.6m by the FSA for failing to adequately screen clients, which may have resulted in financing terrorism. As the BBC reported, the list of terror finance organizations in the UK in 2001 included around 1,400 people and 500 organizations. National Criminal Intelligence reported: "organized crime in the UK is a multi billion pound industry."[3]

---

1 *The Guardian*, 17 August 2010.
2 Ibid.
3 "Serious and Organized Crime Strategy", Presented to Parliament by the Secretary of State for the Home Department by Command of Her Majesty, October 2013.

Moreover, BBC reported 930 organized crime groups in the UK, majority of these are indigenous, British-born gangs. They are involved in crime and terror related activities. Illegal immigrants from Asia and Africa are going to Northern Ireland. As they have no right to work, they have no option but to act as drug smugglers, procurers and transporters. They gradually settle in Northern Ireland, in search of jobs and shelter. Illegal money comes from the trade across the UK, and is sent to the militant groups of various Muslim states. A Home Office report revealed: "The scale of the illicit drug trade in the UK is large." It was recently suggested there were 300 major importers into the UK, 3,000 wholesalers, and 70,000 street dealers.[1]

The smuggling of narcotics provides huge money to the terror networks on monthly bases. The revival of ethnic and sectarian culture and its links with criminal mafia, and narco-dollars, highlights serious problems facing the UK law enforcement agencies. The proscribed terror and militant groups, overtly or covertly, started working with new names, their tacit support to the terror networks of Northern Ireland and extremist groups in England and Scotland can bring more destruction to the society in near future. Britain's Security Services Chief warned that: "the country is facing a new wave of terrorist attacks. Britain faces terror attacks on two fronts from a new generation of al Qaeda extremists and Irish Republican militants who could strike on the mainland."[2]

On Sep 24, 2010, CNN reported Britain's warning over Irish-related terrorism. MI5 Chief claimed a rise in Northern Irish terrorist activity. Security Service raised threat level to "substantial" while Home secretary announced Irish-related threat assessment balance in staying alert but not alarmed. About the Terror threat assessment, *The Telegraph* reported Home Office warning: "to encourage people to be alert to the increased threat from Irish-related terrorism." The threat is high as hundreds unemployed and poverty stricken legal and illegal young people were expected to join the IRA terror network.[3]

---

1 "The illicit drug trade in the United Kingdom", Home Office Online Report 20/07, Matrix Knowledge Group.
2 *Telegraph*, 05 January 2011.
3 *CNN Report*, 24 September, 2010.

There are many networks in the UK, but new ones keep popping up and shifting and evolving. The Israeli fake passport story and stories of underground espionage all are interlinked. Extremists are getting stronger and black market networks are flourishing. Fake marriages are providing an avenue by which professional criminals can enter the country through Asian and African marriage bureaus. Pakistani marriage centers, and European girls facilitate terrorists and criminal mafia groups in the country. They facilitate terrorists, foreign agents, criminals, espionage masters, drug mafia and extremists to live here and continue their terror related activities. Cheap weapons are no problem: they can prepare IEDs in their houses and offices. In addition, weapons are being smuggled from Pakistan to the UK.

On 04, June 2011, Press TV reported the Police Service of Northern Ireland (PSNI) examined a bomb blast in Londonderry which damaged several buildings in Brandy but caused no injuries. "These explosive devices, no matter how small they are, can maim and kill," Chief Inspector Jon Burrows said.[1]

However, a local newspaper reported that in response to the government's anti-radicalization measures extremists have merely gone underground. Now, as the government is focusing 90% of its attention on international terrorism, no priority is given to home-grown extremism and the local burgeoning of international terror networks, which goes on apace. In 2011, the Commissioner of the Metropolitan Police (CMP), Sir Paul Stephenson, warned that terror attacks in the country remained severe and could take place any time.

On 18 February 2011, *Daily Telegraph* reported Northern Ireland's Chief Constable saying, almost a quarter of a billion pounds of extra security funding will give momentum in the battle against terrorism. In his New Year message, Prime Minister David Cameron warned that security services were facing a daily struggle to stop plots that would do terrible harm to the citizens and the economy.[2]

A recent warning from the security agencies to manufacturers and retailers indicates that terror groups have intensified their war against the state. CPNI, which works in partnership

1 *Press TV*, 04 June 2011.
2 *The Telegraph* 18 February 2011.

with MI5, has also warned about possible terror attacks. In the past, terror groups have attempted to contaminate food in the UK, and intelligence reports say this can happen again in the near future. The multifarious threats of terrorism are extraordinarily complex, but no more effective approaches have been proffered for curtailing the problem. On 24 January 2013, BBC reported that the Prime Minister was challenging Northern Ireland's parties to do more themselves to build a "shared future" and break down barriers.[1]

Sectarian violence in Northern Ireland continues to make headlines in print and electronic media across Britain. Violence in the province is often seen as intractable, mainly because of the nature of the conflict and the failure of both religious groups to reach a permanent settlement. Significant failures of the local administration in tackling the issue through negotiation and community level in the past, caused misunderstanding about the conflict resolution mechanism of the central government. The issue of peace walls now has become the main focus of debate in intellectual forums, as they have created more clefts and distrust, greater distances between groups, and greater alienation and communal differences.

Racial walls have never been considered an effective instrument of peace in any religious conflict of modern history. Walls cannot separate a brother from brother, mother from son and friends from friends. Walls cannot divide minds, hearts, ethnic and linguistic relations. We can separate human beings by any means, but we must not undermine human values, relationships and traditional ways of life. Walls in Northern Ireland are an ugly blot in the face of Britain's social history; they present an intolerant picture of the United Kingdom abroad.[2]

Walls mean that political and religious leaders of the country are unable to settle disagreements through negotiations. They are proof of the incompetency of the police and intelligence infrastructure to maintain law and order. If all engagement techniques and strategies have failed in bringing stability, then we need to study the administrative experiments of Asian and European states to learn how they have tackled religious and po-

---

1 *BBC*, 24 January 2013.
2 *Daily Outlook*, 30 July 2012.

---

litical violence and what mechanisms they have put into use.[1]

The walls that separate communities, sects and cultures have badly set back the evolution of British society. These walls must end now, Peter Robinson warned in his 25th November speech in Castlereagh. Robinson warned: "We cannot hope to move beyond our present community divisions while out young people are educated separately. The reality is that our education system is a benign form of apartheid, which is fundamentally damaging to our society."[2]

In June 2011, Reuters reported Prime Minister David Cameron demanding the end of segregation between communities:

"A crucial area where I believe we need to move beyond the peace process is in tackling the causes of division within society here." The Prime Minister criticized the increase in so-called Peace Walls and said: "Given the history of Northern Ireland, I don't for one minute underestimate the scale of the challenge, but it is a depressing fact that since the 2006 St. Andrews agreement, the number of so-called peace walls has increased from 37 to 48."[3]

These flawed administrative measures have put British society in deep water. The future of our children is bleak as sectarian conflict remains deeply rooted. No doubt, The Good Friday Agreement and other peace efforts brought some positive changes, in bringing sectarian communities to a close, but the issue of segregated housing and unequal access to housing (in other words, homelessness) still needs to be settled.

Even the banking system has to change its position. Deputy Prime Minister Nick Clegg argued that British banks need to keep balance but complained that banks are holding black people back from the last frontier of racial economic equality.

Low quality and sectarian education, sectarian feelings at the school and college level, terror attacks, bomb blasts, all these contribute to a sense of insecurity in the streets, markets and parks. Greater danger is approaching as the issues of ethnicity,

---

1 Ibid.
2 *The Guardian* 24 November 2011
3 In June 2011, Reuters reported Prime Minister David Cameron demanding the end of segregation between communities.

racism and sectarianism have taken hold across the country.

The recent clashes between loyalist and republican, police and sectarian elements in Northern Ireland left large number of police officers injured. According to the *Northern Ireland Peace Monitoring Report* for 2012: "There is no occasion in Northern Ireland when people stand together to experience the sense of being one people with a single, shared identity." This precarious reverse of confrontational politics is an immediate warning for both the law enforcement and local administration. Government and its administrative machinery are in hot water as the street violence across the province has threatened peace process.[1]

Sectarian violence in Northern Ireland is complicated, and cannot be separated from political, geographical and cultural contexts. There are many paths to reconciliation and the elimination of violence and the deepening social crisis, but the local government would need to adopt a multidimensional security approach. The United Kingdom is offering technical support and mechanisms for peaceful resolution of ethnic and sectarian conflict to several Asian states including Afghanistan and Pakistan, but meanwhile the country's successive governments have never been able to eradicate the roots of extremism, international terrorism, racism, ethnic and sectarian violence in Northern Ireland and Scotland. We often read heartbreaking statements from police and intelligence chiefs about the looming threat of international terrorism and cyber attacks, and we have experienced numerous changes in the National Security Strategy since 2007, but no proper solution has so far been sought.

In 2012, Home Secretary Teresa May once again warned that the law enforcement agencies must prepare to tackle a lone gunman or Mumbai-style attack on the streets of Britain. Extremist and terrorist networks are very strong and often challenge the national security of the country, but Home Secretary and her administration have failed to control them. The recent wave of sectarian violence in Northern Ireland has now become a bigger national security challenge, where terrorists and anti-state elements target the police and innocent civilians. Author Mari Fitz Duff in her book *Conflict Resolution Process in Northern Ireland*

---

1 *"The Northern Ireland Peace Monitoring Report, 2012"*.

(2002) has also analyzed the basic roots of violence in the province and revealed some important facts.[1]

In July 2012, former MI5 Chief Jonathan Evan warned that the new tactics of IRA and revealed about the existence of some terrorist groups, and their possible attacks in Britain. On 26 July 2012; *The Guardian* reported the merger of three main dissident republican terror groups in Northern Ireland. This was a new and an irksome development after the 1998 Good Friday Agreement. Security expert were much anxious about this new development in a sensitive time, the UK security agencies were dealing with Olympics security.[2]

Britons have already experienced the fatalities of Improvised Explosive Device in parts of Northern Ireland. Terrorists targeted security forces, police and public properties, they warned to target police stations, regional headquarters of Ulster Bank and government properties. In a *The Guardian* report, new IRA warned: "Irish people have been sold a phony peace, rubber-stamped by token legislature in Stormont." The security of British airports, rail tracks and public transport was a particular matter of concern ahead of the Olympic Games.[3]

Artificial barriers which physically separate Catholic and Protestant homes are not considered more effective, because both the communities live in the same city, work there and have established businesses there. If walls have been effective in preventing violent clashed in the past, then there would need to be more walls built in the business areas to separate Catholic and Protestant businesses.

In future, there may be more walls in Belfast but peace will not return to the city unless the issue is addressed at the community level, or the local state institutions are re-organized. The process of reorganization will gave an opportunity to the local sectarian and ethnic minority groups to experience an employment life. Across Belfast, there are more religious differences between the two sectarian communities and, as experts say, one can hardly assume that such a division is not reflected in conflicting loyalties within the law enforcement agencies.

1 Mari Fitzduff, 2002, *Conflict Resolution Process in Northern Ireland*
2 *The Guardian*, 26 July 2012.
3 *The Guardian* 26 July 2012.

In June 2011, more than four hundred sectarian elements attacked police stations, houses, shops and government installations with petrol and paint bombs. Officers responded by firing 66 baton rounds and water cannon. Masked men, whose identity was not known, attacked the police vehicles and fired directly on them. These organized attacks on police and residential areas show that sectarian terrorists have received advanced military training, and there might be terror elements in their ranks.[1]

Young children of sectarian parents add to the security problem as they go violent on both sides. These young and newly-trained people have complicated the security situation in Northern Ireland. As these terror elements are attacking police and government installations, the question arises whether they are in contact with international terror networks, for instance in Pakistan, Waziristan or Afghanistan. Recently, sectarian elements have emerged with growing expertise in the use of Improvised Explosive Devices. Thus the Protestant and Catholic communities still face a future of segregation or communal violence.

Protestants and Catholics: Segregation

Sectarian violence in Northern Ireland continues to ruin the lives of Irish people. The separation of communities by the so-called walls is a weak and failed approach to conflict resolution mechanism. In 2011, the Prime Minister also expressed reservations about the 90 walls that have divided communities of Northern Ireland into pockets.[2]

On June 21, 2011, *The Guardian* reported sectarian clashes involving hundreds of dissidents in Belfast city. The nature of the attacks, mob organizations and masked men attacking the houses of Catholics, obliged the British government to take the issue seriously. *The Guardian* reported gunshots, petrol bombs, fireworks; bricks, stones and smoke bombs were fired as violence broke out in the Lower Newtownards Road and Short Strand areas. The Police Service of Northern Ireland (PSNI) confirmed that officers fired a number of AEP or stun-grenade rounds.[3] The

1 *Daily Mail* 22 June 2011.
2 *Daily Times*, 25 October 2012.
3 *The Guardian*, 21 June 2011.

Northern Ireland Peace Monitoring Report (2012) termed the conflict as a lesson for the warring factions whose warlordism changed the political calculus of violence.[1]

The Queen's historic visit to Northern Ireland couldn't change mind of dissidents and sectarian elements. They continue to attack the police and residents in markets and streets. In Britain's one-hundred-year history, this was the first such royal visit. After her visit, some people believed that there would no longer be war or violence in the provinces, but the June 2011 attacks proved that rival groups don't want peaceful resolution of the conflict in Northern Ireland. The Queen returned to London in despair.[2]

Segregation between the Protestant and Catholic communities is a future danger of communal violence. David Mckittrick gives us more details about peace walls:

> In the West and North of the city, the most violent areas during the troubles, these walls still delineate neighborhoods. Most of them are ugly, although a few, for example around Ardoyne, have been prettified and artfully camouflaged with shrubs and climbing plants. Sometimes these are sardonically referred to as "designer peace lines." In a society where hate, sneers and violent dislike cross its limits, no iron or clay wall can intercept clashes and bloodshed.[3]

The way ethnic and sectarian antagonism in Northern Ireland is tackled is no more effective. Government and local administration cannot bring peace and stability by constructing big walls. If walls were an effective way of separating communities or sects, the Berlin Wall would have remained in place. These walls in Northern Ireland and Scotland have only created new law and order problems.[4] Recent violent attacks on various communities and their expulsion from their housing indicate that terrorists have adopted new strategies.

The Chief Constable of Northern Ireland once said, he needs vastly more financial support for the fight against the dissident

---

1 *The Northern Ireland Peace Monitoring Report*, 2012.
2 *Daily Times*, 25 October 2012.
3 *The Prospect Magazine*, 24 May 2011.
4 *Daily Times*, 25 October 2011.

republican terror groups.[1] On 18 February 2011, *The Telegraph* reported him as demanding almost a quarter of a billion pounds of extra security funding to tackle terrorism, extra detectives, more equipment and ground and air transport. "A total of £199.5 million will come from London and £45 million from the Executive's reserves over the next four years," he said.[2]

Moreover, head of the Northern Ireland Police Federation demanded more officers to tackle violent sectarianism, but the Chief Constable said, more people were charged in terrorism offences and the pressure would continue with an increased street presence. The Chairman of the Northern Ireland Affairs Committee at the House of Commons, Laurence Robertson, said he was pleased the extra money had been provided.

In Scotland, the government has been active in addressing the scourge of sectarianism since 1999. In January 2006, *the Scottish Executive* published an action plan on tackling the issue of sectarianism.[3] The same year; the Home Office published "Respect Action Plan" for tackling anti social behavior. All these actions and steps had limited utility since the basic roots of extremism were not properly addressed.[4]

There have been sectarian attacks on various religious and non-religious places in Northern Ireland from 1994–2002. Various properties including churches were attacked more than 600 times. Some 6,500 incidents of criminal damage, assaults and disturbances have been seen in Northern Ireland from 1994–2003. In Antrim, Armagh, Down, Fermanagh, L'Derry and Tyrone, there were 450 sectarian incidents from 1994–2003. During this period, over 14,000 residents demanded re-housing and

---

1 Ibid.
2 *The Telegraph*, 18 February 2011.
3 On January 2006, the *Scottish Executive* newspaper published an action plan on tackling the issue of sectarianism. *Scottish Executive*, January 2006.
4 Anti-social behavior measures were first introduced in the mid 1990s, and since this time more powers and measures have been added to give local authorities, the police and others a toolkit of measures with which to tackle incidents of anti-social behavior. House of Commons Committee of Public Accounts Tackling Anti–Social Behavior Forty-fourth Report of Session 2006–07, Report, together with formal minutes, oral and written evidence. Ordered by The House of Commons to be printed 09 July 2007.

1,500 claimed to have been intimidated.[1]

And it bears repeating, the violence is by no means limited to the Christian communities who are not quite ready to embrace their fundamental precept of brotherhood. On 24 June 2010, *The Guardian* reported on race-based attacks in Northern Ireland:

> Isolated families in loyalist areas having their homes ransacked, their belongings destroyed and their lives threatened is a phenomenon now occurring with sickening regularity. In the latest incidents, a mob attacked two homes in the loyalist Village area of south Belfast and in White abbey; cars belonging to Filipino and Indian families were burned. The attacks come a year after a hundred Roma people were forced to flee Northern Ireland after racist petrol bombings, also in south Belfast.[2]

In its report, the Northern Ireland Council for Ethnic Minorities concluded: "the Province's criminal justice system was blighted by 'institutional racism' and those who worked in it had not learnt the lessons of the Stephen Lawrence inquiry." Another report, by the University of Ulster, revealed that: "Northern Ireland has the highest proportion of bigoted people in the Western world." This research had been based on the survey of 32,000 people in 19 Euro states plus Australia, Canada and the US.52[3]

According to a report of the Institute for Conflict Research and Breen Smyth Consultants, there are twenty-seven areas, where sectarian violence takes the lives of residents. Some sources revealed about this violence may be organized by paramilitary groups.

---

1 *Beyond Violence: Conflict Resolution Process in Northern Ireland.* Mari Fitzduff, United Nations University Press, 2002, and also, *Belfast Telegraph*, 16 October 2010, also, *The Guardian* 29 November 2011.
2 *The Guardian*, 24 June 2010.
3 Belfast Forum, 29 May, 2012, and also, "Northern Ireland Heads Western Bigotry Index", 7th February 2007, University of Ulster.

CHAPTER 9. INTELLIGENCE AND SURVEILLANCE MECHANISMS

On 24 January 2014, RT news reported the court of Strasbourg ordered British Ministers to provide evidence on mass surveillance of GCHQ, to find out whether the agency surveillance activities went against the European Human rights Convention. British secret intelligence came under fire, when four Euro Human Rights groups filed cases against its surveillance mechanism in European states. The agency denied the allegations and categorically stated:

"in accordance with a strict legal and policy framework which ensures that our activities are authorized, necessary and proportionate, and that there is rigorous oversight, including from the secretary of state, the interception and intelligence Services commissioners and the parliamentary intelligence and security committee."[1]

The revelations of Mr. Edward Snowden also sparked widespread outrage not only in Germany but also sounded an alarm in other European states about the illegal surveillance mechanism of NSA and GCHQ. With this, an intelligence war between all the Euro-states started on the UK soil. A government

---

1 *RT news*, 24 January 2014

security document published in *The Telegraph* warned that the UK is a high priority target for 20 foreign intelligence agencies. Intelligence reports revealed that Iranian, Korean, Serbian and Syrian intelligence agencies have roots in UK society, while the intelligence agencies of some European states, such as France and Germany, are also present in the field.[1]

Security Service, MI5 warned that the threat of espionage did not end with the collapse of Soviet Communism in the early 1990s. Espionage against UK interests continues, and is widespread, insidious and potentially very damaging. The security service, on its website, also warned about the vulnerability of institutions to foreign intelligence agencies:

"The UK is a high priority espionage target. Many countries actively seek UK information and material to advance their own military, technological, political and economic programs. The activities of intelligence agencies identified as posing the greatest threat are subject to particular scrutiny. The threat against British interests is not confined to within the UK itself. A foreign intelligence service operates best in its own country and therefore finds it easier to target UK interests at home, where they can control the environment and take advantage of any perceived vulnerabilities."[2]

The *Sunday Telegraph* reported Whitehall's concern about the Russian spying network in the UK. According to the newspaper report, Britain's European neighbors, including Germany and France, were also engaged in industrial and political espionage within the country.[3] Now the UK and other European states blame each other for spying on their citizens and leaders. The flames of this conflagration can ignite the violent fire of a crucial intelligence war.

---

1 *The Telegraph*, 07 February 2009, and also, Security Service website, https://www.mi5.gov.uk/home/the-threats/espionage.html.   The Influence of Intelligence-led Policing Models on Investigative Policy and Practice in Mainstream Policing 1993–2007: Division, Resistance and Investigative Orthodoxy. James Adrian, University of Portsmouth 2012, also; Intelligence-Led Policing: "The New Intelligence Architecture". US Department of Justice Office of Justice Program, Marilyn Peterson, September 2005.
2 *The Telegraph*, 07 February 2009, and also, *Daily Times*, 07 January 2014
3 Ibid.

In this secret war, the UK might face an uneven situation if the European intelligence infrastructure enters into revenge politics. In the near future, this intelligence war may make the UK more vulnerable to hostile secret networks. The police may face an uncontrollable situations involving serious organized crime, and intelligence agencies may face difficulty in countering unexpected invisible forces.

The war of intelligence started between European states and the UK when France, Germany and Spain summoned both the UK and US ambassadors to explain the motives behind their surveillance policies. Germany became very angry when it found that the Berlin-based UK embassy was involved in alleged eavesdropping.

Authors and research scholars in Britain have contributed greatly to the development of intelligence mechanisms in the country. In modern Britain, we have several intelligence-gathering infrastructures, to collect information and classify it; but hardly any means to process it professionally. The intelligence agencies use unreliable sources of information and target specific communities, which have increased distances between the state and citizens. The social and ethnic role of the intelligence community has also fed misunderstanding between whites and other communities.

The Intelligence and Security Committee doesn't fulfill its constitutional duty in overseeing intelligence mechanisms and the controversial role of our agencies. From 2007 to 2013, major security concerns were terror-related incidents and the failure of the intelligence apparatus to identify terror elements before they took deadly action.

The Security Service, MI5, and Secret Intelligence Service, MI6, are well-known components of the British intelligence machine, but these are just two parts of the machine; command and control operates through no fewer than four entities. The Cabinet office has its own important role. The Intelligence and Security Committee (ISC) was established in 1994, to oversee the expenditures of MI5, MI6 and GCHQ. It was reformed through the Justice and Intelligence Act 2013. Normally, national oversight practices vary greatly in terms of how much power is granted to intelligence services, and how they are accountable for their actions.[1]

In most European states, the democratic accountability of intelligence agencies is considered to be of great importance. Executive control, parliamentary oversight, judicial review, internal control and independent scrutiny are the ways democratic accountability is ensured.[2]

As a multicultural society, Britain has established a wide-ranging intelligence infrastructure to tackle extremism and international terrorism. Over the past forty years, specifically, technological advancement confined human being to limited activities. With this advancement, the power of the state also increased to carry out surveillance upon its citizens. Knowledge and surveillance management, compared to policing policy, has received a surprisingly high amount of attention. Intelligence has always been of primary importance for security and law enforcement agencies.[3]

With the introduction of the Special Irish Branch in 1883, the work of intelligence has been central in the operations of many police operational units. Intelligence is a well-classified, analyzed and processed knowledge, which plays important role in the preparation of security plans of a state. Intelligence is knowledge, a decision-oriented and action-oriented knowledge.[4]

Without decision-oriented knowledge and action-oriented knowledge, no knowledge and information can help security agencies in the protection of state security. Intelligence takes many forms, like national intelligence, strategic intelligence, tactical intelligence, signal intelligence, signature intelligence and foreign intelligence.

All these agencies are working under Intelligence Act 1994, Security Service Acts 1989 and 1996. Established in 1909, MI6 gathers foreign intelligence and is responsible to the foreign of-

1 *Securing the State*, David Omand, 2012.
2 *The Influence of Intelligence-led Policing Models on Investigative Policy and Practice in Mainstream Policing 1993–2007: Division, Resistance and Investigative Orthodoxy*. James Adrian, University of Portsmouth 2012.
3 *Securing the State*, David Omand, 2912.
4 "The United Kingdom Intelligence Machinery", November 2010, https://www.gov.uk/government/uploads/system/uploads/attachment_data/file/61808/nim-november2010

fice of the country. Another well reputed secret service, MI5, established in 1909, operates under the 1994 Intelligence Act, working closely with the local police. Britain's intelligence agencies cannot do their job without the consent of their ministers. Their hands are tied with Ministerial rope. Richard M. Bennett and Katie Bennett in their well-written report on British intelligence revealed some important facts about their accountability and responsibility:

> Britain has a complicated and rather bureaucratic political control over its intelligence and security community and one that tends to apply itself to long term targets and strategic intelligence program, but has little real influence on the behavior and operations of SIS and MI5. Not so much 'oversight' as blind-sight. Despite the domestic changes of recent years and their formal establishment as legal government organizations, there is still little true accountability for their action or valid test of their overall efficiency. This myriad of organizations include the four main elements of the UK intelligence community; Secret Intelligence Service (MI6) responsible for foreign intelligence, the Security Service (MI5), responsible for internal security and counter espionage within both the UK and Commonwealth countries. The GCHQ, Government Communication Headquarters, SIGINT and COMSEC agency and the DIS, Defense Intelligence Staff, responsible for the intelligence and security activities within the UK armed forces. They report to the JIC and through then to the civil Service (PSIS) and finally the Ministerial Committee (MIS).[1]

According to the author of Intelligence and Intelligence Analysis (2011): "Collectively, a number of oversight bodies, including the role of the UK Home Office, Her Majesty's Inspectorate of Constabulary (HMIC) and the Association of Chief Policing Officers (ACPO), and the National Policing Improvement Agency (NPIA) have achieved a lot more influence on the development of the UK policing intelligence capabilities than their counterparts in other countries discussed in this section." In the Annual Report of the intelligence and security committee for 2012–2013, some legal decisions have been taken to improve

---

1 "Richard M. Bennett and Katie Bennett report", August 2003.

the performance of intelligence agencies.[1]

In army circles, Britain's Defense Intelligence Staff (DIS) plays an important role in security related issues. This agency is part of the Defense Ministry, but helps other government departments. DIS was established in 1964 with staff members of other agencies and civilian experts. The agency supports the Ministry of Defense in security and intelligence matters. The Defense Intelligence Staff has three branches of intelligence services, including the Defense Geographic and Imagery Intelligence Agency (DGIA) and Defense Intelligence and Security Centre (DISC). All these intelligence services play a vital role in the national security of the United Kingdom; and another very important intelligence agency, one that plays an important role in tackling cyber terrorism, is GCHQ, which operates under the intelligence act 1994.[2]

The Government Communication Headquarters (GCHQ) is responsible for the protection of critical infrastructure. The National Security Strategy for 2009 defined the most important factors of the British security threat levels. The Security strategy specifically pinpointed the threat posed by the growth of Indian and Chinese economies; international terrorism; and weapons of mass destruction.[3]

On 13 May 2014, the *Guardian* reported GCHQ's illegal surveillance activities by developing spy programs that remotely hijack computers' cameras and microphones without the user's consent, the newspaper reported. The activities of GCHQ breach the right to private and family life under article 8 of the European convention on human rights and the 1990 Computer Misuse Act, Privacy International alleged. Eric King, deputy director of Privacy International, said: "The hacking programs being undertaken by GCHQ are the modern equivalent of the

---

1 *Intelligence and Intelligence Analysis*, Patrick Welsh, 2011, and also, annual report of intelligence and security committee for 2012–2013

2 "GIS in the Defense and Intelligence Communities". Defense Intelligence Staff, Ministry of Defense. https://www.gov.uk/defence-intelligence-services, and also, GCHQ aims to protect critical private networks from hackers. Christopher Williams, *The Guardian*, March 2011.

3 "The National Security Strategy of the United Kingdom: Security in an Interdependent World". Cabinet Office, London, March 2008.

government entering your house, rummaging through your filing cabinets, diaries, journals and correspondence, before planting bugs in every room you enter. Intelligence agencies can do all this without you even knowing about it, and can invade the privacy of anyone around the world with a few clicks," the *Guardian* reported.

Since the London underground terror attacks in 2005, the risk of international terrorism has not yet diminished, and the main threat to national security comes from home-grown militant groups and their networks. On the issue of home-grown extremist networks across Europe and the United Kingdom, co-operation among intelligence agencies and other security forces of these countries has taken a new form, with surveillance being given top priority; the watch-dog system puts prevention ahead of reactive responses.

As mentioned in the national security strategy paper, in the near future attacks may well be delivered through cyberspace. In Britain, MI5 has set up a Centre for the Protection of National Infrastructure (CPNI) to provide a reasonable security to the critical infrastructure of the country, while GCHQ is playing central role in the protection of national infrastructure.[1]

GCHQ and Signal Intelligence have a key role in protecting CPNI. To protect the basic infrastructure of a state, it must be born in mind, that national security measures must be based on traditional secret sources, open sources and personal data that is supposed to be protected. The issue of intercepting communications has become more complicated. Complaints have come in from various circles about intrusions into their privacy and family life. The law of terror or the Regulation of Investigatory Power Act 2000 (RIPA), Communication Act 1985 and the Police Act 1997, allow the state security agencies to intercept communications. The surveillance laws have been amended time and again, but in spite of all these technological efforts, no specific progress has been made in the interception of extremists' e-mails, even those that emanate from outside the country.

On 16 June 2013, *The Guardian* published a comprehensive report about the role of British intelligence agencies in intercept-

---

1 Ibid

ing communications which revealed that these agencies not only set up fake Internet cafes to secure information on diplomats but RIPA allowed agencies to use every conceivable means of information collection:

> The powers that allow British's intelligence agencies to spy on individuals, including foreign diplomats, were set out in the 1994 Intelligence Services Act (ISA). They were framed in a broad way to allow those involved in espionage to conduct all manner of operations with ministerial authority, and the type of technique used during the G20 summit four years ago suggest a creativity and technological capability The powers that allow Britain's intelligence agencies to spy on individuals, including foreign diplomats, were set out in the 1994 Intelligence Services Act (ISA). They were framed in a broad way to allow those involved in espionage to conduct all manner of operations with ministerial authority, and the types of techniques used during the G20 summit four years ago. After GCHQ, MI5 and MI6 were given their remit through the ISA; the Regulation of Investigatory Powers Act (RIPA) gave the agencies more precise tools to gather intelligence through techniques such as targeted interceptions. Under RIPA, the director general of MI5, the Chief of MI6 and the Director of GCHQ are among 10 very senior officials who can apply for warrant to either the foreign or home secretary.[1]

Criticisms of the interception of communications in the United Kingdom have been a central theme in the media and intellectual forums since 2001. There have been many complaints in public and government circles regarding phone tapping, bugging, e-mail hacking and privacy violations, but according to the Regulation of Investigatory Power Act 2000 (RIPA), and, specifically, Interception Communication Act, police and intelligence agencies have legal authority to intercept communication. Orla Lynskey described the legal control of data sharing with the United States and elucidated the legal aspects of privacy of British citizens in her recent article:

> Following the revelation that US intelligence agencies are engaged in widespread surveillance of internet

---

1 *The Guardian*, 16 June 2013, and also, *Domestic Security, Civil Contingencies and Resilience in the United Kingdom.* Paul Cornish, Chatham House, 2007.

communications using the so-called 'PRISM' program, President Obama's guarantees that PRISM does not apply to US citizens and it does not apply to people living in the US is unlikely to reassure many of this side of the Atlantic. PRISM gives the US National Security Agency (NSA) access to both communications contents and traffic data held on servers of global internet communications heavyweights such as Google, Facebook and Apple. The PRISM revelation quickly led to the concern that the UK's Government Communications Headquarter (GCHQ) was gathering data on UK citizens via PRISM, thereby circumventing the protection offered by the UK legal framework. William Hague, appearing before the Commons, was quick to refute this claim, describing it as 'baseless'.[1]

According to the RIPA's section 12, Secretary of State can authorize the relevant authority on the issue of interception. Some people, including parliamentarians, filed complaints regarding their telephone monitoring, but there are laws that allow monitoring telephone calls. Some laws that authorize state security agencies to conduct such monitoring are the Regulation of the Investigatory Power Act 2000 (RIPA), Telecommunications Interception Act of 2000 (TIA), Data Protection Act 1998 (DPA), and Telecommunication Regulations of 1999 (TR).[2]

In the Annual Report (2012) of the Interception Communications Commissioner (ICC), presented to Parliament pursuant to section 58 (6) of the Regulation of Investigatory Power Act 2000, it has been suggested that the media and the public still need to understand RIPA and the way it defines the remit of the commissioner, the Lawful Interception of Communication and the Acquisition of Communications Data (LICACD). Part 1, Chapter 2 of RIPA provides the power to acquire com-

1 "Looking through a legal PRISM at UK and US intelligence agency surveillance." Orla Lynskey described the legal control of data sharing with the United States and elucidated the legal aspects of privacy of British citizens in her article, in The London School of Economics and Political Science blogs, 13 June 2013, http://blogs.lse.ac.uk/politicsandpolicy/archives/34140.
2 Surveillance and counter Terrorism. How to make applications under the Regulations of Investigatory Power act 2000 (RIPA) and how the government respond to terrorist incidents and also, "Home Office March 2013. Interception Communications Code of Practice". Pursuant to section 71 of the Regulation of Investigatory Power Act 2000.

munications data. The RIPA bill was introduced in the House of Commons on 9 February 2000, and completed its parliamentary passage on 26 July. RIPA regulates the manner in which certain public bodies may conduct surveillance and access a person's electronic communications. The role of the Interception communications Commissioner has been defined in RIPA.[1]

Interception has been long established practice in the UK, but before 1985, there was no specific law or framework governing it. Ordinances had been governing the practice. From 1957 to 1981, government in the United Kingdom had three official reports available to the public: the 1957- Becket Report, the 1980-White Paper and the 1981-Dip Lock Report. In 1985, government hinted about the introduction of an Interception of Communications Act. Later on, following the White Paper, the same year, the Interception of Communications Act was introduced.[2]

In 2008, some reports revealed the government's Interception Modernization Program (IMP). According to the Home Office details, IMP is a cross government program established to maintain the ability to obtain communications data. In 2009, a Consultation Document was released, nominally to protect the public in a changing communication environment. Later on, the Home Secretary explained that the government wanted to minimize intrusions into people's private life.[3]

Britain has a complicated and rather bureaucratic political control over its intelligence and security community and one that tends to apply itself to long-term targets and strategic intelligence programs. The UK National Intelligence Service Hand-

1 "The Annual Report (2012) of the Interception Communications Commissioner (ICC)", presented to Parliament pursuant to section 58 (6) of the Regulation of Investigatory Power Act 2000, and also Investigatory Power Act 2000 (RIPA), Telecommunications Interception Act of 2000.
2 "Regulation of Interception of Communications in Selected Jurisdictions," 2 February 2005, Prepared by Thomas Wong Research and Library Services Division Legislative Council Secretariat. Moreover, Orla Lynskey describes the legal control of data sharing with the United States and elucidates the legal aspects of privacy of British citizens in her recent article. London School of Economics and Political Science
3 Consultation Document, 2009, and also, Investigatory Power Act 2000 (RIPA), Telecommunications Interception Act of 2000

book, Volume 1, Strategic Information Activities and Regulations (2013) have defined the role of the Prime Minister, Ministers and Secretaries in controlling intelligence agencies and their
operations:

> In their day-to-day operations the Intelligence and
> Security Agencies operate under the immediate control
> of their respective Heads who are personally respon-
> sible to Ministers. The Prime Minister is responsible
> for intelligence and security matters Permanent Secre-
> taries' Committee on the Intelligence Services (PSIS) -
> Civil Service control. Ministers are assisted in the gen-
> eral oversight of the Agencies by the Permanent Secre-
> taries' Committee on the Intelligence Services (PSIS).
> Members include the PUS to the FCO, MOD, HO and
> Treasury as well as the CO Intelligence Co-Coordina-
> tor representing the JIC. SIS is directly administered
> through the Permanent Under-Secretary's Department
> of the FCO in Downing Street.[1]

Successive Governments have gradually developed a techno-
logically-advanced system. According to the *Daily Times report*,
the Royal Academy of Engineering produced a report in March
2007 on the dilemmas of privacy and surveillance and the rapid
changes in technology; they made various recommendations.[2]
Meanwhile, nothing is confidential anymore; not only have we
done away with secrecy or secret planning and infiltration, we
live under constant surveillance at home, at the office, in the toi-
let, at the bus stop, on the sidewalk and in the streets, in airports, rail stations, shops and houses of worship. We are living
in a surveillance society.

Intelligence and Security Committee of Parliament in its annual report 2012-2013 has elucidated the arrangement for intelligence agencies and public bodies to access data:

> In June 2012, the Government published a draft
> Communications Data Bill which was intended to mod-

---

1 *"National Intelligence Service Handbook* Volume 1" Strategic Information
Activities and Regulations, 2013, and also, "the Annual Report of the
Interception Communications Commissioner 2012."
2 "Surveillance and counter Terrorism. How to make applications under the Regulations of Investigatory Power act 2000 (RIPA) and how
the government respond to terrorist incidents". Home Office March
2013.

ernize the existing arrangements for the Agencies and other public bodies to access this data. A Joint Committee of Parliament was established to conduct formal pre-legislative scrutiny of the draft Bill. It published its report in December 2012. The ISC undertook a parallel investigation, concentrating on the use of communications data by the intelligence and security Agencies. The ISC's report was sent to the Prime Minister in November in 2012, and was published in February 2013.[1]

There has been an overall loss of privacy protection around the world, and most specifically in the United Kingdom. We have no privacy safeguard system; we are open to everyone, everywhere across the country. With the introduction of identity and fingerprint databases, no one can remain anonymous; no one can simply be an innocent pedestrian. Governments check us everywhere, like livestock; they have reach to our private life, our financial records, bank accounts, bedrooms and even our pockets. Institutional fraud, password theft and population terrorism are the reasons behind all these surveillance preparations.

Telephones have become the enemies of individuals: cameras, handsets and cell phones, all watch us day and night. Even setting aside the CCTV cameras all over the streets and highways, we are watched wherever we go by our own mobile phones. With their discreet lenses they can transmit images to other cell phones. The 2007 report of the Home Affair Select Committee, the Secretary of State report presented to the parliament in 2008, and others suggest that surveillance of citizens' activities in the United Kingdom is only going to increase, and significantly.[2] According to some reports, we have over six million surveillance cameras in the country, recording a staggering 600,000 images in 1 hour.

Before this, in 1998, some legal progress was made in limiting surveillance and data use. These progresses were: The Human Rights Act 1998, the Data Protection Act 1998, and the Regula-

---

1 "The Government draft Communications Data Bill, June 2012".
2 "Protecting the Public in Changing Communications Environment, Summary of Responses to the 2009 Consultation Paper". http://webarchive.nationalarchives.gov.uk/+/http:/www.homeoffice.gov.uk/documents/cons-2009-communication-data/cons-2009-comms-data-responses2835.pdf?view=Binary.

tions of Regulatory Powers Act, 2000. The Basic Outline of the Data Protection Act has been laid in the report of the House of Lord Select Committee on Surveillance for 2008–09 as follows:

> The use of personal information is regulated by the Data Protection Act 1998 (DPA) which covers the circumstances under which personal information can be processed by public authorities and private organizations. Under the provisions of the DPA, any individual or organization engaged in the handling of personal information is required to ensure that all information is: Fairly and lawfully processed. Processed for limited purpose, adequate relevant and not excessive, accurate and up to date. Not kept for longer than is necessary, processed in line with rights of data subjects under the act.[1]

In our modern world, intelligence plays an important role in the decision making process. Britain's Security Service (MI5) is responsible for domestic intelligence. In the past, MI5 personnel could not initiate law enforcement activities, but in recent years, it helps the police in many ways. The role of intelligence in tackling foreign threats is of particular importance. The main duty of intelligence in tackling international terrorism is to know about the particular state, its geography, politics, ethnic composition, religion and its policy towards its neighbors. Keeping in view this role, the Security Service in the United Kingdom needs to change the way it tackles internal security threats. At present, terrorism, sectarianism and extremism are not effectively handled. As we know, the network of foreign intelligence and terror groups keep getting stronger, and they receive financial support from various underground networks, some within the country.

If the information once secured were only analyzed, discussed and shared with the other relevant institutions, it could have a positive impact. For an intelligence agency, in my opinion, it would be essential to establish and work to a "nationally owned" and led vision of security. If the reform process for

---

1 "Surveillance and counter Terrorism. How to make applications under the Regulations of Investigatory Power act 2000 (RIPA) and how the government respond to terrorist incidents", and also, Home Office March 2013, and also, "Dilemmas of Privacy and Surveillance". Royal Academy of Engineering, March 2007.

the security sector is not "nationally owned," it shows a lack of knowledge and experience. This is the foundation; states must develop a solid security system and security policy framework.[1]

In the national security strategy report for 2008, the Government identified the key threats facing the United Kingdom as: terrorism, weapons of mass destruction, trans-national organized crime, global instability, civil emergencies and state-led threats. As a result, the role of the Professional Head Intelligence Analysis (PHIA) was created "to provide a 'champion' for analysts and to establish a distinct career specialism for this group."[2]

In addition to this, the Government established more joint intelligence working groups to tackle the issue of terrorism from a technical standpoint: The Joint Terrorism Analysis Center, Center for the Protection of National Infrastructure, Joint Intelligence Committee and Assessment Staff and IT Centre, under the supervision of GCHQ. The Intelligence and Security Committee reported: "the Defense Intelligence Staff (DIS) is a critical part of the country intelligence community, and a single largest intelligence analytical capability in the UK."[3]

The Home Office in its study report has claimed that Internet-protocol-based communications will render the UK's domestic interception capabilities obsolete over the next decade. However, the Home Secretary told the committee:

> We do recognize the changing technology that we are facing, the way in which both the collection and dissemination of information Britain's National Security Challenges and data will change fundamentally, and it will change more quickly in this country then it will in many others . . .The impact of that will be to massively degrade (unless we make big changes) out ability, not just to be able to intercept, but actually potentially to

1 "Regulations of Investigatory Power act 2000 (RIPA)", and also, Home Office March 2013.
2 "National security strategy report for 2008".
3 "Guidance of Defense Intelligence: roles", Ministry of Defense, 12 December 2012. https://www.gov.uk/defence-intelligence-services, The DIS's task is to analyze information, from both overt and covert sources, and provide intelligence assessments, advice and strategic warning to the Joint Intelligence Committee, the MOD, Military Commands and deployed forces, and also National Intelligence Machinery, September 2001, https://www.gov.uk/government/uploads/system/uploads/attachment_data/file/250868/0114301808.

be able to collect the communications data in the first place in order to be able to target the interception.[1]

In this chapter we have analyzed the performance and responsibilities of the British intelligence community in detail; now, let's compare the checks and balances of certain European intelligence agencies and the system of checks and balances at MI5 and MI6. If we study the culture of intelligence community in France, we will find the same culture that Britain's intelligence community follows. In 04 July 2013, Reuters reported that the French intelligence agencies were spying on French citizens' phone calls, emails and social media activities.[2]

The French intelligence agency DGSE intercepts signals from computer and telephones within the country and between France and other states. According to a report in *The Guardian*, British intelligence has the same spying program on international phone and internet traffic, and shares what it gathers with the United States. Germany's hysteria over the allegations regarding the NSA spying network in Germany, reached a genuine fever pitch. In France, the intelligence services alleged that NSA was spying on the citizens of the country.[3]

French intelligence agencies have adopted the same intelligence mechanisms the UK intelligence pursues. The General Directorate of External Intelligence (DGSE), Central Directorate of Interior Intelligence (DCRI), Directorate of Military Intelligence (DRM), Directorate of Defense Protection and Security (DPSD), Intelligence and Electronic Warfare Brigade (BRGE), French Network and Information Agency (ANSSI), Judicial Police (DCPJ) and National Commission for the Control of Secu-

1 "Intelligence and Security Committee Annual Report 2007-2008". Intelligence and Security Committee, UK, 2009.
2 *Reuters* report, 04 July 2013, and the Security Service website. https://www.mi5.gov.uk.
3 The *Washington Post*, 10, June 2013, the Realities of Intelligence: The French View November 2, 2013, http://20committee.com/2013/11/02/the-realities-of-intelligence-the-french-view/ *Foreign Policy*, 14 February 2014, National Strategy for Combating Terrorism. 2003. "Fresh Leak on US Spying: NSA Accessed Mexican President's Email", By Jens Glüsing, Laura Poitras, Marcel Rosenbach and Holger Stark, *Speigel online International*, 20 October 2013. http://www.spiegel.de/international/world/nsa-hacked-email-account-of-mexican-president-a-928817.html.

rity Interception (CNCIS) have been praised for their successes in preventing planned terrorist attacks since 2001. All these institutions have established their own intelligence networks. There are many boards of oversight that scrutinize the actions of the intelligence apparatus and aim to ensure accountability.

In Romania, the intelligence community changed its approach and culture after the collapse of communist bloc in the 1990s. Intelligence reforms brought about positive changes in the country, while domestic and foreign intelligence were reformed through different legal practices. The Romanian intelligence community consists of six services and ministerial substructures that are specifically changed with covert intelligence collection. In December 1989, the former fourth Directorate for Military Counterintelligence and the fifth Security and Guard Directorate and the sixth Criminal Investigations Directorate were ultimately dissolved. Moreover, 3,000 personnel were dismissed. Before the formation of the new parliament in Romania, parliamentary oversight was designated as an issue of first priority. The SRI Director was responsible to submit a regular report regarding his agency's activities.[1]

---

1 *Democratic Control of Intelligence Services: Containing Rogue Elephants*, edited by Dr Hans Born, Ashgate Publishing, Ltd., 2013, and also, "European approached to Home Land Security and Counter Terrorism". 24 July 2006. "CRS Report for Congress, Congressional Research Service". https://www.fas.org/sgp/crs/homesec/RL33573.pdf

CHAPTER 10. INTELLIGENCE WAR IN CYBERSPACE: THE ART OF FIGHTING WITHOUT FIGHTING

Five Eyes, TEMPORA, PRISM, ECHELON and the politics of Intelligence war received extensive coverage in the print and electronic media across Europe and the United States. In response to the uprisings that swept the Arab world, North Africa, Syria and Ukraine, concerns about the possible cyber attacks on State computers, or cyber exports, have been amplified in the media, sparking a debate as to the appropriate course of action. Western states have invented the most dangerous cyber technologies that can destroy the data of a state within minutes. Electronic Frontiers Foundation in its recent paper warned:

> The reach of these technologies is astonishingly broad — governments can listen in on cell phone calls, use voice recognition to scan mobile networks, read emails and text messages, censor web pages, track a citizen's every movement using GPS, and can even change email contents while en route to a recipient.[1]

1 "Mass Surveillance Technologies", The Electronic Frontier Foundation Report, https://www.eff.org/issues/mass-surveillance-technologies, and also, Cyber terrorism in the Information Age: A Comparative Analysis of the U.S. & UK State Sponsored Strategies August 15, 2007. *Black Ice: The Invisible Threat of Cyber-Terrorism*, DanVerton, McGraw-Hill 2003, also, *The Impact of New Technologies on the Military Arena: Information Warfare*. Captain Paulo Fernando Viegas Nunes, Portuguese Army

Western spy agencies build 'cyber magicians' to manipulate online discourse, according to the Russian Television report (RT, 25 Feb 2014). Secret units within the Eye-Five intelligence alliance engage in covert on-line operations that aim to invade, deceive, and control on line communities and individuals through the spread of false information and use of ingenious social science tactics.[1]

Germany cancelled its Cold War era pact with the UK, while European intelligence agencies have become more vigilant about UK surveillance mechanisms. The US National Security Agency (NSA) and the UK Government Communications Headquarters (GCHQ) had prepared a comprehensive list of target individuals and institutions including the European competition commissioner, buildings and NGOs that provide financial assistance to Africa.[2]

Brussels reacted furiously to claims that the NSA and GCHQ spied on the European commissioner. The European commissioner has access to highly confidential commercial information. The commissioner's spokeswoman said, "This is not the type of behavior that we expect from strategic partners, let alone from our own member states."[3] Now, the EU decided to create its own intelligence agency by developing new surveillance drones and spy satellites. The Italian Prime Minister attacked British Prime Minister David Cameron over allegations that the UK was intercepting secret Italian communications and passing them on to the NSA. The latest revelations from Edward Snowden show that the NSA and GCHQ spied on 100 top officials from 60 states, including the Israeli prime minister, European policy makers and several aid groups.[4]

Document, 5 March 2001, *Air & Space Power Journal*. Also see, *World News*, November 2008.

1 *RT News* report, 25 Feb 2014, and also, "In the Cyber Arena", *Indian Express*, 03 April 2013. *Cyber Terrorism: A Guide for Facility Managers*, by Joseph F. Gustin, Marcel Dekker Publisher, 2003.

2 "Cyber Terrorism: Logic Bomb versus the Truck Bomb". *Global Dialogue*, Dorothy Denning. Vol, 2, Number-4, 2000.

3 "State of the Art: Attackers and Targets in Cyberspace". John B. Sheldon. *Journal of Military and Strategic Studies*, Vol. 14, Issue-2 2012.

4 *Countering Threats in Space and Cyberspace. A Proposed Combined Approach*. Lorenzo, Valeri, Luiss Guido Carli, Chatham House, January 2013.

In the UK, parliamentarians and politicians expressed deep concern over European leaders' complaints against the UK's intelligence policies. In the end of 2013, the Chiefs of the three UK intelligence agencies — MI5, MI6, and GCHQ — appeared before the Intelligence and Security Committee to explain the way intelligence operates.[1]

The US and UK are members of the Five-Eye intelligence sharing alliance, including Australia, New Zealand and Canada, but their method of surveillance clearly violates the principles of the alliance. French intelligence is cooperating with the Five Eyes alliance by systematically providing them with information. Sweden, Israel and Italy are also cooperating with the NSA and GCHQ.

Cyberspace has become decisive arena of modern information warfare. It opens up new dimensions to conflict.[2] Cyber terrorism and hacktivism are the art of fighting without fighting; of defeating enemies without spilling their blood or your own. Hackers break rules to retrieve information. They are breaking the law of targeted country. These techniques are updated in an ongoing way. Technological advancement has also enabled cyber-espionage to reach sensitive data despite sophisticated protection software.[3]

Computer worms and drone attacks are facilitated by powerful software which is easily available on the Internet. In 2008, British Prime Minister Gordon Brown presented white paper to Parliament, which served as the first attempt to distil a National Security Strategy for the United Kingdom. The starting point for the strategy was the existence of a fixed and unwavering obligation on the part of government to protect its citizens and the in-

---

1 *Cyber Security and the UK Critical National Infrastructure*: Chatham House, Paul Cornish David Livingston, Dave Clement and Clair Yorke. September 2011.
2 "Cyber Security Strategy for 2009", and also, *BBC*, June 25, 2009. Assessing the risk of cyber terrorism, and The Handbook No-1 (A Military Guide to Terrorism in the Twenty-First Century) of the US army, which is a basic terrorism primer prepared under the direction of the U.S. Army Training and Doctrine Command, Assistant Deputy Chief of Staff for Intelligence Threats.
3 *Daily Tech News*, 13 March 2013. Yahoo News, 11 March 2013. Truther.org.http://truthernews.wordpress.com/2013/03/31/chinese-kamikaze-done-attack-on-pearl-harbor-hawaii-imminent/.

terests of the state. In February 2013, Chatham House published a comprehensive report on cyber security and global interdependence, in which the vulnerability of Britain's National Critical Infrastructure has been highlighted with different perspectives:

> Security of the cyber layer is of great societal importance, yet the dense interconnection between sectors—facilitated by cyberspace—makes it harder to decide what to protect. As transportation intertwines with food distribution and telecommunications, and as these and many other sectors are supported fundamentally by the finance and energy sectors, it is more difficult to draw clear boundaries between critical areas. In the United Kingdom, the centre for the protection of National Infrastructure says that there are certain 'critical' elements of infrastructure, the loss or compromise of which would have a major, detrimental impact on the availability or integrity of essential services, leading to severe economic and social consequences or to loss of life.[1]

Terrorist groups, nations and non-state actors are trying to benefit from cyberspace. In his articles, published in Journal of Military and Strategic Studies (2012), John B. Sheldon has warned that nation states and criminal groups pose a real threat to our national assets:

> Nation-states, terrorist groups, criminal organizations and hactivists all benefit from the unique characteristics of cyberspace that make the threat the pose real, or in many cases, help inflate the threat they pose in the minds of others. Cyberspace is the domain in which cyber operations take place; cyber power is the sum of strategic effects generated by cyber operations in the form of cyberspace. These effects can be felt within cyberspace, as well as the other domains of land, sea, air and space, and can also be cognitively effective with individual human beings.[2]

Cyber attacks play an important role in changing the environment of war. Several states used cyber attacks against rival.

---

1 "Chatham House report", February 2013, and also, *Drone Warfare: Killing by Remote Control*. Medea Benjamin. 2013. *Daily Tech News*, 13 March 2013.
2 *Journal of Military and Strategic Studies* 2012, and also, Strategic Conflict Inevitable between China and US, Prof. Wang Jisi, "Global Research", 6 August 2010.

Russian attacked Estonia, Pakistan attacked India and Syrian government used cyber attacks against rebels. Cyber war between China and US and between Britain and China can be viewed as a modern technological or information war in the cyberspace. In a Centre for Strategic and International Studies paper on cyber war, James A. Lewis (2010) has outlined the strategic implication of cyber attacks in war and peace:

> To understand the role of cyber attack in war, we must ask of it the same question we would ask of any other weapon system: range, destructiveness, cost effect, and the political implication of use. Cyber attack has both tactical and strategic implications. It can be use against deployed forces or against strategic targets in the opponent's homeland (e.g., those that contribute to an opponent's ability to wage war. Its range is practically unlimited, in that it can be used anywhere the global network extends.[1]

The emergence of cyber terrorism tactics are changing ways every year that can make it more dangerous and difficult to counter. Hackers retrieve secret information from exploiting the other side's carelessness. They are given the task to acquire (i.e., steal) confidential information. *Daily Tech News* reports revealed that it had found information indicating that China is building one of the world's largest drone fleets aimed at attacking the United States in the event of a war.[2]

An addition to cyber attacks, drone warfare is also considered a modern technological war in cyberspace. The drone technology could act as decoys, use electronic warfare to jam communication and radar, guide missile strike on carriers, fire missiles at enemy targets. Inflammatory war propaganda and diplomatic tension between US and China indicates that a World War III scenario between the two states is taking shape.[3] The issue of cyber terrorism is testing the relationship between China and America, prompting President Barack Obama to raise concern

1 The Centre for Strategic and International Studies, "On cyber war", 2010, and also, "Obama Orders US to Draw up Overseas Targets List for Cyber Attacks". *The Guardian*, 7 June 2013.

2 *China's Drone Swarms Rise to Challenge US Power*, Jeremy Hsu, *Tech News*, 13 March 2013, and also, *Huffington Post*, 24 March 2013.

3 *US in Cyber War arms Race with China, Russia*. Rick Wilking. 21 February 2013, Indian Strategic Studies.

over the expanding Chinese cyber networks across the globe. China and Russian have trained thousands of cyber warriors and use them against the West.

The United States and Britain see the biggest and quickly growing cyber intelligence networks of China, Russia and India as a threat to their world dominance, but all sides, from China's Liberation Army (PLA) to the US army, CIA, Pentagon and GCHQ, have been unable to defeat each other in the war in cyberspace for the past decade. To retrieve information about advanced technology, the PLA has exploited security flaws in software and email attachments to sneak into the network of various institutions and companies. According to recent reports, hackers of both US and China are well-trained who know what to do and how to attack across the border.[1]

Russia is part of the game. It has also developed a strong cyber warriors networks. The case of Russian cyber operation is indicative of the potential pattern of cyber intelligence operations in near future.[2] Russia holds a broad concept of cyber warfare, cyber intelligence, and cyber counter intelligence, degradation of navigation support, psychological pressure and propaganda.[3] The Russian Secret Agency (FSB) recently received directions from President Putin to develop a new system to secure Russian networks and detect cyber threats.[4] Western cyber war experts are of the opinion that the Russian cyber network is stronger than China. The ongoing intelligence war among China, the US, the UK, and European states, India, Pakistan and Russia is now being played out in cyberspace.

New cyber weapons and signal intelligence technology are among the most recent developments in Asia, Europe and America. India has developed modern technology too, attacking Pakistani institutions, while Pakistan's army (with the help of

---

1 "Chinese Intelligence in US, Global Security", March 2011, the *New York Times*, 13 January 2013, The *Washington Post*, 14 January 2013.
2 *The New York Times*, 23 April 2013.
3 *Russian Cyber Operations, Potomac Institute for Policy Studies*, Brenner S, 2009, *Cyber Threats: The Emerging*, Fault Lines of the Nation State, Oxford University Press. Cyber Attack: Top US Security Report, Tom Gjelten, 12 March 2013, *Los Angeles Times*, 12 March 2013.
4 *International Policy Digest*, 26 January 2013. *Russia's Top Cyber Sleuth Foils US Spies Helps Kremlin*, Pals, Noah Shachtma, http://www.brookings.edu/research/opinions/2012/07/23-cyber-security-kaspersky-shachtman.

China) has developed its own cyber technologies. China is striving to drill into the US and UK's technology by attacking their institutional networks, military industry and financial sectors, while Russia is doing the same. The United Kingdom and America are not in a position to effectively counter Chinese and Russian cyber networks, because the techniques used by Chinese secret services to recruit and train new cyber warriors are quite different from the West and Europe.[1]

This new industry of information theft now sends its trained members across the world. Their tools are not tanks and guns; they are missiles that target the institutional assets from safe distances. Western societies have become totally dependent on information technologies; therefore, attacks on computers have increased. Recently, Britain's security agencies are struggling to cope with the emerging threat of cyber terrorism and cyber attacks.

The emergence of technological threats from China and Russia, Iran, India, North Korea and their day-to-day increasing attacks on computers in the UK and Europe has threatened business communities and created a climate of fear. Britain is an easy target of cyber terrorism as various institutions recently reported the vulnerability of their computer data.[2] Government and the private sector are under threat. This is a new chapter in international security policies. New strategies require allocation of huge funds; and hectic efforts to protect the private sector is one main objective of the country's cyber security strategy, but GCHQ and its cyber force need more time to improve its countering strategies. The GCHQ and its experts are frankly scrambling to meet the growing fear of cyber terrorism.

During the last ten years, the UK Ministry of Defense, FCO, Border Agency, Home Office and Metropolitan Police experienced numerous cyber attacks, which ranged from terror attacks to hacktivism, professional criminals and terror groups or those that they sponsor. National security, business, economic security and the market economy have come under attack from these groups time and again, but the response from the counter terrorism department has been very dismal. In April 2013,

1 Ibid.
2 *The Independent*, 23 April 2013.

Britain's Cabinet Office Minister Chloe Smith warned that the government faces around 33,000 cyber attacks each month from state sponsored groups.[1]

Cyber attacks remain one of the top four threats facing Britain's national security. Terrorists also use cyberspace to facilitate traditional forms of terrorism such as bomb attacks. Britain has a well-established office of cyber security and information assurance (OSCIA), which supports the Minister for Cabinet Office and the National Security Council, but it, has failed to respond to the present cyber threat satisfactorily. China has recently attacked Canada's important computers. In the end of 2010, series of events and rapidly developing threats of cyber terrorism across Asia and Europe created alarming situation. To counter the looming threat of cyber terrorism, many states decided to have some immediate amendments in their cyber security strategies.

Most private and state owned computers connected to the Internet are vulnerable to infiltration and remote control. In 2000, a police department in Japan reported that it had obtained an illicit software program that could track vehicles.[2] Similarly; e-mail bombs can harm or make vulnerable nuclear installations. In 2009 and 2010, China attempted to get inside the UK foreign office computer 1000 times.

The recent success of Pakistan's army in the field of IT and cyber warfare diverted attention of many states, including US, UK and Germany towards the creation of a strong cyber command to deal with the challenges emanating from the cyberspace. In 2012, in Pakistan's Punjab province, efforts are under way to establish a cyber security unit but, according to DIG Malik Khuda Bakhsh Awan, the government needed trained people to counter the Indian cyber attacks. The recent terror attacks in Pakistan and the vulnerability of its military industry has worried nuclear

1 *China's Cyber Power and America's National Security.* Colonel Jayson M. Spade. US Army War College. 2012. http://www2.gwu.edu/-nsarchiv/NSAEBB/NSAEBB424/docs/Cyber-072.
2 *Express Tribune*, 8 June 2013. *The News International*, April 2013. Cyber Secure Pakistan's Initiative Launched. Pakistan Information Security Association (PISA) launched cyber secure initiative for strengthening the efforts of the government of Pakistan in securing the cyber space. *Strategic Security and Defense Review* published in October 2010.

experts; the challenges Pakistan faces are significant. Terrorist Taliban and other groups want to recruit their IT experts in the field of nuclear and cyber attacks. Any rival state or firm can provide their members with the training of cyber attacks.

Cyber terrorism has already been a grave threat to UK state institutions. Taliban and extremist groups are already planning to target military installations in the country. They have acquired the expertise to use the internet as a way to promote their cause and to conduct their terrorist operations. In 2008, Pakistan set the death penalty for cyber terrorism. According to the country's cyber ordinance: "Whoever commits the offence of cyber terrorism and causes death of any person, shall be punishable with death or imprisonment for life." [1]

The ordinance also sets punishment for electronic fraud, electronic forgery, system damage and unauthorized encryption. Most experts worry about the weak counter measures of the country and complain about the ineffectiveness of Prevention of Electronic Crime Ordinance, introduced in February 2009. Currently there is no law in the country to tackle the recent wave of cyber attacks on state institutions. In recent years, governments and international organizations have focused on cyber security and are increasingly aware of the urgency. In the United Kingdom, cyber security featured prominently in the National Security Strategy and the Strategic Security and Defense Review published in October 2010. Cyber warfare is arguably at the most serious end of the spectrum of security challenges posed by — and within — cyberspace. Just like the tools of conventional warfare, cyber technology can be used to attack the machinery of state, financial institutions, the national energy and transport infrastructure and public morale.

However, while some actions may appear aggressive and warlike, they may not necessarily be intended as acts of war. It is important, therefore, to distinguish between warfare and non-warfare in cyberspace. The action and its warlike properties matter as much as the actor. For example, not all cyber activities of terrorist groups, spies and organized criminals necessarily constitute acts of cyber warfare.[2]

1 Ibid.
2 *BBC*, 8 October 2010.

A large-scale conventional military attack on the UK is rated only as a "tier three" priority alongside disruption to oil and gas supplies and a large-scale radioactive release from a civil nuclear site.[1] In a joint foreword to the Strategy, Prime Minister David Cameron and Deputy Prime Minister Nick Clegg said that there needs to be a "radical transformation" in the way that Britain thinks about and organizes its national security. "We are entering an age of uncertainty. This strategy is about gearing Britain up for this new age of uncertainty — weighing up the threats we face and preparing to deal with them," they said.[2]

Home secretary Theresa May said:

> As technology becomes an increasing issue for terrorists as they become more advanced [in how they use it], our capacity in dealing with it as a threat has to be constantly enhanced. The new counter-terrorism strategy is our response to the continuing and evolving threat we face as a country, she added. "It is both comprehensive and wide-ranging, dealing with grand strategic issues and detailed technological points.[3]

In 2013, the governments of the United Kingdom and Australia announced a partnership to meet the challenges of cyberspace. The recent Wiki Leaks exposure, attacks on various websites and the data infringement incidents stress the need to strengthen cyber security. Here in Britain, defense researchers are of the opinion that the data of the military industry and other departments is under threat from hackers of various states. The chiefs of the country's most powerful intelligence agencies, GCHQ and MI5, warned that government institutions, colleges, industries, defense and intelligence networks face a constant threat from cyber warriors.[4]

---

1 23. *China's Cyber Power and America's National Security*. Colonel Jayson M. Spade. US Army War College. 2012. http://www2.gwu.edu/-nsarchiv/NSAEBB/NSAEBB424/docs/Cyber-072.
2 *The US-China Economic and Security Review Commission. Capabilities of the People Republic of China to Conduct Cyber Warfare and Computer Network exploitation.* Krekel Bryan. Virginia, 2009.
3 *The Computer Weekly*, 12 July 2011, and also, CNN, 29 July 2011.
4 *Strategic Fragility: Infrastructure Protection and National Security in the Information Age.* By Robert A. Miller and Irving Lanchow, Center for Technology and National Security Policy National Defense University,

The recently announced National Security Strategy gives a frightening picture of future cyber terror threats. Prime Minister David Cameron said, "This is what UK defense needs." The Chief of the GCHQ warned that cyber terrorism might target the critical infrastructure in the near future. "Cyberspace has lowered the bar for entry to the espionage game for states and criminals."[1]

Electronic attacks on institutions offer many advantages. First, they are cheaper and the action is very difficult to track. Second, they can use the method of distributed denial of services to overburden the government and its agencies' electronic bases. A recent detailed investigation of the Indian government revealed that a cyber spy network is operating out of China, which is targeting the Indian business, diplomatic, strategic and academic interests. India complains about Pakistan's cyber attacks as well.[2]

Cyber war between Iran and the Arab world is another interesting story. Iranian hackers have been trying to retrieve sensitive data from the computers of state institutions of various Arab states for a long time. Meanwhile, seeking to destroy the Iranian nuclear program, Israel sends strong viruses to the computers of Iranian nuclear installations. Russia attacked the government computers of Estonia and Georgia in 2007 and destroyed important defense and infrastructural data.

Attacks on military industry, infrastructure, communication, police networks and financial markets pose a rapidly growing but little understood threat to the security of a state. Information warfare among the states of Asia and Europe and between China, UK and US can further disrupt the economic cycle of the global economy.

Protecting the Critical Infrastructure against Terrorism, Presentation by: Colonel (ret.) Ed Badolato, CEO, Integrated Infrastructure Specialist in Resources and Environmental Policy, May 26, 2009.

1 *BBC*, 13 October 2010, Director GCHQ, Iain Lobban, made cyber speech at the International Institute of Strategic Studies, 12 October 2012, Mr. Iain Lobban, Director GCHQ, set out GCHQ's broad perspective on cyber security. Speaking to the International Institute for Strategic Studies, he outlined how cyber is not just a national security or defense issue but is something which goes to the heart of our economic well-being, and national interest. http://www.gchq.gov.uk/press_and_media/speeches/Pages/Cyber-speech-at-the-IISS.aspx.
2 *BBC*, 30 April 2012.

This will become a weapon of choice in future conflicts. Cyber warriors use different viruses to disable and meddle with the military data of another country. After the development of the cyber weapons in Asia and Europe, experts say the days of foot soldiers are numbered. The use of computer viruses as weapons against a rival state has now become routine. General Sir David Richard hinted about the establishment of a Cyber Command to protect the country from online strikes and launch its own attacks.

In October 2010, the UK Defense Ministry debated the role of the internet in modern warfare in its Strategic Defense and Security Review. Defense and other departments in the UK and US are feeling a strong threat from Chinese, Russian and Indian cyber warriors. The Chinese People's Liberation Army and the Russian military, like other advanced states, mostly depend on electronic warfare, attacking an enemy's networked information system. In the United Kingdom, the Science and Technology Strategy for Countering International Terrorism for August 2009 highlights technological measures for countering terrorism:

> The UK Security and Resilience Industry Suppliers Community (RISC) provide a focal point for the government to communicate with industry about it counter terrorism needs.[1]

According to *The Guardian* news report, Harry Raduege, former director at the Pentagon, said, cyber attacks were growing in intensity and sophistication. "We have experienced a number of attacks against the financial sector, on the power grid and against our defense capability." Likewise, the Director General of French Information Security said that he had nightmares about attacks on the electricity system, transport, water supplies, the financial sector and hospitals, which are dependent on computers.[2]

1 "The United Kingdom's Science and Technology Strategy for Countering International Terrorism for August 2009", and also, Future Global Shocks. OECD/IFP Project on Cyber Warfare. 14 January 2011.
2 "NATO Cyber Alliance", 20 September, 2010, http://defensetech. org/2010/09/20/a-nato-cyber-alliance/#ixzz31F28hGTn. Defense. org, *The Guardian* 05 May 2010, and also, *Daily Outlook* Afghanistan, 20 December 2011.

The recent comprehensive report of the International Commission on Nuclear non-Proliferation and Disarmament warned that terrorist organizations have the potential to use the Internet and private network infrastructures to stage a nuclear attack. The report has quoted cyber attack on Russian nuclear network. According to the report, cyber warriors could hack into government emails and private networks, eliminating the need to attack a nuclear command and control center directly.

The police chief of the Indian Punjab warned that cyber-terrorism is considered a serious threat at par with nuclear, bacteriological and chemical weapons. The police chief warned that Indian cyber criminals have adopted computer technology with the sole objective of evading the tight conventional surveillance systems of the Police and Intelligence agencies.[1]

India recently suggested a close partnership with the US in cyber security, particularly against cyber terrorism, as the two countries take their economic and technological collaboration to the next level. Indian Minister of State for Communications and Information Technology Sachin Pilot suggested a close cooperation with the White House.

The recent discovery of the "Stuxnet" computer worm cyber-weapon apparently designed and used to infect Iran's nuclear development control systems, presents a very powerful and dangerous new threat to our current way of life. Links between computer hackers and terrorists, or terrorist-sponsoring nations may be difficult to confirm. Membership in the most highly-skilled computer hacker groups is sometimes very exclusive and limited to individuals who develop, only with each other.

Some experts believe that cyber attacks against multiple networks, including target surveillance and testing of sophisticated new hacker tools, might require from two to four years of preparation, but recent reports indicate that some states have already developed these skills. The Canadian government departments initially targeted are evidence of this. The uneasy question of how to deal with cyber-aggression is looms over the internation-

---

1 *The Tribune*, Chandigarh, India – Punjab, 26 July 2010, and also, Cabinet Office Minister Chloe Smith warned that government faces around 33,000 cyber attacks each month from state sponsored groups. *The Independent*, 23 April 2013.

al community. In the absence of feasible prevention, deterrence of cyber terrorism may be the best alternative.

The more sophisticated a nation's infrastructure, the more vulnerable it may become. According to a paper by Robert S. Owen, "Damage to non-critical infrastructures could inflict considerable economic damage and could cause an existing or emerging technology to lose acceptance in a targeted region or society." Military planners with goals of economic damage or decreased quality of life could achieve these ends at relatively low cost without attempts to physically attack the critical infrastructure itself. Interdependencies between electrical power grids, accessible computerized systems and other "soft" targets allow for potential terrorist intruders. [1]

A top UK electronic espionage expert claimed that: "cyber attacks present a 'real and credible' threat to the UK and have already caused 'significant disruption' to government computer systems." Director General of the UK Secret Electronic Intelligence Agency, GCHQ has warned that: "the internet had opened up opportunities for cyber attacks from both criminals and hostile nations, adding that it would be 'very, very hard' to tell which state was behind the attack."[2]

The United Kingdom is not the only state under cyber threat. The Defense Signal Directorate of Australia recently reported various attempts on its military networks. According to a Government report, more than 20,000 malicious e-mails are attempted on various institutions every month. Cyber terrorism is the most disruptive form of war short of military attack. Some UK military experts believe that terror cells in the country and hostile states using this violent weapon can target critical infrastructure, such as nuclear power stations, electricity supply, water communication and transport systems. Keeping all these threats in view, Turkey is struggling to establish a strong Cyber Security Command to counter cyber-terrorism attacks against

---

1 Ibid.
2 *Cyber Warfare and Cyber Terrorism*, Lech Janczewski, Andrew M. Colarik, Idea Group Inc (IGI), 2008, and also, *Cyber Security Threat Characterization: A Rapid Comparative Analysis*. Neil Robinson, Luke Gribbon, Veronika Horvath, Kate Robertson. RAND, 2012. *Infrastructures of Cyber Warfare*, Robert S. Owen Texas A&M University, USA. http://www.irma-international.org/viewtitle/7437/.

the country.[1]

The Ukrainian Central Election Commission's servers were attacked in March 2006 by hackers but notwithstanding, some 29,000 attacks on the system, the servers continued to operate.[2] In 2007, the Russian cyber military command attacked Estonia. In Georgia, the Government complained about cyber attacks, for example, the defacement of President Saakashvili's website.

In 2012, debates on the security arrangements for the Olympics in view of the threat of terrorism raised many questions about the cost and massive deployment of army and police forces in London.[3] Political commentators and community leaders asked why people were feeling insecure in spite of the allocation of a massive budget to the police and its intelligence units. These debates also led to the commissioning of a number of studies in government and private research institutions to help the government design a better security plan for the Olympic Games. The army prepared its own security plan involving the deployment of Royal Navy's largest ship, the 22,500-ton helicopter carrier HMS *Ocean*, in Greenwich for the duration of the games, and an assault vessel in Weymouth where the sailing events were to take place.[4]

Moreover, ground-to-air missiles were deployed; this was the first time such deployment was taking place. Most security measures were police-led but the army had its contribution to make as well. According to the Ministry of Defense, some 5,000 troops would support the police, up to 7,500 provided venue security and 1,000 provided logistic support. The UK police also deployed more than 12,000 officers with the operation being planned on the basis that security threat level would be set at severe.[5]

---

1 *BBC*, 13 October, 2010, "Home Office: Cyber Crime Strategy", Presented to Parliament by the Secretary of State for the Home Department by Command of Her Majesty, March 2010.
2 *Daily Times*, 22 February 2011.
3 *Critical Threats, Russia and the Cyber Threat*, Kara Flook, 13 May 2009, http://www.criticalthreats.org/russia/russia-and-cyber-threat. Also, *Hacking nuclear command and Control*, Jason Fritz, paper available at the International Commission on Nuclear Non-proliferation and Disarmament.
4 *The Times*, 29 March 2009.
5 *Daily the News International*, Pakistan.

The Intelligence and Security Committee report and Chief of MI5 Jonathan Evan called the Olympic Games a huge event and said: "We are going to be pulling at least 150 intelligence staff out of other roles across the services to put them back into intelligence work at the frontline."[6]

In such a large public event, the threat of a terror attack couldn't be ruled. Maintaining the security of 8 million spectators was a difficult task. Government and law enforcement agencies were increasingly concerned about possible cyber attacks, foreign hackers and intelligence networks seeking to carry out actual terrorist attacks or simply disruption. Chief of GCHQ also warned about the cyber threat to UK security. Mr. Loban warned that the country was witnessing the development of a criminal market place, where cyber dollars are traded in exchange for people's credit cards details.

In this global marketplace, the Internet empowers a growing list of revenue-generating e-business activities. In the near future, cyber terrorism and economic jihad could ultimately target all Britain state institutions, showing that it can be just as destructive as it has been constructive. The Internet has been a driving force behind the modernization of Russia, China and Indian economy and military industries worldwide.

NBC News revealed that the London Olympic Technology Operation Centre was expected to rely on 9,500 computers with more than 1,000 to run the security infrastructure including communication channels and transport networks.[7] According to the director of the Research Control Risk Group: "London has become the pre-eminent terrorist target in Europe, because extremists' threat in the past had been vague and undefined war against the West."[8]

Terrorists may use computers not only to inflict damage to the security infrastructure but to disrupt the whole communication system. These groups have frequently stated that they will launch large scale attacks. They will try to create panic and fear by using IEDs, specifically peroxide and fertilizer, as they already used in Norway in July 2011. According to intelligence

---

6 *Express Tribune*, 8 June 2013.
7 *Daily Times*, 22 February 2011.
8 "Worst Indian Government Websites." *The Times of India*, 20 June 2012.

reports, these non-state actors have acquired advanced technology and they recruit young people in small cells where they use Internet and other communication means. Intelligence reports in Russia have revealed that extremist forces can export radio-nuclear materials or dirty bombs. If they succeed in their plans, there could be massive destruction in London.

The UK Home Office has experienced severe cyber attacks, while in its website the office notes that during a terrorist attack, it is the Home Secretary who leads the government response, according to his/her responsibility for countering terrorism in Scotland, England and Wales. On April 8, 2012, cyber terrorists from unknown base challenged the government and its relevant institutions, saying that they are capable of hacking any website within the country. In my own previous articles and research papers, I warned about future cyber terror attacks on UK state institutions, and this has now become a reality.

The emergence of well trained cyber groups are the biggest threat to corporate information security. These highly skilled groups are collaborating to discover new vulnerabilities in the financial markets and government-run institutions. Cyber attacks on UK state and private institutions have risen with the cost estimated to be £26 billion and in the US one trillion dollars. The GCHQ is considered to be the guardian of Britain's vulnerable financial assets and National Critical Infrastructure. Everyone is affected; on March 20, 2012, the Chinese government complained about cyber attacks against state and private institutions. *China Daily* reported that millions of computers were affected by these attacks.[1]

Now this war has reached a breaking point. To combat the forces of financial jihad, Britain's Cyber Security Strategy was published in November 2011, which underlined the technical aspect of the threat faced by the country's institutions from economic jihadists and state-sponsored cyber forces. The basic objectives of the UK Cyber Security Strategy are to introduce a culture of partnership and transparency both across business and within the international community in an effort to meet the

---

1 *Daily Times*, 7 November 2008, *Daily Telegraph*, 6 November 2008, *Daily Mail* and Register newspapers also reported death penalty for cyber terrorist in Pakistan.

growing cyber threat.[1]

In a London Conference on Cyberspace, experts converged to confront the growing threat to information security from several states waging economic jihad. In his speech, British Foreign Secretary William Hague issued a stern warning to countries involved in financial terrorism against other states and said this undeclared war is unacceptable.100 Prime Minister David Cameron warned that this warfare is against Britain's interests.[2]

Former British Minister for Counterterrorism Baroness Neville Jones said China and Russia were certainly involved in this sort of war. This undeclared war against the financial and military assets of the country has resulted in significant economic losses due to the theft of critical or secret data from important institutions and the cost of protecting against it. Given the increasing availability of malicious software tools, in 2010 and 2011 various private and government institutions experienced cyber attacks.

In 2011, the United States Office of Counterintelligence Executive (ONCIX) released a comprehensive report which documented the loss of billions dollars in intellectual property and classified information every year. The report (Foreign Spies Stealing US Economic Secrets in Cyberspace) suggested that the Russians and Chinese are systematically targeting government institutions and businesses.[3] The *Washington Post* reported that the US Defense Advance Research Project Agency (DARPA) envisions building the cyberspace equivalent of an armored tank to engage on the global battlefield of digital warfare.[4]

---

1 *Daily Times*, 22 February 2011.
2 "National Security Strategy and the Strategic Security and Defense Review", published in October 2010.
3 "Chatham House Report-2010".
4 Ibid, and also, *BBC Channel 4*, 18 October 2010. In the United Kingdom's Science and Technology Strategy for Countering International Terrorism for August 2009, the government highlighted the technological measures for countering terrorism. *Daily Times*, 22 February 2011.

CHAPTER 11. THE POLITICS OF INTELLIGENCE SURVEILLANCE IN BRITAIN

There is an ample evidence that countries around the world are using software that enables the filtering and blocking of online content, technologies produced by Western world that help governments spy on their citizens. Many such companies are actively serving autocratic governments as "repression's little helper." According to the Electronic Frontiers Foundation paper:

> The reach of these technologies is astonishingly broad; governments can listen in on cell phone calls, use voice recognition to scan mobile networks, read emails and text messages, censor web pages, track a citizen's every movement using GPS, and can even change email contents while en route to a recipient.[1]

Over the past year, and partly in response to the uprisings that have swept the Arab world, concerns about cyber exports have been amplified in media reports and by digital rights organizations, sparking a debate as to the appropriate course of action.[2]

---

1 Mass Surveillance Technologies, "Electronic Frontiers Foundation". https://www.eff.org/issues/mass-surveillance-technologies.
2 Ibid. and also, *Intelligence Agency Attorney on how "Multi-communication Transactions" allowed for domestic surveillance.* Parker Higgins, 21 August

In late 2012, the US government authorized certain programs that sought to gather information data on a large scale. Some aspects had been declared illegal. In NSA's traditional intelligence alliance with 100 companies, PRISM is considered as a special source operation since 1970s. Immediately after 9/11, a terrorist surveillance program was implemented (PRISM), but it was severely criticized and challenged as illegal, because it did not include warrants obtained from the foreign intelligence surveillance court. Thus, PRISM was eliminated by the Protect America Act 2007 and by the FISA Amendment Act 2008.

Obviously, whether one views these innovations as something positive or something negative depends on his/her position. According to the CNN report, dozens of activists in Syria have had their computers infected with malware that allows supporters of Bashar al-Assad to thwart their efforts to overthrow his government which, however we may view it, remains the legitimate government in a country that holds presidential and parliamentary elections. In Bahrain, where there is no hint of democracy, Trovicor helped install and still maintains sophisticated "monitoring centers" used to surveillance democratic activists' emails, text messages and phone calls despite ample evidence of human rights violations. Almost two dozen former political prisoners testified to the England and Wales lawyers association that they were beaten and subsequently interrogated while being shown transcripts of emails and text messages. There have been at least 140 documented allegations of torture in Bahrain in the past last year.[1]

In Tunisia, Trovicor was also one of many companies selling equipment to former President Ben Ali, whose system was so advanced, it prompted the new head of the Tunisian Internet Agency Moez Chakchouk to say, "I had a group of international experts from a group here lately who looked at the equipment and said: 'The Chinese could come here and learn from you.[2]

The revelations of American whistleblower Edward Snowden

2013. Electronic Frontiers Foundation. https://www.eff.org/issues/mass-surveillance-technologies.

1 *Spy Tech companies & their authoritarian customers, part-III Spy Tech Companies & Their Authoritarian Customers, Part II*: Trovicor and Area SPA. 21 February 2012.

2 *The Guardian* 5 June 2013.

and his shocking allegations about the US and UK surveillance-related activities alarmed people in both states. European security officials say that in 2014, they have noticed an "alarming acceleration" in the number of European jihadists travelling to Syria to obtain combat experience with Islamist groups linked to al-Qaeda. France, Germany and the UK may have the largest foreign fighter contingents in Syria, but Denmark, Norway, Belgium and Austria have contributed a much higher proportion of their population.

The modern UK–US relationship was created during the Second World War in a 100-year pact, and since then all Britain policies — especially foreign policies — have followed the US policy. In 1952, both countries signed mutual defense pact which allowed US to transfer nuclear secrets in the UK. The CIA and GCHQ signed an agreement to share all information and work together against the Soviet bloc and make a strong wall against China. This relationship became stronger during the cold war, as both countries worked to gather bilaterally and within the North Atlantic Treaty Organization (NATO), to counter the growing threat of Communism. Both the UK and the US are permanent members of the United Nations Security Council and are the founding members of NATO.

In every war started by the US, the UK participates without making its own policy; it has been an unconditional participant. The UK has backed US wars going back to the Vietnam conflict and even the Korean War (1950–1953), up to the war in Afghanistan.

In the 1980s, the US and UK made a mutual alliance and the then Prime Minister, Margaret Thatcher, and US President Reagan had very close political relationship, especially concerning the Communist bloc. And when the UK Prime Minister sent warships to attack Argentina on Falklands Islands in 1982, the US President didn't oppose it, but technically the US should oppose UK actions against Argentina because it was a breach of the charter of the Organization of American States (OAS).

After Saddam Hussein invaded Kuwait in August 1990, the United Kingdom supported the US policy against Iraq. Great Britain quickly joined the US to build the strong coalition of Arab states to put pressure on Iraq to withdraw its forces. Prime

Minister John Major worked very closely with the George H W Bush. The UK was the most important ally of the United States in the first Gulf War.[1]

In the 1990s, US President Bill Clinton and Prime Minister Tony Blair led their Government as US and UK troops participated along with other NATO nations in the 1999s intervention in the Kosovo War. Former UK Prime Minister Tony Blair established a personal relationship with both UK presidents Bill Clinton and George W Bush and these relationships led Britain in unfinished domestic war on terrorism within the country.[2]

The UK also quickly joined the US in the "war on terror" after 9/11. British troops joined American troops to invade Afghanistan in 2001 and to invade Iraq in 2003. After the invasion of Iraq, Britain troops made their base in the city of Basra. Soon after, British PM Tony Blair's popularity went down among the British people as well as his party. Blair faced increasing charges that he was simply a puppet of George W. Bush. In 2009 Mr. Gordon Brown, the successor of Tony Blair, announced the end to British involvement in the Iraq war. Later on, Britain faced the threat of terrorism within the country and a great risk of recession due to having adopted US foreign policy.[3]

The UK and the US are home to major financial centers in the world and their investment relationship is the largest in the world. However, their economic relationship suffered a significant negative impact during the global financial crisis of 2008. Economic growth has been weak ever since. Economic and financial issues have been the central domestic challenge facing the coalition so far. In recent years, some observers have suggested the US and UK relationship is losing strength due to economic issues in the US which are more severe than in the UK.

Most analysts believe that US–UK intelligence and counter terrorism cooperation is close, well established and of mutual beneficial: however the two countries' differ in other policies. In recent years, multiple terrorist operations have been reportedly disturbed by the mutual US–UK intelligence and counterter-

---

1 *TBR News*, 6 July 2013.
2 *New Directions in Surveillance Privacy*, edited by Benjamin J. Goold, Daniel Neyland, Willan Publishing, 2009. USA.
3 *New Ham Monitoring*. 25 June 2013.

rorism cooperation; however, there have been some occasional tensions regarding a different pattern of intelligence mechanism and about extradition arrangements. The relationship was damaged by public accusation of Britain's involvement in US-led torture of its nationals in different countries. The British Government faced criticism publicly over extradition arrangements and the public argued that UK nationals should face prosecution in British courts before being extradited to any other country.

Rendition is also considered the intelligence sharing between the US and Britain, without the consent of the citizens. Government and courts separately initiated inquiries into this scandal, but the truth still eludes us as to the country's involvement in rendition and torture.

Writer Benjamin Ward (2014), Deputy Director of Human Rights Watch in Europe and Central Asia, has analyzed the role of British intelligence in rendition and other intelligence operations:

> In July 2010, the British Prime Minister, David Cameron, made a stirring statement to Parliament about his determination to get to the bottom of allegations of UK complicity in overseas torture and rendition. This was vital, Cameron insisted, because "[t]he longer these questions remain unanswered, the bigger will grow the stain on our reputation as a country that believes in freedom, fairness and human rights."[1]

On the issue of abuse and torture of Zeeshan Siddiqui, and Binyamin Mohamed, Benjamin Ward noted:

> Zeeshan Siddiqui, a British citizen, was arrested in Pakistan in May 2005, on suspicion of involvement in terrorism. He was deported to the UK on January 2006. During his detention in Pakistan, Siddiqui said, he was repeatedly beaten, chained, injected with drugs and threatened with sexual abuse and further torture. Pakistani security officials confirmed to Human Rights Watch (HRW) that Siddiqui's arrest had been based on a tip-off from the British intelligence services and come at their request. . . Another episode involved Binyamin

---

1 Writer Benjamin Ward (2014), Deputy Director, Human Rights Watch in Europe and Central Asia, analyzed the role of British intelligence in rendition and other intelligence operations, 20 January 2014.

Mohamed, a British resident detained and tortured in Pakistan and, with the involvement of the US government, in Morocco. He was later sent to Afghanistan and then to Guantanamo, where he was again subjected to ill-treatment.[1]

On 19 December 2013, the *Guardian* reported the UK involvement in rendition and torture of its citizens in the so called war on terrorism. This involvement still remains unanswered. The newspaper reported the interim report of Sir Peter Gibson which raised 27 questions about the involvement of the country's intelligence in rendition operation. According to the *Guardian* report:

> Other questions that Gibson said demanded answers included "whether there was an apparent willingness, at least at some levels within the agencies, to condone, encourage or take advantage of a rendition operation" conducted by other countries. He also questioned whether the British government and its intelligence agencies became "inappropriately involved" in such renditions.[2]

On 19 December 2013, BBC News reported Sir Peter Gibson reviewed 20,000 top secret documents after allegations of wrongdoing by intelligence officers in the wake of 9/11. According to the BBC report, he found no evidence of MI5 and MI6 involvement in rendition cases. Sir Peter told reporters: "It does appear from the documents that the United Kingdom may have been inappropriately involved in some renditions. That is a very serious matter. And no doubt any future inquiry would want to look at that."[3]

Mr. Snowden's disclosure of the communication interception program targeting the United Kingdom's intelligence agency was described by Germany as "nightmarish." On 5 June 2013, *The Guardian* reported a secret US court order forcing a telephone

---

1 *The Professionalization of Intelligence Cooperation: Fashioning Method Out of Mayhem.* Adam D.M. Svendsen. Palgrave MacMillan, UK. Open Security. *Conflict and Peace building. Truth still eludes on UK involvement in rendition and torture.* Benjamin Ward, 20 January 2014.
2 *The Guardian*, 19 December 2013, and also, *Dawn*, 27 February 2013.
3 *BBC News*, 19 December 2013, and also, "Counterterrorism and Intelligence Cooperation," Derek S. Reveron. *Journal of Global Change and Governance. Vol-1 Number-3, 2008.*

company (Verizon) to provide the telephone data of its entire customer base to the NSA. Thus, the Foreign Intelligence Surveillance Court allowed the FBI to obtain three months of data and use it for intelligence purposes. Then, on 6 June 2014, *The Guardian* and *Washington Post* reported NSA and FBI's access to Microsoft, Yahoo, Google, You Tube, Face-book and other internet companies to monitor web traffic of people outside the US. This process was already continued in Britain under the interception of communications law and Regulations Investigatory Power Act (RIPA).[1]

Journalist S.P. Seth wrote a detailed article on US and UK surveillance in a Pakistani newspaper in which he described the furor over the tapping of German Chancellor Angela Markel's personal phone. This act of NSA and GCHQ damaged the trust and undermined the foregoing spirit of cooperation: The furor over the tapping of German Chancellor Angela Markel's personal phone by the US intelligence agencies dramatized spectacularly what Edward Snowden had revealed. On 28 January 2014, *the Guardian* reported the GCHQ mass surveillance:

> GCHQ's mass surveillance spying programmes are probably illegal and have been signed off by ministers in breach of human rights and surveillance laws, according to a hard-hitting legal opinion that has been provided to MPs. The advice warns that Britain's principal surveillance law is too vague and is almost certainly being interpreted to allow the agency to conduct surveillance that flouts privacy safeguards set out in the European convention on human rights (ECHR). The inadequacies, it says, have created a situation where GCHQ staffs are potentially able to rely "on the gaps in the current statutory framework to commit serious crime with impunity."[2]

In another report, *The Guardian* revealed a white structure on top of the British embassy in Berlin that contained spying equipment. British ambassador in Germany was called in for a meeting to Foreign Office to explain allegations that Britain had been using its embassy for covert surveillance against Germany, which was deeply resented:

1 *The Guardian*, 6 June 2014, *Daily Times*, 25 March 2013.
2 Ibid, 28 January 2014

German officials pointed out that it was illegal to use embassy premises to wiretap a host government, and the new report has deepened Berlin's sense of exclusion from the tight eavesdropping alliance known as Five Eyes, consisting of the US, UK, Canada, Australia and New Zealand. The Snowden files make it clear that membership of the club offered some protection against being spied on by another member. They also show that non-members are considered fair game for extensive surveillance, in the form of bulk monitoring of mass communications, and eavesdropping on the call and emails of top officials.[1]

However, when word of the PRISM program broke out, Britain's GCHQ was using the same software through a program code-named TEMPORA, for collecting web data, emails contents and file transfer information from Google, Face book, Apple and YouTube. Thus, British agencies had access to the world communications systems storing countless amounts of emails, telephone calls, conversations and online communications. The Foreign Secretary was unable to comment on the details of PRISM.[2]

RIPA (Regulation of Investigatory Power Act-2000) was under fire for interception of communications and the acquisition and disclosure of communications traffic data. The basic function of the United Kingdom and US intelligence infrastructure has developed partly organically and by design. The changing nature of the security environment led to some immediate changes and developments in their system of intelligence information collection. The PRISM revelation in 2013 and GCHQ's role in data collection, and a weak response by government, are considered a bigger secret game. Citizens of Britain didn't like this game, and several privacy groups filed legal action against the mass surveillance of British citizens. This dubious method of maintaining security and law and order has created distances between young people and their parents, wife and husband, brother and sister and the government and communities.

---

1 *Daily Telegraph*, 20 October 2013.
2 *Fixing Intel: A Blueprint for making intelligence relevant in Afghanistan.* Major General Michael T. Flynn, Captain Matt Pottinger and Paul D. Batchelor, Centre for a New American Security.

Being watched all the time destroys even the sense that one has a private life. It is invasive. In fact, RIPA (Regulation of Investigatory Power Act-2000) protects Britain's citizens against such surveillance by the UK intelligence agencies but it cannot protect Britons from American surveillance under the Foreign Intelligence Surveillance Act (FISA). Senior officials in British intelligence circles have been very anxious about the GCHQ decision to tap into transatlantic cables in order to engage in bulk interception of phone calls and internet traffic. Now, the issue has become more complicated as the public has showed deep anger over the violation of their privacy. Across the border, intelligence surveillance has left negative impacts on Britain's diplomatic relations when Germany expressed deep concern over the British spying of its citizens.

Secret surveillance of people of all sections of society and retrieving their data, every last bit, where they sleep, where they are going to dinner, who they meet there, is an open violation of the rights of free citizens. The *Guardian* newspaper presentation of PRISM documents raised many questions about the way intelligence information is gathered by British intelligence agencies. From Microsoft, FaceBook, YouTube, Google, Twitter to Skype, and LinkedIn, they follow every step and action of social media day and night, but they haven't been able to defeat the prevailing criminal culture, extremism, challenges of hate preachers and the networks of international terrorism across the country.

A strong surveillance camera network also impairs the privacy of citizens. CCTV (Close Circuit Television) cameras are deployed all over England and with particularly high density throughout London. This is the most common way of intelligence surveillance in the United Kingdom. Recent research reports revealed the fact that there are up to 6 million closed circuit television cameras in the country, including 760,000 in sensitive locations. In his recent report, interception communications commissioner revealed about an intelligence failure while six people were arrested on wrong intelligence formation. Another technique of intelligence surveillance concerns mobile phones, the tapping of both phone and people's computer-based local area networks (LAN). Biometric data is also collected, even on international travelers who happen to transit England without intending to step outside the airport.

In 2012, intelligence and surveillance authorities made over 570,000 requests to read the text messages, e-mails and telephonic conversations of citizens. All these efforts of the British intelligence and surveillance community badly failed when terrorists were able to behead a soldier in East London in May 2013.[1]

Communities across the country view British society as a surveillance society. This way of controlling the mind, thought, social, political and religious moments of citizens has raised grave concerns about the increasing levels of police surveillance powers, which turned our modern society into a walled prison.

On 25 June 2013, the New Ham Monitoring Project released a press statement against the intrusive surveillance of London Police Special Demonstration Squad (SDS). In its press release, NMP stated: "It is alarming that a Metropolitan Police Undercover Surveillance Unit targeted NMP and serves as a reminder of the level of misuse of power within the police that we have tirelessly campaigning against for years." This is not the only one example of police spying program, National Domestic Extremism Unit of the London Police is monitoring and keeping records of more than 9,000 people across the country.[2]

Finally, surveillance is intrusive if it involves the presence of either an individual or a surveillance device on private premises or in a vehicle. In these circumstances, every British citizen has a theoretical right to register his/her complaint with the Investigatory Power Tribunal against the Police, Serious Organized Crime Agency, HM Revenue, intelligence services, Ministry of Defense Police and British Transport Police. However, normally enquiries against these organization go nowhere because it is very difficult for a common British citizen to provide solid evidence of intrusive surveillance against the above cited powerful forces.

---

1 US Intelligence report predicts failure in Afghanistan 6 January 2014. http://www.examiner.com/article/us-intelligence-report-predicts-failure-afghanistan.
2 *Washington Post*, 2 March 2014.

CHAPTER 12. INTELLIGENCE COOPERATION IN AFGHANISTAN

The United States and Britain's intelligence failure in Afghanistan raised many questions, including the development of Taliban intelligence networks in major cities. The professionalization of intelligence cooperation among CIA, MI6, ISI, NDS Iranian intelligence and NATO intelligence Units, or at least efforts leading in that direction, became increasingly necessary when the Tehreek-e-Taliban Pakistan (TTP) and Afghan Taliban extended their terrorist networks beyond their spheres of influence. Heightened, sustained vigilance and a coherent approach to a professional intelligence mechanism were considered of deep importance by NATO allies to effectively counter the Taliban's way of misgovernment.[1]

Intelligence relations between the United States and Britain have entered crucial phase since CIA and MI6 have started sharing intelligence through Five Eyes program. During World War II, Armed Forces of the United States developed independent foreign SIGINT relationships with the United Kingdom. This intelligence relationship evolved and continued across the decades. However, with the signing of the BRUSA Intelligence Sharing Agreement (05 March 1946), cooperation between the

1 *The Professionalization of Intelligence Cooperation: Fashioning Method Out of Mayhem*, Adam D.M. Svendsen, Palgrave Macmillan, 30 Aug 2012.

two armies reaffirmed the World War II cooperation. On 14 June, 2013, the *Christian Science Monitor* reported:

> The British intelligence organization's close ties to the US National Security Agency have come under scrutiny amid the controversy over the NSA's PRISM surveillance program revealed by whistleblower Edward Snowden. But Snowden's whistle-blowing over the NSA's PRISM program has brought the extent of cooperation between GCHQ and the NSA under unprecedented, and apparently unwelcome, scrutiny. GCHQ has reportedly had access to since at least 2010 and has used to generate 197 intelligence reports last year — raising questions about whether GCHQ used US-gathered intelligence to dodge strict UK rules on government surveillance.[1]

Researcher Adam D.M. Svendsen has also focused on the US and UK intelligence cooperation. Highlighting the importance of this intelligence relationship, he noted:

> Widely recognized as being one of the 'best' examples of international intelligence cooperation, UK–US intelligence relations appropriately form the focus of this book. Alongside the nuclear relationship, they have supplied one of the key 'pillars' for the wider UK–US relationship or 'special' relations for over 60 years. . . Moreover, the UK–US intelligence relationship is already, to date, the most 'globalized', 'homogenized' and 'internationally standardized' liaison relationship. In part, this reflects the patchwork of long-enduring agreements that collectively compose the UKUSA arrangement and the numerous parallel agreements (MoUs) relating to human intelligence and defense intelligence dating from 1940s. These facilitate many of the wider patterns of international intelligence liaison that exist today, and (in their subsequently updated forms) demonstrate the potential optimum form of liaison that can currently be achieved.[2]

According to Richard J. Aldrich, intelligence co-operation

---

1 *The Christian Science Monitor*, 14 June, 2013.
2 *Intelligence Cooperation and the War on Terror: Anglo-American security relations after 9/11*, Adam D.M. Svendsen, Routledge. 2010, also, "US–European Intelligence Co-operation on Counter-Terrorism: Low Politics and Compulsion," Richard J. Aldrich, *the British Journal of Politics and International Relations*, 2009 VOL 11.

between allies is rarely affected by disagreements over ideals or strategy. This is because the world of intelligence is remarkably factious and fissiparous. Dr. William Rosenau has also described the importance of intelligence in the global war on terrorism. He also discussed the US intelligence relations with the Unite Kingdom and other European states:

> International cooperation is and will remain an important element of the intelligence component of the campaign. Collaboration on counterterrorism did not begin after 9/11... As George Tenet, the director of central intelligence, told congressional investigators in 2002, "[w]e worked with numerous European govern- ments, such as the Italians, Germans, French, and Brit- ish to identify and shatter terrorist groups and plans against American and local interests in Europe.

The issue of professionalizing intelligence cooperation in Afghanistan has received little attention since the majority of foreign intelligence agencies (CIA, MI6, ISI, NDS, RAW and Iranian intelligence) in the country do not sincerely cooper- ate. Afghan intelligence agencies operate inside Pakistan, while Pakistani intelligence agencies operate in Afghanistan. Thus the issue of intelligence sharing remains a paper truth, not a ground reality.

The activities of the Afghan National Directorate of Security (NDS), and Riyasat-e-Amniyat-e-Mili Afghanistan (Directorate of National Security) (RAMA), different Indian agencies, and the Israeli MOSSAD in various parts of Afghanistan, particularly along the Durand Line, have long been the subject of conjecture and supposition. These agencies usually adhere to their national interests; they do not necessarily want to share their collected data with the US Central Intelligence Agency (CIA), and oth- er NATO agencies, or the Pakistani Inter-Services Intelligence (ISI). In his 2011 speech, US Defense Secretary Chuck Hagel ac- cused India of financing problematic groups against Pakistan and Afghanistan.[1]

Such statements further increased the gulf in trust between Kabul and Islamabad. Islamabad also complained that two of its neighbors, India and Iran, were secretly bidding to destabilize

---

1 *Daily Times*, 19 March 2014.

Pakistan from bases on Afghan soil. India rejected these allegations and stated that they were nothing more than an attempt to pressure India to scale back its activities in Afghanistan. India understands that its presence in Afghanistan has promoted it to a regional power in global terms. In 1999, Pakistan enjoyed the same position, but now India has become a rising global power. These allegations and the war of words halted the process of intelligence sharing among India, Iran, Pakistan and Afghanistan.

The International Security Assistance Force (ISAF) established different intelligence units, but most of its secret operations are carried out by individual states in Afghanistan. The CIA does not share all information with its allies, while German intelligence agencies have their own operational role in Kabul and northern Afghanistan. The ISI is no doubt a professional organization but its changeable loyalties have made it suspect in the eyes of most Pakistani citizens. The ever-changing shape of its alliance with the CIA does not help inspire confidence locally.

Outside the Middle East, intelligence cooperation and sharing partners have been instrumental in the roundup of terror leaders in the subcontinent. With Pakistan's proximity to Afghanistan and its links with insurgent groups, its intelligence support has been critical in the War on Terror in Afghanistan. As a full-fledged partner of the US, Pakistan provided an air corridor, logistics, and intelligence support. Mutual trust between the two states remained fundamental in their critical intelligence cooperation.[1]

Despite this, intelligence cooperation between Pakistan and the US represents one of the most significant challenges in Afghanistan. The exponentially growing terrorist networks of the TTP and Afghan Taliban in Pakistan and Afghanistan necessitate increased cooperation among the intelligence agencies of ISAF-NATO and the ISI, NDS and Iranian intelligence, but in reality, none is willing to share their intelligence with any other. The present new emphasis on intelligence sharing between the CIA and ISI creates new challenges.

The CIA relationship with the ISI has arguably been one of the most complicated intelligence partnerships in South Asia.

---

1 Ibid.

Challenges persist in fostering closer CIA and ISI cooperation on Afghanistan, though both states appear publicly committed to fostering closer relationship in the areas of counterterrorism, law enforcement and border control.[1]

After the Swat and Abbottabad operations in 2009 and 2011 respectively, the CIA–ISI relationship raised serious questions. Suspicion grew, the two sides became near adversaries. The arrest of Raymond Davis in Lahore, and the US's unfriendly attitude towards Pakistan, further complicated relations between the two states. Meanwhile, intelligence sharing and cooperation between the intelligence communities completely stopped. As far as Afghan intelligence is concerned, in fact, extending intelligence cooperation to the ISI was not in its control — external powers hold the remote-control for the Afghan game. US intelligence officials recently disclosed that their country's intelligence network is one of the largest in the world — the Agency has more than 1,000 personnel, including operatives and technical staff in Afghanistan.

Moreover, there are a number of intelligence sub-units, like the Serious Organized Crime Committee (CCSC) and Military Counterterrorism Investigation Group, with 3,000 soldiers from the Afghan army, working under the CIA across Afghanistan. All these units, Blackwater, NDS, and other private intelligence companies, have different rules and cultures. Their relations with the main CIA are also strained. Russian intelligence experts recently articulated the over-sized capabilities of the CIA in Afghanistan, and said it does not allow any wider role to the intelligence agencies of other NATO and ISAF member states.

In assessing information, the US and UK officials faced problems of selection and interpretation, especially given the huge volume of data, so much of which is fragmentary or inconsistent. Interviewees highlighted the lack of contextual understanding, especially in historical, political, social, tribal and religious affairs. A former US ambassador to Kabul noted: "The problem is not a lack of information, it's understanding what you're looking at ... often we don't see the context, don't understand an event's meaning, especially when we are not of their culture."[2]

1 Ibid.
2 Ibid.

A further problem is a proclivity towards brevity, with ambiguity, information gaps or dissenting opinions inadequately reflected in intelligence or other assessments. As one of UK Foreign Office analysts put it, speaking of coalition intelligence reporting: "We tend to overstate how much we know. Who wants to say otherwise?" According to a US intelligence officer, there is "a tendency to fit the facts to accepted paradigms or models." This bias is at least partly attributable to the contamination of intelligence by narratives articulated by political and military leaders, which leads to a "blurring of propaganda and analysis."[1]

The deficit of data needed by high-level analysts does not arise from a lack of reporting in the field. There are literally terabytes of unclassified and classified information typed up at the grassroots level. The most salient problems are attitudinal, cultural, and human. The intelligence community's standard mode of operation is surprisingly passive about aggregating information that is not enemy-related and relaying it to decision-makers or fellow analysts further ups the chain. It is a culture that is strangely oblivious of how little its analytical products, as they now exist, actually influence commanders. Afghan forces "struggle due to the lack of intelligence, surveillance and reconnaissance," as well as expertise and technology for countering improvised roadside bombs.

Afghan President Hamid Karzai criticized that the specious distinction the US has drawn between al Qaeda and the Afghan Taliban to justify its efforts to clinch a deal with the latter, insists that Qaeda is "more a myth than a reality." In fact, the birth of the Afghan Taliban—fathered by ISI—was midwife by the CIA in the early 1990s.[2]

Disagreements between EU member states and the CIA have also negatively affected the professionalization of intelligence cooperation. Fundamental divergences regarding the way terrorism should be tackled, and the US's unprofessional approach to the wars in Iraq and Afghanistan, estranged partners and hin-

---

1 "System failure: the underlying causes of US policy-making errors in Afghanistan", Matt Waldman. A Chatham House research paper, 26 February 2013. http://www.chathamhouse.org/sites/default/files/public/International%20Affairs/2013/89_4/89_4_02_Waldman.
2 *Escaping Afghanistan, the graveyard of empires*, Brahma Chellaney, *Japan Times*, 21 January 2012.

dered the advance of intelligence cooperation. In Afghanistan, the CIA and MI6 closely worked with Northern Alliance war criminals and drug smugglers. Therefore, the roots of Afghan intelligence are in northern Afghanistan. Pashtuns were marginalized and the Taliban who accepted the new administration were targeted. Intelligence was skewed to meet immediate operational needs, rather than directed to build up a multidimensional picture of key actors, context and dynamics.

The ranking US commander in Afghanistan, Major General Michael Flynn, in his report complained about poor intelligence cooperation in Afghanistan. Military officers and civilians working with ISAF are non-cooperative and do not share a single word with each other. There is no common database, no common strategy and no common thinking among the ISAF allies. The lack of digital networks available to all participating states raised serious questions about their partnership.

It is no secret that the US, NATO and MI6 do not always get things right, and their analysis leads policy makers and military commanders to wrong conclusions. Their poor data, inaccurate intelligence information about Taliban activities, their sources of unreliable information and their misinterpretations and flawed strategies often cause civilian casualties and needless infrastructure damage.

In Afghanistan, the CIA and MI6 mostly retrieve intelligence from newspapers, the internet, military and law enforcement agencies, and civilian informers. Moreover, intelligence gathered by private intelligence and security companies almost always proves to be misleading. In view of their inability to provide accurate information, in October 2013, British intelligence, MI6, immediately called for reinforcements in Afghanistan amidst fears that the country would become an "intelligence vacuum" where terrorists would pose an increased threat to Britain.[1]

As we all know, the US intelligence approach in Afghanistan has been incoherent for the last 12 years as they failed to collect true military and civilian intelligence from most districts in eastern and western Afghanistan, and the tribal regions of Pakistan. When we study the role in Afghanistan of NATO intelligence

---

1 *Daily Telegraph*, 20 October 2013, and also *Daily Times*, 11 March 2014

agencies, the CIA, Russian and Chinese intelligence, Defense Clandestine Intelligence and the Pentagon, we come across several stories of intelligence failures in the country, as they have never been able to stabilize the country or counter the Inter-Services Intelligence (ISI) effectively.

For US and NATO intelligence agencies, the information needed by their military commanders to conduct a population-centric counter-insurgency operation in Afghanistan was very important, but they could not retrieve it from the majority of remote districts. When intelligence is ignored or is twisted to produce a desired result, it is truly a failure. Since the war in Afghanistan, the failure of US foreign policy has created many problems, while the intelligence community is resisting becoming a party to the fabrication of falsehoods — witnesses the recent pushback over the issue of counter-insurgency.[1]

The CIA and MI6 approach to cooperation on civilian and military levels with Afghan intelligence agencies and the ISI in Baluchistan and Kunar province, the tribal areas and Waziristan has never been satisfactory. They failed to gather information about insurgent cells in remote mountainous areas where insurgents prepare to attack coalition forces.

The roles of the CIA and British intelligence, and their strategies, have been deeply contradictory, particularly since the re-emergence of Taliban networks and their attacks across the Durand Line. They failed to professionalize intelligence cooperation, operations, collection and processes or to provide military and strategic guidance to NATO commanders. For a professional intelligence network to be relevant in counter-insurgency operations, it needs to supply wide-ranging military information from the war zone to commanders and policymakers.

That information, along with much else including realistic presentations setting out the entire range of possible outcomes, the time needed to achieve objectives and the intractable issues tied to information collection, must be presented so they are fully integrated into the design and planning of the intervention itself.

In January 2010, a US commander in Afghanistan, General

---

1 *American Conservative, CIA's 'Colossal Flop'*. Philip Geraldi, 17 December, 2013, and also, *Daily Times*, 11 March 2014

Mike Flynn, prepared an intelligence report that revealed some of the worst intelligence failures of the campaign. General Flynn complained that intelligence was working hard but it was doing the wrong job. Later on, he suggested the separation of counter-insurgency strategy (COIN) from intelligence operations. In *Fixing Intel*, General Flynn sought to drive home the concept that US intelligence needs to collect information about the population of Afghanistan. US military commanders admitted to having very little knowledge of Afghan culture and Taliban insurgents.[1]

They showed a predilection for military-led approaches to problems, including those that were essentially political. Research scholar Matt Waldman has also described the flawed policies of the US and its allies in a recent article, saying, "In the eyes of US officials and informed observers, high level US policy-making on Afghanistan was severely impaired by fundamental, structural flaws, many of which are interrelated and reinforcing." Another US commander, General Eikenberry, criticized the counterinsurgency strategy promoted by General Petraeus. The general rejected the COIN strategy as applied in Afghanistan, in his article published in *Foreign Affairs*.[2]

A new intelligence report from the US highlighted the failure of intelligence in Afghanistan. The US National Intelligence Estimate (NIE) warned that the country would quickly fall into chaos if President Hamid Karzai refused to sign a security deal with the US. The NIE, which includes input from 16 intelligence agencies in the US, predicted that the Taliban would become more influential as US forces draw down at the end of 2014.13 Moreover, in response to these allegations, Afghan President Hamid Karzai expressed concern that his country was the victim of a war that only served the interests of the US and its western allies.

"Afghans died in a war that is not ours," President Karzai said in an interview with *The Washington Post*. President Karzai said he was in trouble for war casualties, including those in US

---

1 *Fixing Intel*, General Flynn. In January 2010, a US commander in Afghanistan, General Mike Flynn, prepared an intelligence report that revealed some of the worst intelligence failures of the campaign.
2 A Chatham House research paper, 26 February 2013. http://www. chathamhouse.org/sites/default/files/public/International%20 Affairs/2013/89_4/89_4_02_Waldman.

military operations, and felt betrayed by what he described as insufficient US focus on going after Taliban sanctuaries inside Pakistan. The US and its allies should know that Chinese and Russian agencies seek influence in the country as a means of securing their borders. In reality, the presence of US forces in Afghanistan provided China with a sense of stability.

Beijing understands that finally the US began to focus on terrorist networks in the country, and it is in China's interest to engage NATO and US forces there. China gives reason for optimism on this matter as it, so far, has succeeded in avoiding any link between its friendship with Pakistan and its interests in Afghanistan. China is seeking the ISI's help in stabilizing Afghanistan. China knows that the ISI has influence in Kabul but wants to deal with Afghan security as a separate issue altogether. In February 2014, the killing of 21 Afghan soldiers in Kunar province triggered the anger of ANA generals who never expected ethnic divides to interfere with Afghan military intelligence that spies on ethnic Pashtun generals, officer, soldiers and their families, in and outside military barracks.[1]

In 2013, the Afghan Defense Ministry once warned Pashtun officers and soldiers that they would lose their jobs if they did not shift their families from Pakistan to Afghanistan. The Afghan Defense Minister had received reports that Afghans living in Pakistan work for ISI and other intelligence agencies. This warning further caused mistrust between Pashtuns and non-Pashtuns officers. Pashtun military officers complain that Afghan intelligence is spying on ethnic bases within the army and police forces which caused their alienation, frustration and suspicions.

The killing was termed an intelligence failure by the Defense Ministry of Afghanistan, and fired some military commanders including regional intelligence chiefs. *Daily Outlook* reported the biggest backlash of the Afghan media where President Hamid Karzai's policies towards Taliban were harshly criticized. Interestingly, the President did not attend the soldiers' funeral but cancelled his visit to Sri Lanka. There were speculations within the Afghan parliament and Defense Ministry that because of

1 *The Limits of Counterinsurgency Doctrine in Afghanistan: The Other Side of the COIN*, Karl W. Eikenberry, October 2013.

their ethnicity, the President did not consider it necessarily to attend the funeral of killed soldiers.[1]

In the last four decades, ethnic rivalries between the central government and local ethnic groups have been reported in Afghan press time and again. After the Soviet withdrawal and the fall of Dr. Najibullah's government, the Afghan army and its intelligence infrastructure collapsed and a new realignment of ethnic and sectarian actors emerged with their criminal militias. They established their own ethnic intelligence units to gather information about their rival military activities. Their intelligence units were influenced by the intelligence agencies of neighboring states to further their national interests in Afghanistan. Inter Services Intelligence (ISI) is also trying to influence Afghan army and its intelligence.[2]

The fragmented population of millions of Pashtuns in Afghanistan and Pakistan has been a key factor in the crisis. Perceiving them as formidable ethnic group, ISI and Saudi intelligence agencies often tried to keep them divided. Afghanistan has never been able to support Pashtuns in Pakistan but the country remains the cradle of Pashtun pride. An addition to ISI and Saudi intelligence plans, Iran pursues a policy of its own, shaped by its national security interests. Iranian intelligence supports non-state actors and some groups of Taliban as well. In reality, all Afghanistan's neighbors are busy provoking ethnic and sectarian groups to strengthen their position in the country. Pakistan wants to maintain its influence in Afghanistan and also is trying to stabilize the country to secure its own territory but, unfortunately, Afghanistan has been in trouble due to its complicated ethnic politics for decades.[3]

The sad incident in Kunar province is considered an intelligence failure, because Afghan civil and military intelligence agencies unnecessarily focused on targeted killings in Baluchistan province. KHAD and NDS operations in Khyber Pakhtunkhwa and Waziristan regions only bring instability to Afghanistan. NDS has started targeting prominent political and religious leaders in these regions. This unnecessary involvement

---

1 *Washington Post*, 28 December 2013.
2 *Washington Post*, 02 March 2014.
3 *Daily Times*, 08 March 2014.

raised many questions about their killing business. The Kunar province is mostly controlled by Taliban forces where Afghan intelligence has no access to collect intelligence information about the dissidents. Speaking at the funeral ceremony, Defense Minister, Maulana Bismillah Khan Muhammadi criticized the controversial role of Taliban, ISI and his own country's military intelligence.[1]

Maulana Muhammadi regretted the failed and non-professional strategies of his country's civil and military intelligence agencies, and ethnic faces of his military commanders who intentionally or unintentionally allowed Taliban fighters to safely enter the fort and kill soldiers, not officers. We have often been told that corruption and illegal use of powers, nepotism, regionalism, ethnicity and sectarianism within the quarters of Afghan National Army have divided the loyalties of ANA officers. Such accusations harmed the reputation of ANA officers as well. There are no checks and balances in the armed forces. The recent incident is an eye opener that should impel us to put into practice the necessary laws for keeping proper checks and balances at the top levels of police and national army.[2]

Relations were further strained between the government and its intelligence agencies as the Taliban intensified their efforts to inflict more harm on the Afghan army and the police and take then large numbers of hostages. The recent investigation of the Afghan Defense Ministry proved that intelligence has failed to counter the Taliban infiltration into the ranks of armed forces. The main reason behind all these incidents is the role of ethnic animosities within Afghan intelligence agencies and their target of Pashtun military officers. Since 2001, non-Pashtuns continue to target Pashtun officers in state institutions. These policies have mostly alienated the whole Pashtun population from the state. Pashtun officers are leaving the armed forces and joining Taliban forces by the thousands every year. The army is dominated by mafia groups who use it against ethnic Pashtuns in Western and Eastern parts of the country.[3]

---

1 *Daily Outlook* Afghanistan, 26 February 2014.
2 *Al Jazeera*, 26 June 2012
3 *Daily Times*, 08 March 2014

CHAPTER 13. BRITAIN AND THE PROSPECT OF NUCLEAR JIHAD

In 2013, the United States and Algeria held meetings to discuss the ways to strengthen cooperation in war against nuclear smuggling. The discussion sought to explore ways to prevent, detect and respond to nuclear and radiological material smuggling incidents. In 1980s and 1990s, several states agencies detected nuclear materials in Asia and Europe and arrested smugglers of plutonium and uranium. These detection efforts turned up nuclear and plutonium material for instance in scrap in the Netherlands and in some places in Germany. However, more than 40 cases of detection and the arrest of smugglers proved that nuclear terrorism cannot be stopped by a single country. Experts in Europe believe that preventing such smuggling and keeping nuclear materials out of the hands of extremists and terrorists is one of the greatest challenges of the 21st century.[1]

The Pakistani networks of nuclear smuggling in South and South East Asia, and secret nuclear cooperation with Saudi Arab

---

1 *Nuclear Security Matters, Analysis on reducing the risk of nuclear terrorism.* Harvard Kennedy School, Belfer Center for Science and International Affairs. International convention for the Suppression of Acts of Nuclear Terrorism, United Nations, 2005, *Nuclear Terrorism: Frequently Asked Questions,* Belfer Center for Science and International Affairs, September 26, 2007. *Threat Assessment of the US Intelligence Community, Senate Select Committee on Intelligence.* James R. Clapper, 12 March 2013.

and Iran are more than troubling. Pakistan already marketed its nuclear weaponry and supplied know-how to Korea and the Afghan Taliban in 1990s. The risk that weapons of mass destruction might be in the hands of states like Pakistan and Iran, not to mention rogue non-state actors, has created a climate of fear across the US, Europe and the UK. The wars in Iraq, Syria, Yemen, Somalia, Afghanistan and the campaign of remote-control killings in Pakistan have brought new Muslim opposition fighters to the region, and have snuffed out any desire to cooperate, identify or integrate with the West for most Muslims. Instead, they now openly hate America and its allies.[1]

The threat of nuclear terrorism is alive and well. According to Australia's Network News, "The US President's nuclear security summit opened in Washington with his senior counter-terrorism advisor warning of a growing threat of nuclear terrorism."[2]

ABC News reported on a nuclear security summit of 47 nations in Washington; American officials said they believe they have so far thwarted Osama bin Laden's group's efforts to build an Improvised Nuclear Explosive Device. But John Brennan, Barack Obama's counter-terrorism advisor, said the threat of nuclear terrorism is strong and growing, "with Al Qaeda actively seeking a nuclear weapon."[3]

1 *Uncovering the Nuclear Black Market: Working Toward Closing Gaps in the International Non-proliferation Regime*, By David Albright and Corey Hinderstein, Institute for Science and International Security (ISIS), Prepared for the Institute for Nuclear Materials Management (INMM), 45th Annual Meeting, Orlando, and also, *Detecting and Disrupting Illicit Nuclear Trade after A.Q. Khan*, by, David Albright, Paul Brannan, and Andrea Scheel Stricker. http://csis.org/files/attachments/130828_Detecting%20and%20Disrupting%20Nuclear%20Trade.pdf. "The Annual Report of Intelligence and Security Committee for 2011", and Press statement of the joint committee on the National Security Strategy 2012. Also, *Top Five Threats to National Security in the Coming Decades.* Sandra. Erwin, Stew Magnuson, Dan Parsons and Yasmin Tadjdeh. National Defense Magazine, India. November 2012. Also; Law Enforcement Intelligence, Nov. 2004.
2 The US President opened a nuclear security summit in Washington with his senior counter-terrorism advisor warning of a growing threat of nuclear terrorism. *Radio Australia*, 13 April 2010, "Steps to Prevent Nuclear Terrorism: Recommendations Based on the U.S.–Russia Joint Threat Assessment", Belfer Center for Science and International Affairs, September 2013.
3 "The Nuclear Security Summit". The first Nuclear Security Summit was held in Washington, D.C., April 12-13, 2010. *The Arms Control*

On April 12, 2010, the US president met the Pakistani Prime Minister and uttered a similar warning:

> The single biggest threat to U.S. security, short-term, medium-term and long-term, would be the possibility of a terrorist organization obtaining a nuclear weapon," Obama said. "This is something that could change the security landscape of this country and around the world for years to come," he added. "We know that organizations like al-Qaeda are in the process of trying to secure a nuclear weapon — a weapon of mass destruction that they have no compunction at using.[1]

Pakistan's fight against extremist and terrorist groups in four provinces raised concern about the security of its nuclear assets while observers warned that the country's nuclear weapons could be obtained by terrorist Taliban or extremist groups, as they have already established a strong network in the military establishment. On 22 September 2008, US General Michael Mullen described the concern about Pakistan's nuclear weapons, saying:

> To the best of my ability to understand it—and that is with some ability—the weapons there are secure. And that even in the change of government, the control of those weapons haven't changed, that said, they are their weapons. They're not my weapons. And there are limits to what I know. Certainly at a worst-case scenario with respect to Pakistan, I worry a great deal about those weapons falling into the hands of terrorists and either being proliferated or potentially used. And so, control of those, stability, stable control of those weapons is a key concern.[2]

In the United Kingdom, extremist and terrorist groups can retrieve plutonium and other material to make a bomb. In this chapter, I will try to analyze the issue with international per-

Association, and also, Sovereignty and National Security. Seow Hiong Goh. November 23, 2009.

1 *Pakistan's Nuclear Weapons: Proliferation and Security Issues,* Paul K. Kerr, Diane Publishing, 2010, and also, *Is Pakistan's nuclear arsenal vulnerable to terrorists?* David Case, 13 June 2011, and also, *Daily Outlook* Afghanistan, 11 June 2012.

2 *Modify Iran's Arak plant to reduce bomb threat,* Frederik Dahl, Reuter, 02 April 2014, http://uk.reuters.com/article/2014/04/02/uk-iran-nuclear-arak-idUKBREA311HI20140402.

spective. Terrorists buy nuclear weapon designs from black marketers (in Pakistan or Afghanistan), easing their task of building crude atomic bombs. Lawless regions of the globe could hide efforts by terrorists to obtain nuclear weapons. According to the *Washington Quarterly* (April 2010) report:

> Proliferant states can continue seeking items for their nuclear programs from an abundance of suppliers and intermediaries available to add to their networks. Because of this, there is a general sense that export controls can never keep up; that proliferant states will always find a way to bypass controls or find another trading company or supplier willing to make the sale, and that these states will only be slowed, not stopped, by export controls in their steadfast efforts to acquire nuclear weapons.[1]

Notwithstanding the US pressure, nuclear trade is growing by the day as Pakistan and other states continue to establish more nuclear installations, and cooperate with other rogue states in promoting nuclear black market. *Washington Quarterly* has diverted the attention of international community to this point:

> In fact, the problem of illicit nuclear trade appears to be growing worse as technologies and capabilities proliferate. We could easily find ourselves in a far more dangerous world. With the global spread of technology and rapid growth in international trade, trafficking networks find it easier to ply their dangerous trade. It is simpler now to obtain the materials, equipment, and know-how to produce nuclear weapons than it was ten years ago, and could be simpler still ten years from now.[2]

The existence of powerful extremist and terrorist networks in Pakistan has put in danger the security of nuclear weapons in the country. The networks have already carried out successful attacks on nuclear installations in the country. In his research paper, Michael O'Hanlon has warned about the extremist's infiltration into the ranks of Pakistan army. He has also warned that in case of the state collapse in the country, what the United States would do. The report also highlighted the nuclear danger

---

1 *Washington Quarterly*, April 2010.
2 Ibid.

in North Korea:

> The country as a whole is sufficiently infiltrated by fundamentalist groups — as the attempted assassinations against President Pervez Musharraf and other evidence make clear — that this terrifying scenario should not be dismissed. Were Pakistan to collapse, it is unclear what the United States and like-minded states would or should do. As with North Korea, it is highly unlikely that "surgical strikes" to destroy the nuclear weapons could be conducted before extremists could make a grab at them. The United States probably would not know their location — at a minimum, scores of sites controlled by Special Forces or elite Army units would be presumed candidates — and no Pakistani government would likely help external forces with targeting information.[1]

Policy makers and military experts have longstanding worries about the purported radicalization of Pakistan army, fearing that some extremist elements within the army might support the TTP and other groups to attack nuclear installations. Talibanisation, extremism and marketing of terrorism in the country remain one of the most likely sources of instability in Afghanistan. Commando style attacks of these groups on Pakistan naval base in Karachi, Wah Ordinance Factory in Rawalpindi, Dera Ghazi Khan nuclear base, Sargodha and Aeronautical Complex in Kamra, highlighted once again the poor security infrastructure of the country and the undetected infiltration of extremists into the ranks of armed forces. Indian military experts said these terror attacks were made possible by elements inside the armed forces.

Terrorists might attempt to sabotage a nuclear facility in any number of ways, from attack by a group of outsiders on the ground, to insider sabotage, to attempting to crash a plane into the facility. Jihadists have long sought to acquire and use WMD — including nuclear weapons — against Western targets. Al Qaeda has reportedly possessed a WMD research branch within its organization since the early 1990s. To make a nuclear bomb requires either highly enriched uranium (HEU) or plutonium.

Nuclear smuggling networks are interconnected in Pakistan

---

1 Ibid.

and North Korea. Countries that have developed secret nuclear weapons programs, are acquiring nuclear subcomponents and 'dual-use goods' to operate nuclear facilities on their own. Control of dual-use goods is extremely difficult because suppliers can easily be misled into believing that these items will be used only for civilian purposes. Recent events in Pakistan and its war on terror, extrajudicial killings in Swat Valley and the killings of Pashtuns in Waziristan and FATA regions has seriously raised questions that now trained terrorists and extremist elements or their colleagues within the army may well resort to nuclear, biological, radiological or chemical weapons. On 04 September, 2013, one of Pakistan's leading newspapers reported a 178-page summary of the United States intelligence community about the US intelligence surveillance of Pakistan's nuclear weapons. Pentagon and CIA have focused on Pakistan's nuclear facilities that might come under attack by TTP and other extremist groups. The trafficking of nuclear technologies and materials has been a worrisome issue since the early 1950s but after 9/11 it emerged as a global threat. In 2013, a Washington-based think tank, released a report that named Pakistan and North Korea as 'illicit nuclear trade suppliers.'

Mr. Fredrik Dahl, in a 2013 analysis, stressed the need to intercept jihadist groups acquiring enriched uranium and nuclear weapons, while the British Foreign and Commonwealth Office said nuclear material is becoming more available—partly because more countries are deciding to adopt the benefits of nuclear energy.

The risk of nuclear terrorism from South Asia to Europe and the United Kingdom has increased mainly because of the expanding numbers of nuclear weapons and the expansion of nuclear energy programs. There are more than 400 extremists and sectarian groups linked to al Qaeda and Taliban terrorist networks in Pakistan alone, and they can attack its nuclear installation any time. Their networks in Britain and Europe, and their tactics of nuclear blackmailing, combine with the increasing level of technological sophistication among terrorist groups and their determination to achieve their political goals, makes the presence of nuclear material in Pakistan a very high-stakes gamble.[1]

Terror networks find support, sponsors and training in Pakistan, and terrorists are displaying increasing sophistication in their strikes not only in weapons use but also in ways of carrying out attacks. The availability of a portable nuclear system in the country potentially can be used in attacks on nuclear weapons sites. The Pentagon and CIA have focused on Pakistan's nuclear facilities that might come under attack by TTP and other extremist groups.[2]

Nuclear power plants, research reactors and uranium enrichment plants could come under potential attack from the TTP and its allies, at any time, as they have already established a strong network within the headquarters of the armed forces.[3] Such a potential nuclear attack might be of several types — a commando type attack causing widespread dispersal of radioactive material, an aircraft crashing into an atomic reactor, or a cyber attack that interferes with the proper functioning of a nuclear reactor. All would be disastrous. After several terror attacks on Pakistan's nuclear facilities (Wah, Kamra, Dera Ghazi Khan, Sargodha), it is undeniable that the TTP and other extremist groups can gain access to nuclear facilities with the help of their radicalized allies in the armed forces.[4]

In December 2011, an article in *Atlantic Magazine* labeled Pakistan the "ally from hell." The article warned that Pakistan was transferring its nuclear weapons from one place to another to hide them from the CIA and, further, that the ineptitude of the Pakistani armed forces was evident from the fact, that instead of transferring nuclear weapons in armored vehicles, they were using very low security vans.[5]

During the Taliban regime in Afghanistan, al Qaeda sought

---

1 *Daily Times*, 03 October 2013, and also, "The Annual Report of the Intelligence and Security Committee for 2011–2012". http://www.parliament.uk/business/publications/research/key-issues-for-the-new-parliament/social-reform/broken-britain/.

2 On September 4, 2013, one of Pakistan's leading newspapers (*The News International*) reported on a 178-page summary of the United States' intelligence surveillance of Pakistan's nuclear weapons.

3 *Daily Times*, 03 October 2013, also, on 2 May 2011, *Dawn* reported al Qaeda's warning to Western world in Afghanistan.

4 Ibid.

5 "A Smith Institute research report", Dr Paul Cornish, 2007

nuclear weapons assistance from Pakistan. Pakistani scientists who helped Taliban and al Qaeda groups were Sultan Bashirud-din Mahmood, a retired officer of Atomic Energy Commission, and his colleague, Choudhry Abdul Majeed.[1]

The threat of nuclear terrorism is not new. Before the 9/11 attacks, al Qaeda and Taliban invited Pakistan nuclear scientists to build nuclear sites in Afghanistan. They arrived with new programs in Kabul. Al Qaeda and Taliban seek nuclear weapons and materials—and could plausibly make a crude bomb. Materials can be smuggled from Central Asia or can be obtained on the black market in Pakistan. There is a sense that any day a trained terrorist could attack a nuclear facility or possibly disperse radioactive materials in a "dirty bomb."[2] *Epoch Times*, on 24 March 2010, warned that extremist groups trained in Afghanistan may have already acquired a "dirty bomb" owing to the growing international black market trade in radioactive material.[3]

A Pakistani civil servant and columnist, Orya Maqbool Jan, warned in a TV debate that jihad against India is mandatory on every Pakistani Muslim. India's fear is genuine. On May 16, 2009, an Israeli news website, Debka, reported that Indian Prime Minister Singh warned President Barack Obama that nuclear sites in Pakistan's Khyber Pakhtunkhwa province are "already partly" in the hands of Islamic extremists.[4]

Before this statement, in 2005, Mr. Singh told CNN that his government was worried about the security of Pakistan nuclear assets after Pervez Musharaf stepped down. Seven years after this statement, in 2012, Indian government arrested a group of terrorists planning an attack on its nuclear facilities. They were linked to Pakistan based extremist groups, Harakat-ul-Jihad Islami and Lashkar-e-Toiba.20[5]

In 2001, the military regime of Gen. Musharaf had established the Pakistan Nuclear Regulatory Authority (PNRA), a force of 200 experts, to combat the uncontrolled smuggling of nuclear materials in the 1990s. Now, the threat has evolved and

1 *Daily Times*, 8 Nov 2012.
2 Ibid.
3 *Epoch Times*, 24 March 2010
4 Israeli website, *Debka*, 16 May 2009, and also *Daily Times*, 03 October 2013.
5 *Daily Times*, 8 Nov 2012.

it is coming from within. The country's borderlands have been converted into a battleground. The government of Nawaz Sharif wants stamp out this problem but is mired in domestic politics. The war in Khyber Pakhtunkhwa and Baluchistan is purely an ethnic war—a war against Pashtuns and Balochs.[1]

The annual report of the UK Office for Counter Terrorism warned about the possibility of a dirty bomb attack on UK installations. On 23 March 2010, *Telegraph* warned that the United Kingdom faces nuclear threat from al Qaeda following a rise in the trafficking of radiological material.[2]

At present we know four types of WMD that can destroy the United Kingdom or any other country within minutes. If terrorists use biological weapons, they will use pathogens (disease-causing agents) or they can use biotoxins (poisonous substances), killing or crippling human beings and tainting the food supply, at best. The societal disruption and economic damage from the panic alone would be unfathomable. Even if such weapons were used against "only" the water supply or agricultural plants, it would be disastrous.

We have already discussed various aspects of the possibilities of nuclear terrorism in Britain. I also wish to highlight the availability of other dangerous weapons in what amounts to an open market. Research scholar, Paul Cornish, in his two research papers, warned that public vulnerability to lethal chemical weapons is matter of great concern:

> The availability of precursors has led to chemical weapons being described as "the poor man's atomic bomb," an expression that also capture some of the moral and legal taboo that has historically (albeit not universally) been associated with chemical weapons. Although the production, weaponization and delivery of chemical weapons would be challenging, scientifically and logistically, as well as extremely expensive, a small number of low-yield chemical weapons would be relatively easy to hide and transport and might thus

---

1 *Pakistan's nuclear and WMD Programme: Status, Evolution and Risks*, Bruno Tertrais, EU Non-Proliferation Consortium, non-Proliferation Paper, No. 19, July 2012, also, *Building Confidence in Pakistan's Nuclear Security*, Kenneth N. Luongo and Brig. Gen. (Ret.) Naeem Salik, Arms Control Association, December 2007.
2 *Daily Telegraph*, 23 March 2010.

appeal to a well-organized and well-funded terrorist group.[1]

Chemical weapons can be stolen or can be purchased from some states. There are many options to choose from: chemical weapons, toxic industrial and commercial chemicals, and toxic chemicals of biological origin. The networks of Pakistani extremists in the UK and their illegal activities, like financing terrorists and smuggling contraband, is matter of great concern. The networks of extremist and terror groups in Britain, the globalization of industry and the consequent routines of international transport, containerization of trade, the diffusion of nuclear weapon technology and the availability of the weapons of mass destruction on the black market present an ever-growing threat to national security everywhere. Terrorist groups and, specifically, al Qaeda are working to acquire these weapons and the ability and financial resources to purchase, steal and make these weapons from fissile material.

In a research paper Michael J. Mazarr warned that terror groups in failed states like Pakistan and Afghanistan can easily move to the Middle East and Africa:

> The specified dangers were never unique to weak states, moreover, nor would state-building campaigns necessarily have mitigated them. Take terrorism. The most effective terrorists tend to be products of the middle class, often from nations such as Saudi Arabia, Germany and the United Kingdom, not impoverished citizens of failed states. And terrorist groups operating in weak states can shift their bases of operations; if Afghanistan becomes too risky, they can uproot themselves and move to Somalia, Yemen, or even Europe. As a result, "stabilizing" three or four sources of extremist violence would not render the United States secure.[2]

The nuclear summit in Washington, according to a Pakistani newspaper, *Daily Times*, was the gathering of over 47 states

---

1 "*Assessing the threat of terrorist use of chemical, biological, radiological and nuclear weapons in the United Kingdom, an International Security Program Report*", Chatham House, Paul Cornish, February 2007, and also, another paper, "Britain and security," 2007, Smith Institute.

2 "The Rise and fall of the Failed-State Paradigm: Requiem for a Decade of Distraction", *Foreign Affairs*, Michael J. Mazarr, January/February 2014.

to address the issue of nuclear weapons. The Conference took place after the US and Russian agreement to cut their nuclear weapons by thirty percent. In its report, the Weapons of Mass Destruction Commission initiated by the Swedish Government (on a proposal from the United Nations) warned that:

> Acquiring weapons of mass destruction and usable materials directly from a sympathetic government would significantly simplify the requirement for the terrorists, obviating the need to defeat security system protecting such materials. Such material, the report further warned, might be provided to terrorist groups by a state that hoped to see an IND used against an opponent, but wanted to be in a position to deny its involvement and reduce the threat of retaliation. Today, the greatest sources of concern in this regard are Pakistan, North Korea, and, if it should begin/resume producing fissile material, Iran.[1]

During civil wars, violence or instability in a country like Iran or Pakistan, terror groups can gain control of fissile materials. Insurgent groups like Taliban or sectarian groups of Pakistan can safely penetrate with the cooperation of contacts inside. Even if such an insurrection were unsuccessful, however, nuclear sites could fall behind "enemy" lines, before fissile materials could be removed, permitting their transfer to terrorists or their allies.

The effective use of Improvised Explosive Devices in Afghanistan, specifically in Helmand province, harmed the UK and NATO forces there. The undeniable effectiveness of this threat has influenced public perception. Yet American officials persistently asserted that the military offensive could change the reality on the ground and force a weakened Taliban to the negotiating table. Over the last few years, war has been almost ever-present across Afghanistan. In this period, insurgent groups have continued to intensify their violent activities. According to rights groups and government officials, hidden on roadsides, behind boulders or on cultivated land, Improvised Explosive Devices (IEDs) are killing or maiming dozens of civilians every month.

---

1 *Improvised Nuclear Devices and Nuclear Terrorism*, Charles D. Ferguson and William C. Potter, The Weapons of Mass Destruction Commission, 2006.

POSTSCRIPT

We are living in a country where racism, discrimination, corruption and a criminal culture have terminally damaged the institutions of the state. In Britain, institutions are facing a crisis of confidence, and this relates to parliament, politicians, political parties, and the Police as well. The Government is under severe criticism. Borough Councils are unable to provide housing for residents. The weakness and the growing unpopularity of local governments, coupled with a decline in confidence and trust on the part of the communities, have received considerable attention from the print and electronic media.

British state institutions that supported the creation of the welfare state have weakened over the last forty years. In addition, their approach to the problem of Scotland is inconsistent and incoherent. Scotland's growing demand for independence risks touching off a virtual civil war. The issue of the weakness of the central state has never been resolved, and this fact is exploited by Scottish nationalists. It's a very touchy issue. At the same time, law enforcement agencies have by and large failed to tackle serious organized crime or the various extremist cultures that are gaining ascendance, and there is a growing spirit of jihadism across the country.

State institutions have become deeply divided along ethnic and sectarian lines, leading to an incoherent approach to both domestic and international crises. Racism and inflammatory statements by some politicians and heads of state institutions have alienated minorities which wished to make Britain their home. The British Government has changed many laws applying to the private sector and to governmental institutions, to stop intimidation, harassment and racist practices against minority groups, and have spent millions of pounds promoting social awareness, but the problems only keep growing.

The low living standards, the decline of the justice system, the draconian powers exercised by the police, and the brazen attitude of the bureaucracy and Borough Councils — and their involvement in corruption, exaggerated surveillance, and discrimination — are the most challenging problems. The growing black market economy and the containerized criminal trade are undermining the traditional trade and economy. Meanwhile even the power plants, including both nuclear and fossil fuels are underfunded. The country is going to have to brace itself for power shortages.

Since the 1980s, the country has faced an increasing problem of joblessness, and the inability to earn a livelihood has become an epidemic in some communities, causing deep-seated poverty and uncertainty. Hidden homelessness is at about half a million. Poverty is on the rise, while leaders of all faiths have advised the government to take action to tackle the "national crisis" of rising hunger and food poverty. Anglican bishops and church leaders signed a letter calling on the Prime Minister, Deputy Prime Minister and Ed Miliband (currently the Leader of the Labour Party and Leader of the Opposition) to tackle the causes of food poverty.

The gap between rich and poor is growing; the conflicts between left and right are becoming more heated. Trust in Parliament and state institutions is at an all time low. In British society, influence, power, wealth and self-gratification are drivers behind corruption. The ruction between the Home Office and Police Department over the law enforcement mechanism has deepened. The Home Secretary vowed to control the rogue elements in the police department, but she faced harsh criticism. The depth of the police corruption scandal was revealed when newspapers uncovered a secret investigation into the records of criminal officers.

Recent accusations of sexual harassment against women police officers bring shame on the government and the police department as well. The distrust between ethnic communities and the police is aggravated day by day, signalling a massive challenge not only for the government but for the Home Office and the policing improvement agency as well. On 05 January 2014, *Daily Record* reported 120 police officers were accused of crimes that include rape, abduction and racism. A *Sunday Mail* investigation also reported at least 14 officers were suspended from duty, while alleged offences were probed. The allegations include rape, sex attacks, violence, wife beating, theft, fire attacks, abduction, stalking, disorderly conduct at football matches, racist actions and data breaches. Thirteen of the fourteen suspended were constables and one was a senior officer of inspector rank or above.

In Iraq and Syria, Britain nationals fought alongside their Arab al Qaeda allies. However, on 24 April 2013, Russian security experts warned that Britain itself was at risk from international extremist networks, specifically from the North Caucasus, who have been allowed to live in the UK. Extremist citizens of the United Kingdom, returning from the Middle East, especially Syria, are the biggest threat to the national security. *The Guardian* reported (2014) there were more than 500 extremists fighting in Syria in the past three years. Concerns over the grave threat were confirmed to the *Telegraph* in an un-signed letter from Whitehall, which said: "The threat to the UK comes from a range of countries and groups, but Syria is perhaps the biggest challenge right now".

The British welfare state faces an evolving threat from domestic extremist forces. The killing of a British soldier in East London proved that extremist forces have established strong networks in society. The welfare state is going to shrink and shatter as these groups developed their criminal networks. There are no more funds to support social welfare programs.

On 02 June, *Gulf News* reported nearly a thousand young people were shot or stabbed in London in 2013. The statistics from London's ambulance service reveal that paramedics were called to treat 973 victims under the age of 25, all suffering a gun or knife wound. The majority of cases are believed to be linked to gangs.

The attitude of young Christians, who generally have pursued no specific study of their religion and don't recognize the importance of attending church and religious ceremonies, is more racist than that of their Muslim countrymen. In churches, attendance is poor whereas in mosques, attendance is very strong — and increasing by the day. I think this is the main factor keeping religious identities separate.

Pubs and night clubs have ruined the lives of many young people. The National Health Service is broadly discredited. There are numerous stories of scandals in hospitals across the country. Thousands of elderly Britons are being killed through starvation and flawed or careless medical practices. Corruption has spread into every part of NHS hospitals.

The Liverpool Care Pathway or 'death pathway' has created suspicions of illegal practices by nurses and doctors in NHS hospitals. We have been told that this is the only way to end the lives of elderly patients when they are near death, but neither the government nor the doctor seem to care that it is the elderly who are the guardians of our history. *Daily Mail* has done a great job in exposing shocking cases of humiliation, brutal murder and abuse of innocent citizens by NHS doctors. There is essentially an illegitimate war being waged on patients in the United Kingdom. This war is more brutal than the war on terrorism. In the war on terrorism, civilian populations are being slaughtered from a distance by drones, missiles and bombs, while in the NHS war against patients, innocent patients are being killed one by one, by hand, by withholding basic necessities and by administering lethal injections.

On 15 July 2013, *Daily Mail* journalists=Matt Chorley and Denel Martin's investigative report about elderly patients in NHS hospitals created a climate of fear in the United Kingdom:

Nurses shouted at relatives who tried to give their dying loved ones a sip of water, an inquiry into the controversial Liverpool Care Pathway revealed. Ministers moved to scrap the end-of-life plan after a damning inquiry found it was being used as an excuse for poor care. Dying patients were placed on the LCP without their families knowing, left for weeks and in some cases months, and denied water despite the pleading of loved ones to let them have a drink.

On the inhuman behaviour of the hospital nurses, the report explores a shocking catalogue of patient abuse, and their humiliation at the hands of NHS doctors:

The shocking catalogue of abuse found that some relatives were forced to give their loved ones water secretly when the nurse was out of the room — because medical staff had forbidden it. Baroness Neuberger, who carried out the review, said that hydration problems were the "biggest issue" raised by people who gave evidence to the review. She added: "The same stories keep emerging of poor care, appalling communications and oft a lack of attention or compassion. Among the worst stories were of people on the Liverpool Care Pathway for days going into weeks without communication or review or discussion. And also stories of desperate people who are longing for a drink of water who were, through misunderstanding of the Liverpool Care Pathway and poor care, denied a drink."

According to the *Daily Mail* report; 130,000 patients are being placed on the Liverpool Care Pathway (Death Pathway) every year.

The issues of Northern Ireland and Scotland are going to be more complicated in near future. British Parliament continues to debate the activities of the IRA, and the looming threat of an independent Scotland. The conflict in Northern Ireland has entered a new phase as both the sects (Protestant and Catholic) have adopted new strategies of destruction and violence. The issue of peace walls now has become the main focus of debate in intellectual forums, as instead of forging a reconciliation, they have created more clefts and distrust, greater distances between groups, and greater alienation and communal differences.

Walls have never been found to be effective as an instrument of peace in any religious or racial conflict in modern history. Walls must not separate a brother from brother, mother from son and friends from friends. Walls do not separate minds, hearts, ethnic and linguistic relations. We can separate human beings by physical barriers, but we must not undermine human values, relationships and traditional ways of life. The use of such flawed administrative measures is a blemish on British society.

The future of our children is bleak as sectarian conflict remains deeply rooted.

No doubt, The Good Friday Agreement and other peace efforts brought some positive movement toward healing the rifts between communities of different faiths, but the issue of segregated housing and unequal access to housing (in other words, homelessness) still needs to be settled. The way ethnic and sectarian antagonism in Northern Ireland is tackled, is no more effective. Government and local administration cannot bring peace and stability by constructing big walls. If walls were an effective way of separating communities or sects, the Berlin Wall would have remained in place.

An additional crisis appeared as Britain (with the US) was found to be spying on its own neighbors and allies. A new intelligence war was started between the UK and the European states when France, Germany and Spain summoned both the UK and US ambassadors to explain the motives behind their surveillance policies. Germany became very angry when it found that the UK embassy in Berlin was involved in alleged eavesdropping. On 13 May 2014, the *Guardian* reported GCHQ's illegal surveillance activities that entail spy programs that remotely hijack computers' cameras and microphones without the user's consent. As noted earlier, the US and UK are members of the Five-Eye intelligence-sharing alliance, including Australia, New Zealand and Canada, but their methods of surveillance clearly violate the principles of the alliance. French intelligence is cooperating with the Five Eyes alliance by systematically providing them with information. Sweden, Israel and Italy are also cooperating with the NSA and GCHQ.

Secret surveillance of people from all sectors of society and collecting their personal data, every last bit — where they sleep, where they go to dinner, whom they meet with — is an open violation of the rights of free citizens. The *Guardian* newspaper presentation of PRISM documents raised many questions about the way intelligence information is gathered by British agencies. From Microsoft, FaceBook, YouTube, Google, Twitter to Skype, and LinkedIn, they trace every step through social media day and night, but all these breaches of citizens' rights haven't enabled them to defeat the prevailing criminal culture, extremism, challenges of hate preachers and the networks of international terrorism across the country.

This book covers all the major challenges the British welfare state faces. The book is intended as a wake-up call to the ruling elite and those who serve them, as the complex of social, political, ethnic, financial and sectarian crises now rocking the boat may very well sink the ship of state. Profound internal instability is inevitable in the near future, if major improvements are not made now.

APPENDIX 1. THE GOOD FRIDAY AGREEMENT, 10 APRIL 1998

Agreement between the Government of the United Kingdom of Great Britain and Northern Ireland and the Government of Ireland

The Good Friday agreement was signed in Belfast in 1998, ending direct British rule of Northern Ireland. It proved to be a major political development in the peace process in Northern Ireland.

This agreement also established several joint institutions between Northern Ireland and the Republic of Ireland and between the United Kingdom and Northern Ireland, ensuring power sharing between loyalist and nationalist representatives. Broadly speaking, this agreement brought to an end the 30-year-long sectarian conflict.

The Good Friday agreement consists of two inter-related documents, signed 10 April 1998.

The Agreement between the United Kingdom and Northern Ireland came into force on 2 December 1999.

Here it is in its essence.[1]

---

1 https://www.gov.uk/government/publications/the-belfast-agreement

The two Governments:

(i) recognize the legitimacy of whatever choice is freely exercised by a majority of the people of Northern Ireland with regard to its status, whether they prefer to continue to support the Union with Great Britain or a sovereign united Ireland;

(ii) recognize that it is for the people of the island of Ireland alone, by agreement between the two parts respectively and without external impediment, to exercise their right of self-determination on the basis of consent, freely and concurrently given, North and South, to bring about a united Ireland, if that is their wish, accepting that this right must be achieved and exercised with and subject to the agreement and consent of a majority of the people of Northern Ireland;

(iii) acknowledge that while a substantial section of the people in Northern Ireland share the legitimate wish of a majority of the people of the island of Ireland for a united Ireland, the present wish of a majority of the people of Northern Ireland, freely exercised and legitimate, is to maintain the Union and accordingly, that Northern Ireland's status as part of the United Kingdom reflects and relies upon that wish; and that it would be wrong to make any change in the status of Northern Ireland save with the consent of a majority of its people;

(iv) affirm that, if in the future, the people of the island of Ireland exercise their right of self-determination on the basis set out in sections (I) and (ii) above to bring about a united Ireland, it will be a binding obligation on both Governments to introduce and support in their respective Parliaments legislation to give effect to that wish;

(v) affirm that whatever choice is freely exercised by a majority of the people of Northern Ireland, the power of the sovereign government with jurisdiction there shall be exercised with rigorous impartiality on behalf of all the people in the diversity of their identities and traditions and shall be founded on the principles of full respect for, and equality of, civil, political, social and cultural rights, of freedom from discrimination for all citizens, and of parity of esteem and of just and equal treatment for the identity, ethos and aspirations of both communities;

(vi) recognize the birthright of all the people of Northern Ireland to identify themselves and be accepted as Irish or British, or both, as they may so choose, and accordingly confirm that their right to hold both British and Irish citizenship is accepted by both Governments and would not be affected by any future change in the status of Northern Ireland.

ARTICLE 2

The two Governments affirm their solemn commitment to support, and where appropriate implement, the provisions of the Multi-Party Agreement. In particular there shall be established in accordance with the provisions of the Multi-Party Agreement immediately on the entry into force of this Agreement, the following institutions:

(i) a North/South Ministerial Council;

(ii) The implementation bodies referred to in paragraph 9 (ii) of the section entitled "Strand Two" of the Multi-Party Agreement;

(iii) A British-Irish Council;

(iv) A British-Irish Intergovernmental Conference.

ARTICLE 3

(1) This Agreement shall replace the Agreement between the British and Irish Governments done at Hillsborough on 15th November 1985 which shall cease to have effect on entry into force of this Agreement.

(2) The Intergovernmental Conference established by Article 2 of the aforementioned Agreement done on 15th November 1985 shall cease to exist on entry into force of this Agreement.

ARTICLE 4

(1) It shall be a requirement for entry into force of this Agreement that:

(a) British legislation shall have been enacted for the purpose of implementing the provisions of Annex A to the section entitled "Constitutional Issues" of the Multi-Party Agreement;

(b) the amendments to the Constitution of Ireland set out in Annex B to the section entitled "Constitutional Issues" of the Multi-Party Agreement shall have been approved by Referendum;

(c) such legislation shall have been enacted as may be required to establish the institutions referred to in Article 2 of this Agreement.

(2) Each Government shall notify the other in writing of the completion, so far as it is concerned, of the requirements for entry into force of this Agreement. This Agreement shall enter into force on the date of the receipt of the later of the two notifications.

(3) Immediately on entry into force of this Agreement, the Irish Government shall ensure that the amendments to the Constitution of Ireland set out in Annex B to the section entitled "Constitutional Issues" of the Multi-Party Agreement take effect.

In witness thereof the undersigned, being duly authorized thereto by the respective Governments, have signed this Agreement. Done in two originals at Belfast on the 10th day of April 1998.

Tony Blair
Marjorie (Mo) Mowlam

For the Government of
the United Kingdom
of Great Britain and
Northern Ireland

Bertie Ahern
David Andrews

For the Government of
Ireland

ANNEX 1

The Agreement Reached in the Multi-Party Talks

ANNEX 2

Declaration on the Provisions of Paragraph (vi) of Article 1
In Relationship to Citizenship

The British and Irish Governments declare that it is their joint understanding that the term "the people of Northern Ireland" in paragraph (vi) of Article 1 of this Agreement means, for the purposes of giving effect to this provision, all persons born in Northern Ireland and having, at the time of their birth, at least one parent who is a British citizen, an Irish citizen or is otherwise entitled to reside in Northern Ireland without any restriction on their period of residence.

APPENDIX 2. FIVE EYES INTELLIGENCE ALLIANCE

The alliance of five English-speaking countries (UK, US, Australia, Canada and New Zealand) was formed in 1946 to share intelligence in the battlefield. The main purpose of Five Eyes (FVEY) was to share intelligence, primarily signal intelligence. Signal and other intelligence collection systems are:

ECHELON: this system collects intelligence information through satellite communications.

THINTHREAD: this is an intelligence analysis tool.

TEMPORA: this system collects intelligence information through an undersea fiber optic cable.

XKEYSCORE: an analytical framework that indexes email addresses file-names, IP-addresses, cookies, telephone numbers and metadata. An addition to FIVE EYES, other surveillance partnerships exist. NINE EYES included the names of four other states (Denmark, France, Netherland and Norway. 14 EYES included the names of Germany, Belgium, Italy, Spain and Sweden.

41 EYES comprises all American and European allies in the context of the Afghanistan war.

MUSCULAR: operated by GCHQ and the NSA.

STATEROOM: operated by the ASD, CIA, CSEC, GCHQ and NS. (Privacy International, https://www.privacyinternational.org/blog/the-five-eyes-fact-sheet.)

Five Eyes Intelligence communities.

Canada: Communications Security Establishment (CSEC), International Assessment Staff (IAS), Chief of Defense Intelligence (CDI), Canadian Security Intelligence Service (CSIS), CSIS (note), Integrated Threat Assessment Centre (ITAC).

USA: National Security Agency (NSA), Central Intelligence Agency/ Director of Intelligence (CIA/DI) US State Department/ Intelligence and Research Bureau (State/INR), Defense Intelligence Agency (DIA), Federal Bureau of Investigation (FBI), Central Intelligence Agency/Director of Operations (CIA/DO), National Counter Terrorism Centre (NCTC).

UK: Government Communication Headquarters (GCHQ), Cabinet Office Assessment Staff. (COAS), Defense Intelligence Staff (DIS), British Security Service (MI5), Secret Intelligence Service (SIS) (MI-6), Joint Threat Assessment Centre (JTAC).

Australia: Defense Signal Directorate (DSD), Office of National Assessments (ONA), Defense Intelligence Organization (DIO), Australian Security Intelligence Organization, (ASIO), Australian Secret Intelligence Service (ASIS), National Threat Assessment Centre (NTAC).

New Zealand: Government Communication Security Bureau (GCSB), National Assessment Bureau (NAB), Directorate of Defense Intelligence and Security (DDIS), New Zealand Security Intelligence Service (SIS), (inherent in SIS mandate), Combined Threat Assessment Centre (CTAG). (Canada and the Five Eyes Intelligence Community, James Cox, December 2012. Canadian Defense & Foreign Affairs Institute and Canadian International Council-2012. (http://www.cdfai.org/PDF/Canada%20and%20the%20Five%20Eyes%20Intelligence%20Community

BIBLIOGRAPHY

Aaronson, David E, Diense C. Thomas and Mushino, Michael C. 1984, *Public Policy and Police Discretion Processes of Decriminalization*, Clark Boardman, New York.

Abel-Smith, Brian. 1958. "Whose Welfare State," chapter 14 in *Welfare and the State: The zenith of Western welfare state systems*, Deakin, Nicholas; Catherine Jones Finer, Bob Matthews. 2003. Taylor & Francis.

Abrahams, M. 2006. "Al Qaeda Scorecard: A Progress Report on al Qaeda Objectives." *Studies in Conflict and Terrorism*, Vol 29, No-5.

Adams, Gerry, 1994, *Selecting writings*, Dingle Brandon Books

Akkad, O. 01 July, 2006. "Muslim Teens Seek Belief in its Perfect Form". The *Globe and Mail* newspaper, Australia

Alinsky, S. 1969. *Rules for Radicals, Random House*, Viking Press, New York

Amghar S. Boubekeur A. and Emerson M. 2007. *European Islam: Challenges for society and public Policy*, Centre for European Policy Studies. Brussels.

Anderson, Don, 1994, *The Inside Story of Loyalist Strike of 1974*, Gill and MacMillan, Dublin, Ireland

Archer, M. 2003 *Structure, Agency and the Internal Conversation*, Cambridge University Press, UK

Arthur, Paul, and Jeffery, Keith. 1996. *Northern Ireland since 1968*. Oxford: Basil Blackwell.

Arthur, Paul. 1974. *The People's Democracy 1968–1972*. Belfast: Black staff Press.

Ascher, K. 1987. *The Politics of Privatization*, Macmillan, London

Audit Commission-2008, "Preventing Violent Extremism: Learning and

Development Exercise, Report to the Home Office and Communities and Local Government".

Audit Commission Reports 1988, 1990, 1991. "Papers No-5, 8, and 10".

Bailey, V. 1981. *Policing and Punishment in 19th Century Britain.* Croom Helm. London.

Bamford, James. 2002. *Body of Secrets. How America's NSA and Brittan's GCHQ Eavesdrop on the World.* Arrow Books, London

Barnard, C. 2011. *Using procurement law to enforce labor standards.* Oxford University Press.

Bartholomew, James. 2004. *The Welfare State We Are In.* Politico's publishing Ltd

Beckett, J.C. 1981. *The Making of Modern Ireland 1603-1923,* Faber and Faber.

Beljac, Marko. *Pakistan and the Prospect for Nuclear Terrorism.* 2008. Australian Policy Online. http://apo.org.au/commentary/pakistan-and-prospects-nuclear-terrorism.

Bell, J. Bowyer. 1989. *The Secret Army: The IRA 1916-1979.* Poolbeg, Dublin.

Bishop, P., and Mallie, E. 1987. *The Provisional IRA.* Corgi Books, London.

Bolton, D. 1973. *The UVF 1966-73: An Anatomy of Loyalist Rebellion.* Dublin: Gill and Macmillan.

Bennett, Richard. 2002. *Espionage. Spies & Secrets.* Virgin Books, London.

Brewer John. D and Gareth. 1998. *Northern Ireland, 1921–1998,* Macmillan Press, London.

Brown, John. 1995. *State, Welfare and Social Policy: The British Welfare State.* Wiley Blackwell.

Bruce, S. 1992. *The Red Hand: Protestant paramilitaries in Northern Ireland,* Oxford University Press.

Buckly, A. and Kenny M.C. 1995. *Negotiating Identity: Rhetoric, Metaphor and social drama in Northern Ireland,* Smithsonian Institute Press

Chatham House Report. 2011. "Cyber Security and the UK's Critical National Infrastructure"

Clark, I. and S. Moody. 2002. *Racist Crime and Victimization in Scotland,* Scottish Executive Central Research Unit.

Colarik, Andrew M. 2006. *Cyber terrorism: Political and economic implications.* IGI Global.

Coulter, Colin. 1997. *Contemporary Northern Irish Society: An Introduction,* Pluto Press, London.

Crawford, C. 2003. *Inside the UDA: Volunteers and Violence,* Pluto Press, London.

Crompton, R. 1989, "Class Theory and Gender," *British Journal of Sociology.*

Curtis, Mark. 2012. *Britain's Collusion with Radical Islam*. Serpents Tail, London.

Darby, John. 1976. *Conflict in Northern Ireland: The Development of a Polarized Community*. Dublin: Gill and Macmillan.

Dennis, Norman, George Erdos, and David Robinson, 2003. *The Failure of Britain's Police: London and New York*. Civitas: Institute for the Study of Civil Society. London.

Deucher, R. and Holligan C. 2010, "Gangs, Sectarianism and Social Capital: A Qualitative Study of Young People in Scotland". *Sage Journal of Sociology*.

Deucher, R. and Holligan, 2008, *Territoriality and Sectarianism in Glasgow: A Qualitative Study*, University of the West of Scotland.

Dixon, Paul, 2006, *The Northern Ireland Peace Process: Choreography and Theatrical Politics*. Routledge, London

Dolye, M. 2009. *Fighting Like the Devil for the Sake of God: Protestants, Catholics and the Origin of Violence in Victorian Belfast*, Manchester University Press.

Durston, Gregory J. 2012. *Burglars and Bobbies: Crime and Policing in Victorian London*. Cambridge Scholar Publishing

Ekblom, P. 2010, *Crime Prevention, Security and Community Safety Using the 5Is Framework (Crime Prevention and Security Management)* Palgrave Macmillan.

Elliot, M. 2009. *When God Took Sides: Religion and Identity in Ireland*. Oxford University Press.

Elliott, S., Flakes, W.D, 1999, *Northern Ireland: A Political Dictionary, 1968–1999*, Belfast, Blackstaff Press.

Ellison, Graham, and Jim Smyth, 2000, *the Crowned Harp: Policing Northern Ireland*, Pluto Press, London.

English, Richard, 2003, *Armed Struggle: A History of IRA*, MacMillan, London.

Esping-Andersen, Gosta, 1989. *The Three Worlds of Welfare Capitalism*. Princeton University Press.

Evan, G. and M. Duffy, 1997. "Beyond the Sectarian Divide: the Social Bases and Political consequences of Nationalist and Unionist Party Competition in Northern Ireland". *British Journal of Political Science*.

Fahey, Tony and Richard Sinnott, 2004. *Two Traditions One Culture? A Study of Attitude and Values in the Republic of Ireland and Northern Ireland*, Institute of Public Administration, Dublin.

Farrel, M. 1980. *Northern Ireland: The Orange State*. Pluto Press London.

Fawcett M. 2000. *Religion Ethnicity and Social change*, Macmillan. London.

Feldman, A. 1991, *Formation of Violence: The Narrative of the Body and Political Terror in Northern Ireland*. Chicago University Press.

Fulton, J. 1991. *The Tragedy of Belief: Division politics and religion in Ireland.* Clarendon Press Oxford.

Ganiel, G. 2008. *Evangelicalism and Conflict in Northern Ireland.* Palgrave, Macmillan, New York, USA.

Garnish, Paul, Rex Hughes and David Livingston. 2009. *Cyberspace and National security of the United Kingdom, Threats and Responses.* Chatham House Report.

Giddens, A. 1990, *The Consequences of Modernity.* Cambridge: Polity Press.

Giddens, A. 1998, *Conversations with Anthony Giddens: Making Sense of Modernity.* Stanford, CA: Stanford University Press.

Githens-Mazer, Jonathan. 2008. *Islamic Radicalization among North Africans in Britain.* Political Studies Association.

Glennerster, Howard. 2006. *British Social Policy 1945 to Present.* Wiley Blackwell.

Gopal, S. 2001. Nuclear *Terrorism: Relevance and Prospect in South Asia.* Paper No. 359.

Gottfredson, M. and T. Hirschi, 1990, *A General Theory of Crime.* Stanford University Press.

Goldstein, Herman. 1990. *Problem-Oriented Policing.* McGraw Hill, New York.

Harnden, Toby, 1999, *Bandit Country: The IRA and South Armagh,* Hodder and Stoughton.

Hay, Douglas, and Francis G. Snyder. 1989. *Policing and Prosecution in Britain, 1750–1850.* Clarendon Press.

Hennessey, Thomas. 1997, *A History of Northern Ireland, 1920–1996.* Gill and Macmillan, Dublin.

Herman, Michael. 1996. *Intelligence Power in War and Peace.* Cambridge University Press.

Heskin, K. 1980. *Northern Ireland: A Psychological Analysis.* Gill and Macmillan. Dublin.

Hirst, C. 2002. *Religion, Politics and Violence and Nineteenth Century Belfast,* Four Courts Press, Dublin.

Holland, Jack, 1997, *Phoenix: Policing the Shadows, the Secret War against Terrorism in Northern Ireland.* Hodder and Stoughton

Holland, Jack, and Henry McDonald, 1994, *INLA: Deadly Divisions-the Story of One of Ireland's Most Ruthless Terrorist Organizations.* Dublin: Torc.

Home Office, July 2013, "Advice to parents and cares on gangs."

Home Office, May 2011, "An Assessment of the Tackling Knives and Serious Youth Violence Action Programme", (TKAP) — Phase ll.

Home Office, January 2014, "Review of the operation of injunctions to prevent gang-related violence".

Jackson, Alvin, 2004, Home Rule: *An Irish History, 1800–2000.* Weidenfeld and Nicolson, London

Jarman, N. 2004. *From War to Peace? Changing Pattern of Violence in Northern Ireland 1990–2003,* Journal of Terrorism and Political Violence. Taylor & Francis Online

Jefferson, T. 1990. *The Case against Paramilitary Policing,* Open University Press. London.

Johnson, Douglas H. 2004–2010. *Sources of Intelligence: A Bibliography of the Monthly Sudan Intelligence Report.* Volume 11, Number 1. Northeast African Studies.

Johnston, Les. 1999. *Policing in Britain, Longman Criminology Series.* Longman.

Jones, Margaret and Rodney Lowe, 2002. *From Beveridge to Blair: The First Fifty Years of Britain's Welfare State.* Manchester University Press.

Kapur, Paul. 2008. *Nuclear Terrorism: Prospects in Asia.* Stanford University Press

Kaufmann, Eric, 2007, *The Orange Order: A Contemporary Northern Irish History.* Oxford University Press.

Kuhn, T. 1996. *The Structure of Scientific Revolution,* Chicago University Press.

Lain, Crimson. *2009. Health Policy: A Critical Perspective.* Sage London.

Lawday, David. 2000. *Policing in France and Britain. Restoring Confidence Locally and Nationally.* Franco-British Council. London.

Laycock, G. and K. Heal. 1989. *Crime Prevention: The British Experience.* Routledge London.

Leventhal, Paul and Brahma Chellaney. 1988. *Nuclear Terrorism: Threat, Perception and Response in South Asia.* New Delhi.

Lowe, Rodney. 2005. *The Welfare State in Britain since 1945.* Palgrave Macmillan. London.

Lukes, S. 1974. Power: *A Radical View.* Macmillan, London.

Lustgarten, L. 1986. *The Governance of Police.* Sweet and Maxwell, London.

Mawby, Dr. Rob, and Dr. Alan Wright, 2005. *Police Accountability in the United Kingdom.* Keele University, UK.

McDaniel, Denzil, 1997, *Enniskillen, the Remembrance Day Bombing.* Dublin: Wolfhound.

McGarry, J. and O' Leary.1990, *The Future of Northern Ireland.* Oxford University Press, UK

McKay, Susan, 2000, *Northern Protestants: An Unsettled People.* Blackstaff Press Belfast.

McKearney, Tommy. 2011. *The Provincial IRA: From Insurrection to Parliament.* Pluto Press, London.

Mckittrick, D. Kelters S, Freeny B, and Thornton. C. 1999. *Lost Lives: The stories of the Man, Women and children who died as a Result of the Northern Ireland Trouble.* Mainstream Publishing, Edinburgh.

Ministry of Justice, "Understanding the psychology of gang violence: implications for designing effective violence interventions," March 2011.

Moloney, Ed, 2002, *A Secret History of the IRA.* Penguin Books, London.

Mullan, Don, 1997, *Eyewitness Bloody Sunday: The Truth.* Wolfhound, Dublin.

Mullin, Chris, 1980, *Error of Judgment: The Truth about the Birmingham Pub Bombings.* Dublin: Poolbeg Press.

Musa Khan Jalalzai. 2013. *Punjabi Taliban: The Prospect of Civil War in Pakistan,* Royal Books, Karachi Pakistan.

O'Brien, C.C. 1988. *God Land: Reflection on Religion and Nationalism.* Poolbeg, Dublin.

O'Day, A. 1998. *Irish Home rule: 1867–1921.* Manchester University Press.

Omand, David. 2010. *Securing the State.* Hurst & Company London

Police Service in Northern Ireland. 2010–2011. "Annual Report of Chief Constable, Belfast".

Rogilio, Alonso, 2007, *The IRA and Armed Struggle,* Routledge, London

Rose, R. 1971. *Governing without Consensus: An Irish Perspective,* Faber and Faber, London.

Rowan, Brian. 1995. *Behind the Lines: The Story of the IRA and Loyalist Ceasefires.* Belfast: Blackstaff Press.

Scottish Government. "Gang Membership and Knife Carrying: Findings from the Edinburgh Study of Youth Transitions and Crime", September 2010.

Singh, Maj. Gen V.K. 2007. *India's External Intelligence: Secrets of Research & Analysis Wing (RAW),* Manas publications. India.

Solomon, John. 1992. *Race and Racism in Britain.* The Macmillan Press.

Sreberny, Annabelle and Gholam Khyanani. 2010. *Blogistan: The Internet and Politics in Iran.* I.B. Tauris, London.

Stuart, Adam and Browne James. 2010. *Redistribution, Work Incentives and Thirty Years of UK Tax and Benefit Reform.* IFS Working Paper.

Taylor, Peter, 1997, *The IRA and Sinn Fein.* Bloomsbury Publishing, London.

Taylor, Peter, 1999, *Loyalists.* Bloomsbury, London.

Ukemenam, Joe. 2007. *Policing in Britain: The Racial Discourse.* Book Surge Ltd.

Ulster Political Research Group. 1988. "Common Sense: Northern Ireland and Agreed Process". Belfast.

"United Kingdom and Its Implications for Ethnic Minority Youth," *British Journal of Criminology* 2013.

Walsh, Patrick F. 2011. *Intelligence and intelligence analysis.* Routledge, Taylor and Francis, London.

Ward, Michael. 2011. *Rebalancing the Economy: Prospect for the North.* Smith Institute, London.

Whittle, Giles. 2011. *Bridge of Spies. A True Story of the Cold War.* Simon and Schuster. London.

Whyte, John, 1991, *Interpreting Northern Ireland.* Clarendon Press, Oxford.

Willmott, P. 1987. *Policing and the Community.* Policy Studies Institute, London.

Wright, Frank, 1992, *Northern Ireland: A Comparative Analysis*, Dublin: Gill and Macmillan.